A BIBLICAL VIEW OF PROSPERITY FROM A COAL MINER'S SON

Wayne Wooldridge

DEDICATION

To my three sons:
Christopher, Michael and Joshua. I love you dearly.
I am proud of your successes, your families, and all you have accomplished.
The only thing that could be added to your list of achievements would be for you to
follow the path laid out in this book, and set that example for your family.
You all have exceptional spouses who are also great moms, and I am honored to know
and love them all. Thank you, Sally, Tanya, and Janelle.

Love you very much,
Dad

TABLE OF CONTENTS

Appreciation		vii
Preface		ix
Chapter 1	Big Ideas and Hard Labor	1
Chapter 2	Enterprising and Devising Plans of His Own	3
Chapter 3	Fear Comes in Many Forms	8
Chapter 4	What the Bible Taught HT	10
Chapter 5	Intelligence vs. Wisdom	14
Chapter 6	They Get Away with It. Why Can't I?	20
Chapter 7	Whose Money Is It, Anyway?	27
Chapter 8	That's Not Fair. He Is No Better Than Me!	32
Chapter 9	It Seems They Get All the Breaks	39
Chapter 10	I Can Do This	63
Chapter 11	The Tree	88
Chapter 12	All the Big Companies Are Doing It. Why Can't I?	95
Chapter 13	Keeping God First in Our Lives	104
Chapter 14	Walking Like David	114
Chapter 15	Balancing Your Life	120
Chapter 16	Does Work Have to Be This Hard?	128
Chapter 17	Different Meanings of Blessing	134
Chapter 18	The Teachings of Solomon	141
Chapter 19	The Challenges of Being a Christian	147
Chapter 20	We Are All Sinners	153
Chapter 21	God's Retirement Plan for Us	158
Chapter 22	The Emotion of Guilt	165
Chapter 23	The Pentateuch	170
Chapter 24	Nobody Is Perfect but God	176

Chapter 25   The Fig Tree   181
Chapter 26   Preparing the Ground to Plant a Garden   188
Chapter 27   Tithing   193
Chapter 28   Developing a Relationship with God   201
Chapter 29   Opening the Window to Faith   203
Chapter 30   God's Blessings   209
Chapter 31   Letting Go of the Past   215
Chapter 32   This All Belongs to God   221
Chapter 33   The Power of Wisdom   227
Chapter 34   The Lamb   233
Chapter 35   Trust in the Lord   241
Chapter 36   Pride: The Biggest Stumbling Block   248
Chapter 37   The Book of Job   255
Chapter 38   Living Like Job   261

APPRECIATION

A special appreciation to Vicki Howard, a good friend and former boss, sort of. I worked for her late husband selling cars, and because of his leadership, I became his top salesman, selling more cars annually than some of the dealerships in our area. Vicki offered her expertise and guidance in helping me to bring this book to life, all while recovering from surgery. Thank you, Vicki. I owe you a debt of gratitude and really appreciate all your hard work.

PREFACE

This book was written to try and win my father's approval. His name was Harry Thomas Wooldridge, better known to everyone as HT, but to me, he was dad. As I tell his story, from his humble beginnings to the day he went home to be with his mother and the Lord, I will share a good portion of his life with you.

More than anything in life, I wanted to have a relationship with my dad, but that would never happen. I rebelled as I grew older, and dad was too proud to give in. It was only after his death that I really discovered who he was. Eventually, I turned my life around and followed his footsteps. But it took many heartaches and failures to come to that realization.

To most, HT's life would be considered simple. But to me, it proved what the Bible says about prosperity. Not in the sense that some would have us believe, but by following the richness of the Scriptures and its practical application.

HT was not an educated man. He was taken out of school at age eleven to work in a coal mine, making a dollar a day. His labor eventually supported a growing family that blossomed into thirteen children.

This book will take you on a journey of the role God played in HT's life. It will open your eyes and hearts to see there is prosperity in the verses found in the Bible. We just have to do it God's way.

Many Bible verses are included in this book, and each is broken down and referenced through Strong's Concordance. The purpose is to let you see the meaning of those words and what they meant in the day and time they were written as referenced in the Bible.

In most instances, the word will give a completely different perspective and much greater insight on what God's word is saying. It is not taken out of context, just a deeper meaning of the verse.

It is my prayer that as you read this book, it becomes an adventurous and illustrative experience for you.

CHAPTER 1
BIG IDEAS AND HARD LABOR

It all began in Hurt, Virginia, on a cold January Saturday morning. Hurt is a small farming community, forty miles north of the North Carolina border. Saturdays were usually spent going to town and getting your weekly supplies or working in the barn preparing for the spring thaw. Being a farmer meant that you were anxious to get seed in the ground and work your land, praying for a bumper crop. On this particular morning, God had a special plan.

January 13, 1912 came in as usual. For John, it was making sure the house was warm, getting the two children out of bed, and putting a pot of coffee on to help with the morning chill. Their log home was cold, as there was a lot of its chinking missing, allowing the bitter winters wind to come through.

Laura, John's wife, was expecting anytime. This morning John and Laura would celebrate the birth of Harry Thomas Wooldridge, their third child. Eventually, the Wooldridge family would expand growing to thirteen children in all.

John could see that farming was not going to provide all the necessities for his large family. He heard about the coal mining industry and the wages they paid and decided it was time to make a move.

Shortly after Harry's birth, the family moved to West Virginia in search of a better life. The place they chose to settle was a little community called Dawson. It is not surprising that it was a farming community.

John had big ideas and agreed to purchase a one-hundred-acre tract of land. He figured he could have the best of both worlds; a large parcel of land with lots of fruit trees and a job in the coal mines that would secure his family for life.

He had no idea how hard and labor intensive the coal mines were. Everything was done by pick and shovel. The work was back breaking, the days were long, and there was only one place you could spend your hard-earned pay—at the company store. The mine paid in script and the company store was the only place that took that script.

The family kept growing, which put demands on John to earn more money. He had to make a choice: to cut back on farming, put more hours in the mine, or figure another way to bring extra money into the house.

The coal industry was booming, but for the little guy who had no formal education there was only going to be one place to fit in, and that was at the bottom. Harry, best known as HT, was growing up fast and would soon be eleven. He was good in school and very enterprising. His father took notice and withdrew him from school so he could work and help with the family's finances.

The Christmas holidays were over and it was time to turn the focus back to work. Ten plus years in the coalmine had turned John into a hard man. He was now drinking very heavily, the farm was starting to run down, and Laura was overwhelmed with their thirteen children. With John's ever increasing drinking, the farm was becoming more desolate and demands from the growing family was taking a toll on young HT, who was now considered a major breadwinner.

Dad delivering coal, wood and ice as a side business

CHAPTER 2
ENTERPRISING AND DEVISING PLANS OF HIS OWN

HT was fourteen when he taught himself to drive the family model T-Ford, and by age sixteen he had a second job delivering ice, firewood, and coal. He had matured well beyond his years and was saving his money, helping the family, and thinking about his future. Working in the mine and drinking whiskey seemed to be a way of life for the coal miner. John fit right in for he liked his whisky, which became a priority on payday.

Being a coal miner was physically demanding. The work was hard and practically everything was done by hand. Conditions in the mine were harsh, making tempers pushed to the limit and learning to take care of yourself was a must if you expected to survive.

John was small in stature, standing just a little over five feet tall and weighed less than one hundred forty pounds, but had a reputation of fighting anything that would stand still. To make matters worse, after a couple of drinks, he could fight a bear.

He was a Jekyll and Hyde. When he was sober, there was not a better man. After a few drinks, he became 'Katie Bar the Door.' He had no fear whatsoever, no matter how big or strong the other man was. He was mean to Laura and the children, and they were all afraid of him.

HT saw the fear and pain his mother suffered and vowed he would never treat his wife or family that way. There was an inseparable bond between the young man and his mother, and he would do anything for her.

Laura was a big woman—tall, with high cheek bones and Cherokee blood. HT took after his mother, for he was a tall, good-looking young man, full of

Dad and mom dating

ambition. Dreams of owning a little house, a family of his own, and making his mother proud of him by doing more with his life was all part of his plan. In his desire to get ahead, HT discovered the power of saving his money and how time compounded his efforts. He knew that fulfilling his dream by working in the mines was stable but he would need more, much more.

He took on a second job delivering ice. It provided him spending money for his personal needs, leaving his paycheck from the mine pretty much free. Part of his check went to help his mother and siblings, but the bulk went into savings.

By age twenty-three, he had already worked in the mine twelve years. Never really knowing what it was like to be a little boy drove him to work hard and save harder.

He wanted to marry and have his own family, vowing to give them a life he never had. Work was all he knew, but he was now ready to settle down.

He courted a young lady by the name of Clara for some time and on the day after his twenty-third birthday, they got married. Within a year, their first daughter was born, and a year later they welcomed a second daughter. All his dreams were starting to fall into place. The couple started to look for their first house when the unexpected happened.

HT had celebrated his twenty-eighth birthday when he found himself pacing the floor at the community hospital. Nervously waiting for the doctors to discover what was wrong with his mother, his dreams came crashing down when at age forty-six his mother passed away. A piece of HT died that day as well.

The loss of his beloved mother hit him hard. Time helped heal the scar but there was always an empty void that nothing and no one could fill. He blamed his father in part for his mother's early death due to his heavy drinking, missing work, lack of money, and the stress of a big family.

HT's family eventually grew to three daughters and one son. The early years of his life mirrored that of his father. He began drinking, and when he drank, he fought. Unlike his father, HT was a big man—standing 6'1, weighing about two hundred and five pounds, and was made of solid muscle from his time in the mines and delivering ice.

His drinking took its toll on the family, and his marriage. His wife vowed to leave him if he did not straighten up, as she was now pregnant with their fourth child. In September of 1947, she gave birth to their son.

With the birth of a son, HT's circle was finally complete! A son to teach how to hunt, how to fish, how to work the soil—all the things he loved to do. Yet one day in the spring of 1951, their son became sick. The doctors could not figure out what was wrong and recommended he be taken to a specialist. Unfortunately, the closest one was one hundred miles away.

The young boy was unable to walk. He laid in the back seat of the car the entire trip, only to rise once to look at a passing train. The diagnosis was polio. Fear ran through HT and Clara when the doctors informed them that losing their son was a possibility. It had been eleven years since the loss of his mother but the memory was as fresh as if it were the day before. He could not bear the thought of another loss.

HT made a pact with God that day—he would stop his drinking and change his ways if the Lord would save his only son. God kept his promise and so did he. On his son's birthday, the boy was released from the hospital with no side effects and in perfect health. Although this was a happy day for HT and his family it would change many things forever. Not only did he quit drinking, but also started attending church.

Having very little formal education, his reading skills were minimal, but that would only propel him to learn how to read. His desire to want to know God in a personal way gave him an insatiable appetite. It was sheer determination and desire that he would learn to read the Bible and hunting and fishing magazines. He also became an avid reader of the newspaper, staying abreast of the local and national news. Pushing himself was something he believed in, knowing that if you wanted to get ahead in life, it required action. He felt education was important, even though he had left school in the fifth grade.

HT, now age forty, had put twenty-nine years in the mining industry. His son had just turned eight years old, and HT thought it was time to start teaching him some skills. Since he had been taken out of school at such an early age, playing sports was something he never really had time for. However, he did play baseball on a team that represented some of the miners he worked with.

He was quite good as the catcher for the team, so he wanted his son to follow him and play the game. One Saturday morning, he and his son went to a nearby school for little league tryouts. Like any proud father, HT stood and watched, but to his dismay, his son failed miserably at every position. They left the field that day and things were never the same between the two. There would be no hunting, no fishing and no teaching his son how to grow things. Thus, HT and his son grew worlds apart.

When the boy got older, he rebelled and constantly got into trouble. He began drinking at a very young age that created strife in the family. HT and his wife were always fighting and their son was usually the cause. Dad wanted to discipline the boy, while Mom wouldn't allow it, protecting him. This would drive a wedge between HT and his son that would last a lifetime.

Dad in baseball uniform

CHAPTER 3
FEAR COMES IN MANY FORMS

With chaos and trouble between him and his wife, HT started to focus more on his job. He had an impeccable work ethic, so management recognized his leadership skills and wanted to promote him.

They not only liked his work but the way the other men would follow his lead, convincing them he was management material. The company had its concerns for several state exams had to be passed in order to become a mine foreman. Unfortunately, there were no workbooks or study material to prep before the exam. The company wasn't sure of his ability to read and understand the exam questions.

HT had been working for some time on improving his reading skills and felt he was ready for the test. He assured the people in management they had chosen the right person for the job. The day he sat for the State Mine Foreman's exam, he not only passed, but scored quite well—his lowest being ninety-four. It took two times to pass the exam, but HT was not a quitter.

HT went on to become the Sunday School Superintendent at his Free Will Baptist Church for more than a dozen years, and a deacon as well. He continued to grow in his walk with God and understanding of the Bible.

His family was maturing. The two older daughters were now married and only two children remained at home. HT's desire to stay busy continued so he embarked on a new venture. He was approached to sell tailor made suits, slacks, and jackets. He did so well that for years he never had to buy dress shirts or dress slacks, for the company paid him in clothing instead of money. He was the best-dressed $6,000 a year coal miner in that area.

As his selling improved, so did his management skills. He began to relate what he read in the Bible to his success at work. He believed what he read and practiced what it taught him. He did not borrow money and paid cash for every-thing. He had a savings program, believed in tithing, being a good steward and helping others.

The entire family was conservative. They had a garden and various kinds of fruit trees on the property. They picked berries as they came in season, canning and storing them for winter. The clothing he sold was of very good quality and at times, he would trade a suit or a couple pair of slacks for a side of beef.

HT loved to hunt and fish. There was a big chest freezer on the back porch always full of wild game and ham from his brother-in-law who would butcher a hog every fall. Shopping at the grocery store was not common for HT and his family. Bud his wife was part of a group of ladies that got together and made quilts for themselves and those in need. He lovingly called his wife 'Bud,' saying she could take a nickel and make a dollar out of it.

Every eight years, he traded cars and paid cash for them. He was a Buick man who would shop and pick out the car and then send Bud to do the trading. "I feel sorry for the poor salesman for he has no idea what he is up against," he often said.

HT used the talents and resources God gave him. He was good at what he did and loved his work—giving his all while on the job. The company he worked for knew he was an honest man that never missed a day's work or called in sick. His supervisor offered him another promotion, but it meant moving to a big city. He was excited about the thought of a promotion and when he was told what the job entailed and where he would have to move he thought, *Thank you God for this opportunity.*

At the interview, he was told his new job would take him to Pittsburgh, Pa.—many miles away from the life he had always known. The thought of moving from a small town to a major metropolitan city instilled a fear in HT that was unbearable. He just could not see himself living in a big city, so he turned down the job. When his son would later find this out it would create one more wedge between them.

HT spent a total of forty-eight years in the coal mines, breathing in coal dust, smoking Lucky Strike cigarettes, and loved every minute of it. At age sixty-two, he had to retire due to health reasons and lived another fourteen years. On May 19, at the age of seventy-six, he passed away from black lung that had finally got the best of him.

CHAPTER 4
WHAT THE BIBLE TAUGHT HT

If the principles in the Bible worked for HT, do you suppose they could work for others? Rest assured, he had no rich uncle or favorite aunt but worked and lived by what the Bible taught. He treated those he worked with fairness, kept his promises, and lived according to God's law.

Was he prefect? Far from it! Did he work to improve? Every day. Did he make mistakes? Many. Did he give up? Never! Did God reward him? Greatly! To the onlooker, this family was nothing out of the ordinary. By all standards, they were considered lower middle-class, but had something special you could not put your finger on unless you knew them personally. HT had a dream of doing better, setting a standard of raising the bar for his family. Did he accomplish what he set out to do? Was he met at the Golden Gate and told, "Well done, good and faithful servant?"

HT was my father and as I tell his story, a lump comes to my throat and tears well up in my eyes because I would have loved to have known him better. I wish I could have known what went on inside his mind as he read God's Word. In his mind, which many would call simple, he was an uncomplicated, down-to-earth man, seeking wisdom through Scripture. He refused to clutter his mind, march to the beat of someone else's drum, or get caught up in the fast pace life.

I would like to have heard him explain the verses he read from his King James Bible and what they meant to him as he learned the biblical principles. I would like to have heard him break it down in layman's terms for me. Did God do miraculous things for my father? I would say yes.

He spent forty-eight years in the coalmine industry and never had as much as a hangnail. Many who worked with him had died from roofs collapsing, crushed by equipment, electrocuted, lost limbs, and numerous other tragedies. Even though my father was in management for the majority of his years, he never pushed a pencil and was always in the mine alongside his men. He dearly loved what he did.

A *Biblical View of Prosperity* is meant to be used, not simply read. As you continue reading this book, mark passages that apply to your life, read carefully the "Think About It" sections, and don't forget to jot down your answers to those questions. Take the time to get to know the God my father knew, and in the process, I hope you see the way the LORD works in the lives of those who choose to follow him.

You may be thinking, "I don't see anything special about what HT did—all I see is someone who worked hard, saved his money, and lived wisely."

The simplest comment to that is: the philosophy he chose to live by was from the Bible; his father only taught him to work, drink, and fight. The Bible was where he got his instruction, his reason for living the way he did. He chose to do it God's way. He chose not to borrow. He chose to tithe and work in the summer to store up for winter and plan for the future.

This all came about because of what he read in the Bible. All these instructions came from the words he read and made a conscious choice to follow them, and in doing so, he walked a different path.

On that summer day in 1951, when HT made that vow: "God, save my son's life and I will give you my life," he took the first steps to a deeper relationship with God. He quit his drinking and saved his marriage, which shows that if you put faith to your feet it does make a difference.

What did HT discover? What was that revelation—that 'Aha moment?'

He discovered that reading his Bible, saying prayers, and being nice to those around him did not make him a better person. HT read verses in the Bible over and over, learning how to pronounce the words, then he got a dictionary to see the meaning of those he didn't understand. He knew that this was going to be a journey, not a stroll in the park. But, he had made a promise to God, and anyone who knew HT knew he was good at his word.

Over the years, the more he read, the more he understood. The more he understood, the more he trusted, and the more he trusted, the more it played out in his life and the life of his family. Some may say that HT lived a simple life, therefore, it was easy to accomplish what he did. But, what does the Bible say about prosperity and what did he accomplish? Was it a fluke?

As his journey unfolds, you will find many verses referring to wealth, happiness, peace, and everlasting life, but the most important thing you will discover is 'the lesson.'

Dad and Wayne shortly after Wayne came home from the hospital

The Bible was written over two thousand years ago. Many scholars have put their mark on it. Some agree, some don't, but the one thing they all admit is that, though the words in this book were written long ago, they are timely and apply to our lives today.

It is fair to state that the Bible is for the person who believes what is written in it. If you are like me and are a believer, then you are in for a wonderful ride. However, if you are not a believer, it is my hope and prayer that by the time you finish this book two things would have taken place.

First, God is now first in your life, and second, you have discovered what He says about prosperity. HT followed what he read and proved it to be a workable path. God gave him the ability to reason (discernment), or the sense to look before he leaped.

Though he watched his father's ambition turn to greed, then to alcohol and destruction, and then mimicked that in his own life, it was his desperation of saving his son's life that turned him to God. It's what he did next that made all the difference. HT chose to listen to God and take action.

As we look at the Old and the New Testament, digging deep into God's Word, even in Greek and Hebrew, you will notice how the words have multiple meanings, and different applications in most cases.

This deep study provides a flavor of what God was thinking when He spoke those words. It also offers insight into how the prophet was divinely guided or how the disciples gave direction when Jesus was teaching. It is exciting to see how it all unfolds.

There are many who doubt the Scriptures, or at least question them. In doing so, they may be missing on a blessing. If you ask any athlete what drives them to continue, they will tell you it is the faith and belief they have in themselves. The Scriptures tell us the same thing. They tell us to make a choice and once that choice is made, to act on it.

HT had to have been a blessed man to figure this out without technology, the concordance, and all the reference materials available today. God opened his eyes to help him understand. The saying of "when the student is ready, the teacher will appear," applies to him.

CHAPTER 5

INTELLIGENCE VS. WISDOM

H T was a wise man. But was he intelligent? What's the difference? By definition, the word wisdom means knowing what to do with knowledge, while intelligence means having that knowledge. While wisdom is the quality of having experience, intelligence is the ability to apply knowledge and skill. HT had both. He asked God for discernment, and God gladly gave it to him.

In James 1:5-8 (NIV), we read: *"If any of you lacks wisdom, you should ask God, who gives generously to all without finding fault, and it will be given to you. But when you ask, you must believe and not doubt, because the one who doubts is like a wave of the sea, blown and tossed by the wind. That person should not expect to receive anything from the Lord. Such a person is double-minded and unstable in all they do."*

Here we are told, "Ask and you will receive . . . generously." But in the next breath it warns us, "Don't be double minded." Many Christians today live in a state of compromise. Half of the time they live for God, while the other half is reserved for the things of this world, and the pleasures and treasures it provides. I was like that once.

Think About It

All of us have the privilege of asking Jesus for anything. What would you ask Him for?

After you write down your thoughts, let's break down some keywords to get a better understanding of what James is telling us in the above verse. As you read, notice the key word in bold print. Here we will define its meaning and give insight into the thought behind it. Keep in mind that this is about you—discovering if this biblical prosperity stuff is for real or just a bunch of hot air.

Did HT just get lucky, or did he ask God for wisdom? The word **wisdom** means to s*eek, be cunning and go higher.* Immediately, we are told to seek God, search for Him, and get to know Him better. When I hear the word 'cunning,' the first image that comes to mind is a snake charming its prey before it strikes and traps it.

We need to be cunning and wise in the marketplace. Learning and knowing our trade and all its ins and outs is our first step. Second, being alert to others' schemes and agendas, and recognizing when they are truly on our team, or when they are out to use us to get ahead.

Similarly, we ought to be cunning when learning God's Word so we can be prepared against the lies of this world and those who want to challenge us. Like anything in life, there's good and bad, and being ready for any situation we encounter is just smart.

Read and ask questions, go outside your comfort zone, stay late, come early, and be hungry for more. God knows we won't all be CEO's, but He also knows we all fall way short of the potential He has put in us.

When HT was presented the challenge of joining the ranks of management, he knew he had to be prepared to take the state exams. He talked with the electricians, machine operators, and construction crew and became an expert in all the different areas that helped him ace the exam.

James compares us to the **salty sea.** For many years, 'salt' was used to preserve meat, but once the salt lost its saltiness, it had no further use. In comparing us to the sea, we are given a similar message: "We need to maintain our saltiness."

How do we do that? James tells us we must believe and not doubt, because *he who doubts is like a **wave tossed** back and forth by the **wind.*** The wave is created by the wind pushing down on the water, which in turn causes pressure that forces the water back to the surface. As the motion continues, the waves get larger and they become billows even to the point of rage. James is telling us we will be subject to situations in our life that can cause pressure to the point of rage and we must maintain our composure.

This is where it is so important to seek God first. Then, seek godly counsel, and surround ourselves with strong Christian friends. Pressure will create a sense of urgency and invariably, we will make a hurried decision that can be costly. For that reason, the Bible reminds us not to make a decision when we are under pressure. It is never to our benefit, and very seldom is it ever the right one.

Not only does the wave bring pressure, but we are **tossed** back and forth by it. Another word for tossed is 'agitate' and all of us can think of a time when we were agitated. James warns us not to be the one who changes positions on a decision we have made. We are not to be a person who can't keep a commitment or tell others how it should be but does not follow his own advice.

HT never made a quick decision. He did a little research by going to his favorite book— the Bible. And he always prayed.

The Pharisees, that group or social movement in Jerusalem founded in 167 BC, who became the foundational, liturgical, and ritualistic basis for Rabbinic Judaism, were notorious for having two sets of rules: one for themselves, and one for everyone else.

The men who worked for HT liked him so much because he never asked them to do something he was not willing to do himself. He was also a man who kept his word. What he told you is what he did. Whatever shift he was working always met his quota. The men knew they could take him at his word. If he said, "We need eleven hundred ton tonight. If you finish at 10:30 at night, you are out of here," even though the shift ended at midnight, once the tonnage was met and the men cleaned their work area, they could leave.

On his shift, production was up, accidents were down, and overtime was at a minimum. It became a win-win situation for him, the men, and the company. His job was secured, the men looked forward to coming to work, and the company was making money.

Prior to HT reading and following God's Word, the decisions he made were not always as wise. Each passing year working in the mine gained him valuable experience. But he was always short on confidence; it would only grow after he turned his life over to God. Before then, on more than one occasion, pride would be a stumbling block for HT.

"I know your deeds, that you are neither cold nor hot. I wish you were either one or the other! So, because you are lukewarm—neither hot nor cold—I am about to spit you out of my mouth" Revelation 3:15-16 (NIV).

Being lukewarm is what I call 'a fence-straddle,' a person who refuses to get on one side of the fence when making a decision. You can't depend on this person to stand by it. HT always let his 'yes' be 'yes', and his 'no' be 'no.'

Think About It

It is vital for you to understand that the tossing motion can cause the wave to dash over you. You can easily lose direction, get confused, give up, and even panic. This is God's design to give you strength and focus. So, keeping that in mind, what storms are you facing and what lessons are you learning from it?

_____

_____

Even though waves can cause rage and confusion, by fixing our eyes on Jesus, He becomes the calm in the midst of the storm. God reminds us that being tossed about is merely a character-building session. The lesson we are being taught is how to maintain composure. We do this by maintaining our focus on Him.

There are two forces that cause the motion of a wave. One is the **rotation of the earth** and the other is the **wind.** The wind has so many faces, but none can be seen. It is like an invisible breath, coming from all four corners of the earth, driving those waves. Though we can't see it, taste it, or touch it, we know it is there. The wind can be the destruction in the midst of a violent storm or it can provide a cool breeze on a summer day. We love to see the flowers sway and dance to a summer breeze, which can only be done by the wind.

Our thoughts are different when a storm is brewing and we are alone. As the wind whips or howls, our mind runs rampant and our imagination can stir our fears with each creek or snap.

God is like the wind. Gentle, yet demands respect. It is all around us, but we can't see it and yet, we know it is there. It is just one more part of the puzzle that is provided by God to strengthen us.

HT had a strong back and developed big arms from working in the mines, but what he lacked was strength in wisdom. Through his persistent study of God's Word, he was given wisdom. Prior to knowing God, he relied heavily on his strong back and led by example. There was nothing wrong with this approach, except it was not as productive.

We are told to **think,** to use our heads before we form an opinion, and not just to take things at face value when we are presented with a situation. We are reminded over and over in the Bible to seek God's wisdom, gain knowledge, and get understanding.

These directives require for us to think critically and come to a conclusion. God is not satisfied with us just reading His Word or memorizing verses. He wants these words to become our foundation.

One way to develop this foundation is to get others' opinions, so that we may gain wisdom from a multitude of counselors. The Word also tell us to pay close attention to our surroundings and be wise in the guidance we seek.

HT knew the mine was a dangerous place. The roof could collapse and many a man had suffered broken backs from roof cave-ins. There were heavy power cables on the mine floor and water was always prevalent, or when they drilled at the face of the mine, into the coal seam, and blast it to bring the coal down.

The continuous miner that scooped the coal onto a conveyor belt had huge steel augers to crush the coal. A few men lost their lives by being careless around that machine. Methane gas was a near constant as huge fans moved the air through the mine. The average temperature year round was about 50 degrees. HT had safety meetings on a regular basis to remind his team how important it was to always be aware of their surroundings. But invariably, someone was foolish enough to think it would never happen to him.

Finally, we are told in this verse, "Not to be **double minded.**" Double minded means "two-spirited" and God is very clear on where He stands and expects us to do the same. To be two-spirited means there is a battle going on inside us. Of the two forces that are fighting to take control of our lives, there will be a clear winner. That winner will determine our direction for the rest of our lives.

God knows there will be those who will choose not to follow Him. His heart breaks for them, but because He has made us with free will, some will make a different choice. Double minded also means to evaporate. By choosing not to seek God's wisdom, at some point His direction will no longer be offered. We will find ourselves on the outside looking in, asking what happened. Many will look to blame God for where they are in life. Just remember: choices have consequences. Even in HT's pre-Christian days, his decision was always final. He made it on the knowledge he had gained and stuck to it.

"My son, if you accept my words and store up my commands within you, turning your ear to wisdom and applying your heart to understanding—indeed, if you call out for insight and cry aloud for understanding, and if you look for it as for silver and search for it as for hidden treasure, then you will understand the fear of the Lord and find the knowledge of God. For the Lord gives wisdom; from his mouth come knowledge and understanding"—Proverbs 2: 1-6 (NIV).

Think About It

Search for wisdom, hunt for it, and seek it out. Do you really believe those words? What is your first step when you are about to make a big decision in life?

_____

_____

God sees the heart of man. He knows we are prompted to make our own rules, to set our standards, to go our own way. And yet, He is patient with us. Though we may disappoint Him at times, He is always there, waiting for us to turn His way.

The way HT avoided making the wrong decisions in life was by seeking God's wisdom through His word. He grew up in a house with a lot of turmoil. The children observed a mother under fear and pain and a father who drank too much. This type of environment could have been an excellent breeding ground for failure. He had example after example of wrong choices and seeing what the consequences repeatedly brought. He had a real good road map of what not to do.

There's no doubt that HT was an intelligent man with more than just common sense. But the part and time in his life where he excelled the most came after his introduction to the Bible.

CHAPTER 6

THEY GET AWAY WITH IT. WHY CAN'T I?

Over the years, HT observed many a shift foremen, section boss, or mine superintendent. They cut corners, stole equipment, cheated the company and did things that put their men in danger, and thought they would never get caught. In fact, some of those men were actually rewarded in pay raises and promotions. HT often asked himself "Why can't I get that raise or promotion?"

The Book of Colossians, Chapter 3: 23-24 (NIV) answers that question. *"Whatever you do, work at it with all your heart, as working for the Lord, not for human masters, since you know that you will receive an inheritance from the Lord as a reward. It is the Lord Christ you are serving."*

Paul is very clear in the above verse. We should honor God with our work and give our employer, a full day's work for a full day's pay. We are to treat everything we do as if we are honoring God. We are to be good stewards with all the resources we have at our disposal, including our jobs.

Think About It

On a scale of 1 to 10, with 1 being "not good at all," and 10 being "outstanding," how would you rate yourself as a steward of God's resources?

_____

_____

The first keyword to study closely in the above verse is **whatever.** And that word simply means **"everything."** Here's a challenge for you: for the next two weeks work your particular profession as if God were your boss. Even if you are your own boss, try the experiment. Chart your progress each day for that two-week period, and most probably what you will see is this: in the first two to three days, that person who is your boss may start to notice you. By day five, his attitude toward you may start to change. By the following Monday, he begins to raise his expectations of you. By Wednesday, he is communicating with you regularly. By Friday, he has gained a whole new respect for you.

If your boss has an overseer, he has been telling his boss to keep an eye on you as well. The only problem is you can't go back to your old habits. But if you are being looked at for a raise or promotion, that's a good thing, right?

As you look at the word **whatever** and its meaning: *long, great, many, much and more,* take a look at the significance of each definition, as it relates to this word. Interestingly, each description can either produce a positive or negative effect on your life and its outcome.

The word **"long"** tells us anyone who has been in a skill for a long period of time is considered to be a very good master. Their work experience has allowed them to become seasoned at what they do. They can be depended upon to give good advice or to do excellent work. They are someone others seek because of their reputation and are in demand because they are the best. When looking at the word **"long,"** you automatically associate it with "many, much, more, and great."

The Bible refers to the gray hair on a man's head as a sign of wisdom and should be treated with respect. *"The glory of young men is their strength, gray hair the splendor of the old"* Proverbs 20:29 (NIV).

Does this mean that a young person is not wise? Far from it. But those years of experience have brought some lessons the younger person does not have. That experience can be a benefit, thus letting one avoid having to endure the same trials. Even the person with grey hair may not appear to be wise in the eyes of many. The old can do foolish things as well. You read or hear on the news almost daily of a senior citizen who has been taken advantage of. This is the reason you seek godly counsel—not just counsel.

There are many how-to books written by experts, and depending on the topic, you can find a plethora of them on basically anything. How to start your business, how to manage your money, how to plan your wedding, how to discipline your kids . . . Be sure to check the source, because when there is no alignment with biblical principles in their wisdom, then what sounds good is often flawed.

In the Book of Malachi 3:15 (NIV) we read, *"But now we call the arrogant blessed. Certainly the evil doers prosper and even those who challenge God escape."*

Think About It

Who, in your group of Christian friends can you go to for advice?

_____

_____

When you gain insight about something from non-believers, always be sure to align that wisdom with God's Word. The person who not only seeks to be wise but lives that wisdom out day by day will receive a double blessing. By taking the time to master your skill your rewards will be great and you will be in demand by many. And of course, the reward you receive in heaven blows away anything you could ever receive here. God will bless what you receive if you honor Him.

The harder you work, the luckier you get. In verses 23-24, Paul goes on to explain that we will **"receive,"** which means completion, separation, and departure. When you are on God's team and you're told you will receive something, that itself is a blessing. God chooses His people from all walks of life. We are broken, incomplete, and usually in need of repair. But the good news is He does not look at the current you or me, but the completed finished product. He is all about being the author and finisher, and One we look to make us whole.

We will be separated and singled out, one who others will seek to follow. God wants to separate. He is one who wants the good in a person to shine. He separates the wheat from the chaff, the good from the bad, and is always about His father's business. Being on His team, we are told to break the old habits and get rid of those things that cause us to stumble.

HT made sure he was always early for his shift. He wanted to walk the mine, check conditions, look for possible safety concerns, and see if the conditions in the mine were right for a productive shift. God expects us to always be setting the examples. We never know when He is going to say, "I need you now." If you are going to talk the talk, be prepared to walk the walk. Someone is always watching.

To separate also means departure, and God clearly explains we will depart from our old ways. When choosing to follow God, part of the separation process will include giving up something or someone. Some of your life-long friendships will end. One of the reasons is because they won't understand your new faith. They will reject you and this will be hurtful and cause you to wonder if you made the right choice.

To some, the decision to accept God over friends is too much and so, they will go back to their old ways. God is merciful and He never shuts His door on anyone. So, the invitation is always available to come back, as He wants us for the long haul. He is not interested in our speed, but wants those who are willing to endure.

Vince Lombardi, the head coach of the Green Bay Packers, a three- time Super Bowl winner lived by the basics. There were many articles written about him and was always referred to as "the disciplinarian." He was not a man who backed down, and expected his players to listen and to follow his rules or they would be penalized.

God is a lot like Vince. His rules are easy to understand and He expects us to follow them, but there is a difference. He will not penalize us when we don't obey. He will just let us deal with the consequences and not interfere.

HT didn't always listen to God. He was offered a job with a fellow Christian who was opening a mine. He was asked to be the general superintendent, which was a very big step up. He did not seek godly counsel or check out the persons' credentials, mainly because the man was a member of the church and a big sup- porter. So HT took a shortcut on God and it backfired in a big way. He walked away from a secure position with seniority to a situation that did not pan out. It took him some time to get back in the good graces of his old company, learning a valuable, but costly lesson.

Paul tells us we will receive an **inheritance,** meaning *a partitioning, getting by appointment, by lot, possessor of your share, law, to parcel out.* Our first reaction to these words indicates we will be in receivership of something. We think of it going hand in hand with the thought of plenty.

God is a generous Father. He has no problem rewarding those who do well. There are many examples in the Bible of God's generosity. He was merciful in His portioning—usually giving more than was asked for. When God appeared to Solomon in his dream and asked him what he wanted, Solomon replied, "*Your servant is here among the people you have chosen, a great people, too numerous to count or number. So give your servant a discerning heart to govern your people and to distinguish between right and wrong. For who is able to govern this great people of yours?*" 1Kings 3:8-9 (NIV).

Some scholars say there never has, or never will be one as wealthy as Solomon. The portion God will grant us will always be more than we need or deserve. One of the meanings of inheritance is that it will be given by appointment. Yes, there will be a test. God gave many examples of those He rewarded according to their ability.

In Luke 12:48, we read, *"But the one who does not know and does things deserving punishment will be beaten with few blows. From everyone who has been given much, much will be demanded; and from the one who has been entrusted with much, much more will be asked."*

C.S. Lewis once said, "We are half-hearted creatures and fall way short of our potential." Most are accused of being too greedy, when in fact we could achieve and accomplish much more than we do. The inheritance we receive will be portioned by lot. It will be our share—all we need to do is follow the Law God has written. Does this mean we can't raise the bar and qualify for more? God knows our potential—we don't. It is up to us to work and stretch ourselves beyond what we are accustomed to. We need to get outside our comfort zone and get uncomfortable. God will let us know when we reached our mark.

When HT chose to turn down the promotion that would have taken him out of his comfort zone, he lost much more than he ever imagined. The income he turned down was but a small part of what could have been for him and his family. In essence, his selfishness or fear of moving to a big city was costly to his entire family. Remember, God lets us make our own choices. The difference in the outcome is whether we involve Him or not. This was a lesson that would haunt HT for the rest of his life.

He turned thirty-five in January of 1947. By that time, his mother had been dead for seven years and his third daughter was now seven. His drinking was escalating, things were out of hand between he and his wife Bud, and she discovered she was pregnant. She threatened to leave HT if the drinking did not stop. He agreed to slow down, but he didn't stop. Their baby boy was born in September, and HT was elated! He went to the mine and told everybody he had a son.

For the next three-and-a-half years, things were pretty stable in the Wooldridge household. HT slowed down on his drinking, the oldest sister helped take care of the baby boy and all seemed to be going well. And then came things took a quick turn.

Their son, named Wayne, got sick and no diagnoses could determine his illness. HT and Bud took him to a specialist, who suspected the boy had polio. At the time, polio was a deadly disease, and those who survived were left with permanent nerve damage, leaving a patient confined to a wheelchair. Unfortunately, the closest hospital equipped to treat polio was a little over one hundred miles away.

HT and Bud laid Wayne in the back seat on a pillow, covered him with a blanket, and drove to the hospital. The road was windy and the trip was close to five hours. In the quietness of the long trip, HT made that pact with God. He said, "If you let my son live, I will give you my life." God kept his end of the bargain and so did HT

Over the next six months, many one-hundred-mile trips would be taken while their son was going through treatments to see how he would respond to the newly approved vaccine. In September of 1951, Wayne was released to go home. The doctors said he escaped the crippling effects of polio and the only side effect may be one leg a little shorter than the other. As it turned out, that did not occur. HT changed his ways and God kept his promise.

This inheritance is something we will receive as a **reward,** which is a sign of completion. It is also referred to as 'recompense and we will render.' When one encounters the word 'reward' most would naturally think of some good pleasure. Paul is reminding us that God may recompense us, which carries two meanings: If we do good there is a reward, and if we do wrong, there is a reward. God is in the business of keeping us on the right path. This means chastisement to which God sees as a reward because of the good that will come out of it.

The Bible prepares us for a life-long journey. As God equips us, He in turn expects us to go and equip others. Each step of the journey that we complete is most often so subtle it is never recognized.

HT figured out early on that labor equaled reward, but it took him a long time to see how he could compound his efforts. One day, as we look back and realize what we have accomplished, it will then dawn on us how far we have come. We need to stop and thank the One who made it possible to make that journey. That is all God asks us to do—remember the One who made it possible.

Think About It

God expects us to give up and give back. We give up our pride—the "I" in all we do. The give back includes our time, talents, and resources. In the lines below, write down what you are willing to give up and give back.

We wrap up this verse with the word **serve,** meaning bondage to, tie, binding and must. Paul tells us that we are to serve a God who paid a dear price for us. We need to serve Him with all our heart.

Many people rebel when they are told to do something because they feel they have the right to do what they want. God has given us the freedom to make our own decisions, and do our own thing. However, what if the choice we make turns out to be a bad choice? Then what? Will God come to our rescue? Will he give us a second chance, or will He just let us figure it out on our own?

The answer is actually all of the above. He will come to our rescue and give us a second chance. However, the consequences have already occurred, and we will have to deal with it on our own. He will even give us direction, but we have to take care of it. The ability to choose separates us from every other creation.

The lion sees the cobra and thinks it has to attack, the cobra strikes and the lion dies. Man sees the cobra and knows it is deadly and goes the other way and lives. So when God gives us a directive, He is doing it for our good, not just because He is someone who likes to give orders.

In serving God, we bind ourselves to Him. This is a good thing. He will give us some rope, but not enough to hang ourselves. He is very matter of fact in saying, "We must serve Him and can't have two Gods." He is not a part timer. It is Him —all the way. This is the part many find difficult to accept. They want a God who is convenient at their beckon call but not always looking over their shoulder.

God does not operate that way. His book of rules (laws) is very clear on this. In, *"Thou shalt have no other God before thee,"* is pretty clear, leaving no room for misinterpretation. Then, it just comes down to making a decision of which side of the fence you are on.

In bringing these verses to a close, Paul tells us to do our work for God, not man. Raise your standards higher; not just for the day, but always. Complete what you start. This will separate you from the crowd and set you on the path to plenty with expectations of greatness. God does not have a problem in providing the reward. The real issue is, are we willing to do our part? His rules are really rather simple, but very matter of fact. No shortcuts. Just do it.

HT learned that if you do a good job, you get recognized. The more you get recognized, the more those in charge take notice, and soon a promotion follows. However, he took his eyes off the prize, as he and his wife argued over things. Bud wanted the house to look nicer but HT argued that they didn't have the extra money.

"We would if you had taken that promotion," Bud would quip. And that quickly escalated the tension in the house. There were good times too.

CHAPTER 7
WHOSE MONEY IS IT, ANYWAY?

I grew up in a house where there were three hot meals every day and family time around the table. During the summer, especially during lunch when my father worked the afternoon shift, we all ate together. There was laughter, open discussion, and everyone was involved in each other's lives, unlike today.

At 12 noon every day my mother had the radio on listening to a hard-core preacher on WOAY. I can still picture him. Red-faced, tie loose, pounding the pulpit saying, "Give your life to God or you are going somewhere that you aren't going to like."

You can only hear that so many times before you begin to wonder: *am I surrendering to God out of fear or do I truly want him in my life?* I don't remember if he asked for money. I'm sure he did, but I don't know if my parents sent any to him. But I do know this—there is a stigma attached to ministers and money.

I was invited to have dinner with three gentlemen the other day after we had closed a real estate transaction. The conversation was light and general. We were close in age, and had several things in common. The conversation worked its way around to business ventures as the one gentleman had experienced considerable success.

His brother said, "As a young man, I was told: 'if you want to make big money, become a minister, a banker, or get into insurance.'" That is a prime example of the stigma attached to the church and preachers. People have this barrier built up resisting those who proclaim the gospel feeling, "When is he going to drop the question?"

The whole *name it and claim it* movement of the 90s was such a scam. It was beyond ridiculous! Therefore, the question still remains in the back of many people's minds when they hear a verse quoted, such as the one about to be discussed.

I heard the words to a song one day that went something like this. *The one who leads me by the hand I cannot feel and ask me to walk the path I cannot see. Is this called faith?*

As we look back on what HT accomplished, we can easily say it was not a big deal. Actually, it is not that much at all. But when you take into account that he started out making a dollar a day—$3,120.00 a year—and when he retired at sixty-two he was at $25,000.00 a year—that is more than 80% increase. But more importantly, it is not the increase, but how he managed God's money. That's right, he realized it was not his; he was just a manager for God. God blessed him abundantly.

In HT's early years before he came to know God, a lot of his hard-earned money went for booze, clothing, and cars. That changed once he got married, started raising a family, and the declaration he made when his son became sick.

God has a way of turning the tables on us. What was once considered a necessity becomes frivolous, and what was once considered a must is no longer necessary. As you begin to study the Bible, you will start to understand the principles God has laid out. Once you sense of them, then comes the discipline of following them.

HT remembered the hard work he put in to free himself from under his father's rule and the only way that would happen was to create enough income to be on his own. In time, he learned to live by the Word of God.

"For we live by faith, not by sight," Paul says in 2 Corinthians 5:7 (NIV). This verse is short and to the point. It does not leave much to discussion, so let's explore it.

Paul wrote this letter to the church at Corinth around 55A.D. *We are told to live*, meaning to take a certain direction or **walk**—*proof of ability, completeness, companion, and at large.* In modern day terminology it is often said, "I hear what you are saying, but your actions don't follow your words." Another saying is, "You talk the talk, but I don't see you walking the walk."

Live it out or walk by faith, and show our commitment daily in our actions. That's what Paul said, and he had a passion to tell others about his walk with Jesus for he was on fire for the Lord. He was committed to telling everyone about the gospel as long as he was in his earthly body. Paul lived by the Word of God and his actions proved that daily. He was challenged to the point of imprisonment, but that never weakened his faith.

Paul was never alone. He knew God was always at his side and demonstrated his courage every chance he got. Throughout the Bible, we are told to have faith, and are reminded that God will be at our side even though we can't see Him.

In John 20:18-27, we see when Jesus appeared to His disciples. *"On the evening of that first day of the week, when the disciples were together, with the doors locked for fear of the Jewish leaders, Jesus came and stood among them and said, 'Peace be with you!' After* he said this, he showed them his hands and side. The disciples were overjoyed when they saw the Lord."

"So the other disciples told him, 'We have seen the Lord!' But he said to them, 'Unless I see the nail marks in his hands and put my finger where the nails were, and put my hand into his side, I will not believe.' A week later his disciples were in the house again, and Thomas was with them. Though the doors were locked, Jesus came and stood among them and said, 'Peace be with you!' Then he said to Thomas, 'Put your finger here; see my hands. Reach out your hand and put it into my side. Stop doubting and believe.'"

Our walk is done by **faith,** *truthfulness of God, conviction, and reliance upon Christ.*

All we do should be centered on God. It is like stepping into a strange dark room and feeling along the wall to find the light switch. As your mind imagines, you listen to every sound, your senses heighten, and you have certain anxiousness until you find the switch. Once the switch is found, you quickly turn it on and a sigh of relief comes as the dark becomes light. Your tenacity keeps you going until you find the switch.

God is our switch. Each time we become anxious or our fears overtakes our thoughts, we need to turn to Him. It is so easy to doubt every turn we take and every decision we make, when all we have to do is go to His word and He will provide a peace that surpasses all understanding.

I imagine HT had a difficult time grasping this concept, having only a fifth-grade education. He learned to read the Bible, then figured out what it was saying, being brave enough to step out in faith to see it work. This lesson would be invaluable to HT for once he began to see results nothing would waver his belief.

Many times, we develop tunnel vision believing that it works in one area of your life, but not applying it to all areas. This is what HT did.

HT struggled with verses like, "And the peace of God, which transcends all understanding, will guard your hearts and your minds in Christ Jesus" Philippians l 4:7 (NIV). He began to pay attention to the times he went to God to seek His strength. It may have been a time of trouble or a situation he was dealing with. The more he depended on Him, the more he had peace.

He discovered the more sincerely he took God's Word the more it worked in his life. By seeking His guidance and trusting that He would provide the answer, a peace came over him, regardless of the severity of the concern.

He learned to trust God and, more importantly, to seek His Word to help in those situations. God does not want us to come running to Him only in times of trouble, although it seems that is when most of us do. He wants our dependence on Him at all times. This taught HT an invaluable lesson as well as helped him grow in his walk with God.

Paul then says, *"For we live by faith, not by **sight**"* 2 Corinthians 5:7 (NIV). It is clear as we read this passage that our walk with God is to be taken as a blind man. We need to depend on another and the one we need to depend on is God.

Think About It

God provides insight into what we read in His Word, which in turn develops and allows us to put action to our belief. Test Him on this. Re-read 2 Corinthians 5:7. Write down how your renewed mind has led you to have a new perspective on things.

Today's advertising promises society many things; most often it promises happiness. *Do it your way. I want it now. It is my life.* Companies can influence the way people lead their lives and perceive their needs and wants upon viewing an advertisement. But all of this points to the *Self*, creating in us a very inward focus. God chastises the man whose only thought is of himself.

All his gain, whether great or little, will end in misery. In Proverbs 1:19 (NIV), we read: *"Such are the paths of all who go after ill-gotten gain; it takes away the life of those who get it."*

People are taught to be self-sufficient and independent. God wants the same, except He wants us to rely on Him for all our instructions. Though, man wants to do it his way, God's way is better. Thus, the battle of the mind incurs.

It's like a kid who wants to ride a bike but wants his father to hold on so he won't fall over. But once he gets the hang of it, he wants him to watch from a distance. Then, as he becomes really good at riding his bike, he wants his father to let go and let him ride! But when the father tries to put restrictions on him, the kid rebels, because he thinks he knows best.

Can you imagine how HT must have felt when he was pulled out of school at age eleven and told his school days were over?

"Tomorrow you will start working in the mines," his father told him one day. "We need you to help with the family bills and the income you earn will be to help support the family."

"All work and no play makes Jack a very dull boy," the old adage says And there's a lot of truth to that. Resentment, anger, fear, and sadness were just a few of the emotions HT felt for a long period of time. Since it would be several years before he gave his life to God, one can only imagine the emotional roller coaster his life was on. He did not know or understand how to call on God.

Man is the same as the child learning to ride his bike. He tells God to leave him alone, and God steps out of the picture. But the minute the man gets in a bind, he looks up and says, "how about a little help, God?" So, God pulls the man out of the mess and man takes off only to find himself in another predicament later.

In Romans 1:18 (NIV), we read: *"The wrath of God is being revealed from heaven against all the godlessness and wickedness of people, who suppress the truth by their wickedness."*

This means that this type of behavior will last only so long. Then man will continue to go his perverse ways and toward destruction. This is called, "walking by sight," having no interaction with faith and the end is usually not good. You have the right to say, "I will take my chances" and you definitely have that freedom. But, at what cost?

"You also must be ready, because the Son of Man will come at an hour when you do not expect him" Luke 12:40 (NIV). That is not meant to put fear in us, but to make us think.

Think About It

When we walk by faith and not by sight we have a certain confidence—even a remarkable inward peace that says we know it is going to be okay. Can you look at your life and see where God has increased your faith as you relied on Him?

In HT's pre-Christian days, he relied on his brawn, not his brain, which was not uncommon, as so many men thought strength would overcome their adversity. He grew up fast, and drinking, smoking, and fighting, became a way of life. Very few fights did he come away from on the losing end.

As a result, he became callus and indifferent, thinking only about himself. There would be many more years of drinking before he would come to know God, and many more before he would trust to walk by faith.

HT was a manager who did not push a pencil. He was underground with his men. He knew each of their jobs and explained the duties and the dangers. He always stood by his word. He did not swear or lie to his men. He stuck by what he said and followed God's example. The more he learned about what God's Word said, the more he lived it, day in and day out.

CHAPTER 8

THAT'S NOT FAIR. HE IS NO BETTER THAN ME!

Hard work was no stranger to HT, however being treated fairly didn't seem to be in his favor. He watched as other shift foremen received promotions, pay raises, better working conditions, and so he wondered why he did not get them as well.

He knew these other foremen were cheating on their tonnage reports allowing their men to work in unsafe and unclean working conditions; turning their backs and allowing men to walk off with tools that did not belong to them. He had more than one of his men come tell him of these things and some he had witnessed himself. When he would bring it up to his superior he was told they would look into it. Yet nothing was ever done. And the more he spoke about it to his boss, the more they seemed to distance themselves from him.

He started to feel as if he was the one being punished, and in time, he discovered that the ones he reported to were some who were dismissed. He felt cheated and that his efforts, honesty, and hard work were not being recognized. Bitterness began to creep in, and old memories would rush in, taking him back to the days when he was still living at home and his father would take his entire paycheck, giving him nothing—not even a thank you—and spending most, if not all, of it on whiskey.

HT came to a conclusion that life is not fair and looking out for others does not have much reward. And yet, there was something different about him. Regardless of how he felt about his working conditions or circumstances, he could not bring himself to slack on his responsibilities to his men or the company. God was working on him.

In Matthew 25:15-28, we read where Jesus tells the Parable of the Bags of Gold. *"To one he gave five bags of gold, to another two bags, and to another one bag, each according to his ability. Then he went on his journey."*

After a long period of time, the Master returns and summons his servants to settle the accounts. *"The man who had received five bags of gold brought the other five. 'Master,' he said, 'you entrusted me with five bags of gold. See, I have gained five more.' His master replied, 'Well done, good and faithful servant! You have been faithful with a few things; I will put you in charge of many things. Come and share your master's happiness!'"*

The second servant received the same reward since he doubled his talents. The one who received one talent was afraid of his master. *"So I was afraid and went out and hid your gold in the ground. See, here is what belongs to you."*

"His master replied, 'You wicked, lazy servant! So you knew that I harvest where I have not sown and gather where I have not scattered seed? Well then, you should have put my money on deposit with the bankers, so that when I returned I would have received it back So take the bag of gold from him and give it to the one who has ten bags.

"For whoever has will be given more, and they will have an abundance. Whoever does not have, even what they have will be taken from them. And throw that worthless servant outside, into the darkness, where there will be weeping and gnashing of teeth.'"

Two of the servants were faithful and obeyed, while one did not, so who is at fault? Is it the Master or is it the servant? Most would jump to the rescue of the servant and say the Master is being too harsh. But if we look closely and assess the situation, we find that in the beginning the Master chose three servants whom he trusted and felt were qualified to manage his business while he was away.

Two of the servants saw this as an opportunity to prove to their Master they were qualified, while the third decided to rest on his reputation. His choice was costly. He not only lost his job, but he was stripped of his title and put out into the street as a beggar. Is the Master being cruel or is he making a business decision?

This example of a business decision that had to be made, and the example that was set sent a clear message to anyone who was considering management. "If you do well, the Master really takes care of you, but if you try and slide by, expect to pay the price."

In today's business world you need to do a survey. We as business people need to be aware of our surroundings, be current on our local economy, and be prepared to make the necessary changes. Meaning, we have to create alliances, keep our finger on the pulse, and be ready to switch gears if necessary. In defense of the Master, we must admit the third servant was not creative or sought the help of his teammates at all. There was obviously enough to go around; he was just unwilling to be a team player.

Think About It

Has God entrusted you with a task, job, or assignment? If so, write it down here or on a separate piece of paper as a reminder not to forget it.

I wonder how HT would have responded to this situation? We know he was unhappy with the outcome of how he was passed over and felt he was not being noticed. We also come to find out his consciousness will not let him do less than his best. I think it would be safe to say the Master would have been saying, "Well done, good and faithful servant. You have been faithful with a little and I will put you in charge of much." But, like most of us, HT needed some time to learn this lesson.

The key words in these verses are: **faithful, trustworthy,** and **obey.** The master was going on a long journey and he needed people he could trust who would run his operation exactly as he would. He chose three men whom he thought he could trust and would obey his orders.

This life is always going to be a proving ground of one type or another. There are always going to be challenges (tests). There will be those who will step up, and those who will fail. That is the reality of it. We, as humans, don't like to look at it in those terms because it is too black and white.

But God is exactly like that. He states there is a right and a wrong. To God, there is no grey area, no maybe, no little white lie, and He does not skirt the issue.

Exodus 23:2-3 (NIV) is a good reminder of that.

"Do not follow the crowd in doing wrong. When giving testimony in a lawsuit, do not pervert justice by siding with the crowd, and do not show favoritism to a poor man in his lawsuit."

Matthew next tells us we are to be **servant's** bondsman, slave bind. These words all indicate we belong to someone else. To be in bondage, a slave or bound to another would seem that we are not free to be, or do. But, as we study God's Word, we see the more we bind ourselves to Him, the more freedom we have. The more we lose ourselves of the carnal things we thought we needed to make us happy, the happier we actually are.

Think About It

Freedom from the daily burden you carry is possible if you are willing to study God's Word and gain a deeper understanding. So, what should you do to put those words into practice today?

HT definitely felt he was in bondage. He had felt this way since age eleven when his childhood was robbed from him—having to work very hard and not being allowed to enjoy any of the fruits. Many a weekend would find him drinking, fighting, and getting angry at the world. He felt helpless to do anything about it. He knew he was smart and had talent, he just did not know how to channel it.

Matthew brings to our attention the word **talent, balance, certain weight, uphold, be driven**, and **endure.** These are fascinating words to be associated with. Just imagine your Master has just given you a huge promotion because you have been faithful. Now the day has come and you just received your promotion and are being put in charge of much. Your whole economic picture is about to change in a big way.

A big pay raise is on the horizon. You can now buy the home you have always wanted, send the children to a private school and get rid of that car that has two hundred fifty thousand miles. Your list of wants is huge. There are two cautions that get thrown to the wind every time this scenario occurs. We spend it before we get it, and we spend more than we get. Don't get caught up in reading your own press clipping and forget your Master who has entrusted you with this new-found wealth.

What has now changed? This new position requires counseling, developing new relationships, traveling in new circles, and more demands of your time. Do you remember the schedule you used to keep? The discipline that got you the promotion? This is not a time to slack or let up. You have momentum and need to stay focused.

Focus on the word **talent,** which was what your boss saw in you, and what got you the promotion.

Think About It

The first word associated with talent is balance. So, if you were to get a promotion, how are you going to balance all that is coming at you from your new position?

_____

_____

What do you think HT did when he was approached about joining management? He had to prepare for an exam, so how do you suppose he spent his extra time?

The first thing God wants is balance. And precisely in this order: God, family, and work. We need to spend time daily in God's Word and to continue to hone our skills. This will allow us to maintain the proper perspective: both at home and work. We then can help others to attain their desired dreams. Balance also states our need for family time as a group and time with each individual. Talent also means to continue to increase your skill level to stay on top of your game.

We next look at **certain weight**. Years ago, a lot of people would use this phrase in judging a person's worth in their weight. It may have been said that someone who was considered a good worker, that they were worth their weight in gold.

There is another direction we can go and that is how we handle our priorities. On what do we base who gets attention or what gets done first?

In Acts 10: 34-35 (NIV), we read: "Then Peter began to speak: I now realize how true it is that God does not show favoritism but accepts men from every nation who fear him and do what is right." This means, we all get equal treatment.

HT was noted for fair and equal treatment and his men could count on his word. They knew they all had an equal chance at being recommended for the promotion for the ball was always in their court.

Matthew tells us to **uphold,** meaning you're going to continue to keep the same standards as before the promotion and the same desire to push for excellence. Management has a tendency to let their subordinates do all the grunt work. A good manager is not afraid to roll up his or her sleeves and get in the trenches alongside his people. The strongest characteristic HT had was his skill to communicate with his men. He did that best in the trenches, besides them. They could never accuse him of not knowing the conditions in the workplace, because he was always there.

You also uphold the integrity of the company at all cost and you see that those who work for you do the same. Integrity is high on God's list, also. By following the same principles that got you the promotion and the drive that took you up the corporate ladder, you want to maintain that same principle throughout life.

"Do you see a man skilled in his work? He will serve before kings; he will not serve before obscure men " Proverbs 22:29 (NIV).

God expects our best. By doing the work to please Him, we will please all the others.

Think About It

Endure. Paul says, "I run the race not for the crown, but to finish what I started." Think of your life, and the race that God has given you. What will you do today to ensure you will cross the finish line?

_____

_____

This reminds me of the Olympic runner who was expected to win the four hundred-meter when he pulled a hamstring and his father ran out of the stands wanting to assist. The runner waved his father off indicating he wanted to cross the line on his own. He was expected to take home the gold, but instead he came in last.

"Do you not know that in a race all the runners run, but only one gets the Prize? Run in such a way as to get the prize" 1 Corinthians 9:24(NIV).

Those are all pretty challenging words and call us to a much higher standard than most of us are used to. What do we put most of our time into? Is it that which benefits us, or that which is best for God? If we have trouble distinguishing between the two then we need to spend more time in God's Word and in the counsel of godly men. We should set an example in every aspect of our lives for others to witness.

Certain weight means to have a balance in every aspect of your life and not to overcompensate in one area, because you are weak in another. God expects us to uphold His law and not to be like a two-edged sword. He expects us to talk the talk and walk the walk. We are human and will make mistakes. But, we need to own up to the mistake and take the consequences. We must be willing to learn and set the example for others who may hold us in high esteem.

Don't be a disappointment to others. Instead, be a beacon of light to draw others to you. We are told in the Scriptures to go about your Father's work with zeal. Have passion for the obligations you have committed to. Give your boss more than a day's work. Don't be so concerned with what your coworker does. Focus on what the Lord has entrusted to you, which is much more.

Do you want even more? Then do more! God will let you know when you have reached your limit and when your plate is full. Remember, you are setting examples for others to follow and to encourage those who have low self-esteem, not so that you stand up and beat your chest and say, "Look at me."

"Similarly, anyone who competes as an athlete does not receive the victor's crown except by competing according to the rules" 2 Timothy 2:5 (NIV).

Life throws a lot of curves; each day presents us with challenges. Some days we would like to stay in bed and wait till the sun rises the next day. As the day brings us its obstacles, we need to seek God as our encourager.

Shutting down for just a moment may make all the difference in the world concerning a particular situation. We need to learn to endure: not give up or give in. I like a challenge and when a plan comes together, I love to see a finished product come from something rough, unpolished and rugged. When I coached junior high football one of the greatest feelings I enjoyed was seeing the finished product. As the season progressed and I saw that the seventh, eighth or ninth grader turn into a well-oiled machine, it was worth all the pain.

In the fall, a month before the season began, we had two drills for conditioning and learning the basics. On those hot August days many wanted to quit, but it was my job to be their encourager—to assure them that it would all be worth it if they finished. God is telling us the same things in His word. Stick to it and continue to learn. Yes, there will be days you will want to quit, but hang in there. He assures us it will be worth it.

Why do you suppose HT was chosen to be a supervisor over other men? He may have had the least education, his English was probably not the best, and his writing skills were probably very poor, so why him?

Upper management who observed him from up close and afar recognized he had some excellent skill sets. He was honest, he knew how to communicate to his men, and his production was always up while his costs were in line.

He was trustworthy, dependable, oriented, and displayed a desire to finish strong. Since he was such a hard worker they knew he would improve on his language and his writing skills.

Even though others saw these skills in HT, he did not see them in himself. At this point in his life, everything that he had accomplished was just from pure hard work. He was wise enough to understand his physical strength would not always be his strong suit.

CHAPTER 9
IT SEEMS THEY GET ALL THE BREAKS

Some people get all the breaks, while you are left on the sidelines wondering, *why not me?* Yes, life is not fair. You may work your tail off and it may go unnoticed, while your coworker, who didn't put forth any extra effort gets the promotion. Be careful not to show it. Those who are responsible for moving you forward not only watch your actions, but also your reactions.

HT was beginning to wise up and learned from his mistakes and way of thinking. When confronted by upper management with the comment about his lack of education he could have become defensive, but he chose to take it as a challenge. Instead of feeling sorry for himself or thinking, "I will never get ahead because my father made me go to work at age eleven and quit school," he chose to say, "I can do this. Give me the chance and I will show you."

He was confident in making that statement because he was busy preparing himself for such an occasion. He knew if he expected to get ahead he had to prepare. It was not going to be handed to him.

Two things were happening in his life. First, he was a true leader who helped his fellow workers.. Second, he spent time at night and weekends learning how to read and taking an interest in the affairs of his community. His life continued to change without realizing it, he was preparing for the next step.

Think About It

The Bible teaches us that preparation is a must and the one who does nothing to prepare is a fool. In what areas of your life do you need to prepare or adjust?

_____

_____

As you are thinking about that, consider the powerful words in this next verse:

"Do not judge and you will not be judged. Do not condemn, and you will not be condemned. Forgive, and you will be forgiven. Give and it will be given to you. A good measure, pressed down, shaken together and running over, will be poured into your lap. For with the measure you use, it will be measured to you"

Luke 37-38 (NIV).

Humans are notorious for judging others. We are all guilty of being quick to pass our opinion. In my eight years of coaching, I heard many comments from the stands as to how to do my job. We called them "The Friday night coaches."

Many who sat in those stands gave an opinion and freely judged the coaches on the sidelines. Coaching those young men was a difficult task, but we enjoyed it because of the end result. Our team was full of talent. At almost every position it made it difficult to give the players equal time on the field. We felt it was important to accomplish this knowing these kids may not have this opportunity at the next level. We caught a lot of flack from the fans because of our philosophy. We stuck to our guns, but the pressure was sometimes unbearable. Looking back, it's hard to recall how cruel some people were with their words.

HT experienced this same kind of ridicule from other foremen who were younger, more educated, and who came from, what they considered, better families. Their fathers who taught them how to play baseball, took them hunting, fishing, and attended their Friday night sporting event. All the things HT had never experienced.

Growing up fast, hard, and missing out on his boyhood made him bitter. He had a tendency to wear those feelings on his shoulder, and those who judged him left a mark he carried for many years. In his bitterness, he began to judge condemn, criticize and question another's ability.

Think About It

How does God view judging?

_____

_____

To **judge** is to condemn, determine, or call in question. When we put ourselves in the position of being a judge, two things will occur. We tell others we're qualified to pass an opinion and set ourselves up for others to ridicule us.

Rest assured, once you elevate yourself to a position of authority others will take potshots at you. Rich Devos, the co-founder of the Amway Corporation once said, "When you put yourself upon a pedestal, expect to be knocked off."

What Luke is telling us is that once we put ourselves in the position of judging, we should also expect others to watch us more closely. Once we have condemned another, people are waiting and watching for you to make the same mistake.

We take great pleasure in watching another fall and God addresses the gloater as well. Judging means 'to warn' and this is why God is telling us to be careful. By judging, we are condemning another and when we condemn we are pronouncing a sentence on that individual.

With condemnation comes a label that means something, or someone, is going to carry it for a long time. In other words: a scar that may take a long time to heal. When we condemn someone, realize the rippling effect that it will cause. There may be a time when others will do the same to us. When we bring it upon ourselves to judge, we are in fact deciding to make a determination about another person or situation. Either way the pronouncement of a sentence can be very damaging. As humans, we are quick to judge. It is in our nature to point the finger and bring down the gavel.

Being a judge is a very critical position to put ourselves into because we are calling into question another person's character and integrity. Making sure we have all the information is crucial when calling someone into question. We should keep our own house in order before we go and make claims against others.

Luke wants us to get a complete understanding of the word **condemn,** *to consume, burn down, or against,* taking on a whole different meaning than we previously discussed. We need to look closely at the verse to internalize what Luke wants us to see. Do not condemn (consume) means "To set on fire or burn down."

It is wrong if our judgment takes us to the point of being the judge, jury, and executioner. It is better to go to the one who is accused and confront them directly. By dealing directly with the accused the information one receives is better accessed. We should never take another's word without first checking with the accused.

This does require us to do a complete and thorough investigation of our own. Whatever the circumstances, we should never draw a conclusion without seeking counsel or asking questions. God is not in the business of condemning; He is in the business of forgiving.

Think About It

God has no favorites, and no one is held in higher esteem than another. So why should we? About whom do you need to begin to judge less and love more?

_____

_____

"Whoever is not with me is against me, and whoever does not gather with me scatters." Matthew 12:30 (NIV). We are not in a position to be against another. By choosing to be against someone we make a choice that requires an explanation. This, in turn, gives an opinion to others requiring them to choose sides, and the results can have tremendous impact on someone's life. The more reason to follow God's law and not judge somebody else.

Does this mean we are to turn our backs and look the other way? No. God calls us to be accountable for our actions. We are not to be the judge and jury; instead, we are to do our due diligence by confronting the issue, disclosing the injustice, reconciling the difference, leaving God to heal the wound.

In Jeremiah 22:3 (NIV), we read: *"This is what the Lord says: Do what is just and right. Rescue from the hand of the oppressor the one who has been robbed. Do no wrong or violence to the foreigner, the fatherless or the widow, and do not shed innocent blood in this place."*

When HT heard something said about him. his anger raged, and he was ready to fight. He later learned that fighting only solidified the words that were being said about him.

This school of hard knocks became unbearable. The lesson he later learned was that God's timing was different than his.

Forgiving was hard for him. He had made a mistake by quitting his job and taking the new position because things were not coming together as promised.

So, he went to God and asked for forgiveness, then counseled with some Christian men and talked with his wife. Then he made a decision based on sound counsel.

After telling his wife, he went to the owner, stating his concern. After they talked things through, they came to a resolution and he eventually returned to his former company. God forgave HT but that did not eliminate the consequence of lost wages, time out of work, and tension between him and his wife. This all could have been avoided.

Think About It

What mistakes do you need to bring to God and ask Him for forgiveness?

_____

_____

The apostle Luke tells us to **forgive,** *to free, fully, let go, put away and divorce.* This should be easy to understand, but most of us have a tendency to hang onto feelings. We let them lay dormant in a subconscious state, waiting for the opportune time to unleash them. When we refuse to let go of feelings it is usually the result of emotion mixed with pain. We feel the need to have justice. There is a saying, "Yesterday is gone, tomorrow may never come, all we have is today, take it and give thanks."

There is a great freedom in forgiving. When uncovered, most bitterness comes from unforgiveness. We will inflict ourselves with this torment for years ignoring the only person we are hurting—ourselves. The other person either does not know or has long forgotten the incident.

Forgiveness has to start from two different places: one, addressing the issue, and two, being willing to get past it. If these two issues are never discussed then forgiveness will never be erased from the wounded person's mind. We must put it away. Divorce ourselves from it and bury the hatchet. We can't move forward as long as we are dealing with issues from the past.

H.T's past—his father's drinking, abusing his mother, her untimely death, being pulled out of school at age eleven, no childhood . . . gave him plenty of reasons for not forgiving. His work environment, drinking, and God not being in the picture left him angry and with a deep desire to get even. In everything he did, he viewed everything with a selfish attitude, trying to find his advantage point or what he could get out of it. To forgive, measure, and portion wasn't something he gave much thought.

Luke directs us to **measure,** *a limited portion or degree.* We are a greedy-driven society. The Media tells us what we need and it is ok to get it at any cost. The Scriptures tell us we will only be given so much. We are not just referring to money— this is applicable to every area of our life.

Years ago, on a fine summer evening, I was coming out of a McDonalds in downtown Pittsburgh. There was a man standing outside the door asking for money. I reached in my pocket and took all the loose change I had and put it in his hand. I don't remember the exact amount, but he looked at it and then at me, and made a snide comment.

The look on his face was one of disgust so I asked him to open his hand. I reached to take the change back but he quickly closed his hand and walked away. I gave out of the goodness of my heart but he received with an attitude of ungratefulness.

We need to pay close attention to how we run every aspect of our lives, being thankful to God for everything we have. He keeps a record of what He has entrusted to us, and foolishness will come back to haunt us. Those are subtle reminders when there is a real need and you are a few dollars short. This light comes on in your head and you remember, "If I had not spent that money I had the other day." It happens too often. We buy something on impulse, only to realize later we should have prayed about it first.

I used to make fun of someone when I heard them say, "I need to pray about this decision." Being in sales all my life, I heard that statement on more than one occasion. There were only a few times I can remember that they came back to purchase. I no longer make fun of that comment now. In fact, I practice it myself.

There are several verses in the Book of Proverbs that talk about how man plans his course, but it is the Lord who determines his path. So, *"Commit to the Lord whatever you do and he will establish your plans"* Proverbs 16:3 (NIV).

Godly decisions are a two-part process. First, we seek the counsel of other godly people who are qualified. Second, we seek God and wait on Him when making that decision. The question that comes to mind immediately is, "How do we know when God has answered the prayer?" If you are willing to be patient, God will open the right doors and shut others.

Discernment is not man's strong suit. We can make what we consider good decisions concerning work, our personal lives, and maybe even in business. But compared to what God has in store for us, those decisions are not even in the same league.

Failed marriages are at an all-time high because of man's decision-making. Top executives commit white-color crimes at astounding rates because of poor decisions. Sexually transmitted diseases spread like wildflowers because of poor decisions . . . and the list goes on.

Man's selfish drive leads him to satisfy his own desires. For wisdom, man cannot hold a candle to God's. "Learn from man, but lean on Him," says it all.

Think About It

What good habits do you need to develop to be more discerning about decisions you make in your life? How will you start? When will you start?

_____

_____

There is one thing you could never take away from HT He had a saying, "If you make a nickel, save three cents of it." This philosophy came from his early days of having nothing and that principal stayed with him all his life.

If everyone thought along those lines, where would this country be today? He always saved and when it was time for any major purchase there was never the question of where the money was coming from. The only question he had was, "Where is the best price on the product he needed?"

Cash flow, even in lean times, never became a problem for HT, mainly because he had planned for the occasion. He later learned God's Word clearly stated, *"But seek first His Kingdom and his righteousness, and all these things will be given to you as well"* Matthew 6:33 (NIV).

When our outgo exceeds our income, our upkeep will lead to our downfall. HT had a soft spot in his heart for anyone in need since he had experienced this himself. Giving was easy for him, but for his wife it did not come so easy. She felt that he let people take advantage of him and this became a point of conflict between them.

The Bible says, *"Each man should give what he has decided to give in your heart to give, not reluctantly or under compulsion, for God loves a cheerful giver"* 2 Corinthians 9:7 (NIV). When we give, it must be because we want to, not because we are told to. When giving, it is not unreasonable to take the time to check out what your money is going for. That is not begrudging, it is wise stewardship.

You should even know the programs your church is participating in and be given updates from time to time. Just as God holds us accountable for our giving, He holds the church accountable for the way they handle the funds received.

The black marks of the church with their poor spending habits has created a reputation that will take some time to overcome. Many churches have taken on independent accounting firms to separate themselves from the income received. This has helped assure they are held accountable to the congregation they serve. The days of the church doing as they pleased is over, realizing the congregation will no longer stand still and let things pass them by without question. God expects everyone to be accountable. No one gets a free pass on this.

This was all foreign to HT for church was not in his life yet. His saving habits came out of need, desire, and living through a depression—learning to watch how every penny was spent.

Think About It

How do you manage your money? Do you spend more than you earn? Do you pay with credit or cash? What are the benefits of paying with cash only?

The last word Luke brings to our attention is **pressed,** *to squeeze, arrest, apprehend and crowd.* Squeeze in all you can and make sure every nook and cranny has been filled.

Have you ever had to fill up something that was loose and granular? As you poured the material into the container you had to stop and tap the container to make sure it was settling down. This allowed you to put more in even when the container looked full. Not only did you get to press it down—you got to actually let it run over and spill on the floor.

The other words that define pressed are arrest, apprehend, and crowd—like in pack it in tight. God has given us this kind of abundant measure. It is overflowing and we are expected to take control and use it wisely. The above definitions clearly indicate that we can have way more than we will need; however, we must handle it all according to God's will.

The question becomes, "Will we be good stewards?" God gives and takes away. The take away part is something we actually bring on ourselves. This stems from making bad decisions, and having no counsel or prayer. It is all part of His plan for us to keep Him in the loop.

If you were to summarize these verses in layman's terms, it would read something like this: "Be prepared to have the spotlight put on you if you are going to take the role of a judge." "Be careful in condemning; it has a lasting impact." "Forgive freely, for it not only sets the other person free, it does you as well." "Make sure the cup you measure from is always overflowing."

By pressing down, you are getting the best, and the overflowing only allows you to do more for others. Keep in mind that giving is actually what stimulates the getting, as long as we are doing it for the right reason.

Did HT's cup run over? At this stage in HT's life, his cup was full and it was because of the habits he and his wife had disciplined themselves to. He was not familiar with God's law yet.

Think About It

What in your life do you need to begin to do differently to receive more and to do more for others?

_____

_____

"The one who does not know and does things deserving punishment will be beaten with few blows. From everyone who has been given much, much will be demanded, and from one who has been entrusted with much, much more will be asked" Luke 12:48 (NIV).

These words speak volumes to the one who will accept them. What Luke is saying here is, in our innocence, if we do something wrong, our punishment will be less than someone who knowingly does wrong. Many are quick to jump and say, "But it was done unintentionally; there should be no punishment."

It is because of this kind of thinking that our court systems are jammed with a backlog of cases, wasting judges and jurors' time, not to mention the taxpayer's money. The judicial system was originally designed to protect the innocent and punish the guilty, but nowadays it works the opposite way. Everyone is looking for an angle to beat the system. The saying, "It is not what you know, but who you know" unfortunately applies to the American judicial system. There are many good judges and attorneys, but for every good one there seems to be three that aren't.

In the second half of the verse, Luke focuses on the word **given,** *adventure, minister, have power, bestow, smite, suffer, and yield.* We are to understand that if God gives us something there are promises that go along with that gift. We are to minister to others, to go and be a disciple. He will bestow upon our abilities. There will be times we will suffer, but because we are in His grace, our yield will be great.

As God advances us in His kingdom, He also takes us on detours where there are lessons we must learn. The only way to learn these lessons is to submit to God and follow His lead.

"He redeemed us in order that the blessings given to Abraham might come to the Gentiles through Christ Jesus, so that by faith we might receive the promise of the Spirit" Galatians 3:14 (NIV).

We will be given power through His Word. He tells us, *"Ask and it will be given to you; seek and you will find; knock and the door will be opened to you"* Matthew 7:7 (NIV). He holds nothing from us. We just need to study His Word and we will find the answers.

The word given carries with it the message of minister, if we are in the position of being a giver. People wonder why you are giving and this is an opportune time to share Jesus' story of hope and salvation. Being a giver puts you in the position of power. People are automatically drawn to you allowing you to share God's Word.

Given also says, we will suffer, and have to yield to His command. In the Old Testament, God had no problem getting Israel's attention with a disaster, causing hundreds to die because of being rebellious. But it is hard for us to accept God doing something like that after his Son paid the price of death for our sins.

So why would He smite us, cause us to suffer or yield to His will? It ties in directly with the first half of the verse—the unknowingly who commits a wrong act will be punished. While the faithful are rewarded, the disobedient are disciplined. If you are ignorant in your wrongdoing, your punishment will be a little, but if it is blatant your punishment will be severe.

In essence, it is not God who is doing the punishing, but our own choice of not obeying His law. We are told we will yield—meaning to relinquish or give up. God wants and expects us to be givers. To hold on loosely, because we cannot out give God. The return we will receive is far greater than that which we are told to give. Our greatest reward is not while we are here on earth. This is difficult for most to understand. Myself included.

Yield also means to receive. While we are required to yield to God's will, in return, He will give back, which far exceeds any expectations we could ever imagine. We have one responsibility and God has two rewards—one while here on earth and one when we get to heaven.

Our next word is **much,** *abundant, great, sore, straightly, largest portion.* God will provide for our daily needs exceedingly above all we expect. If we have been given a large portion, God has some expectations of us. He will set us on a straight path so that we will neither stumble, nor waiver to the left or the right.

Many of the Old Testament leaders such as Solomon, David, Samson and King Nebuchadnezzar had God's blessing. They achieved great fame only to fall because they let it go to their heads. It is so easy to fool ourselves into thinking we achieved all this on our own. We, just like the leaders mentioned, need to be reckoned with. My father would say, "God had to bring them down a notch or two."

Is God capable of giving us much? The answer is yes. It is a must that we keep in mind. His expectations are high on what He wants in return. For those of you who think this is a negotiating point, you can forget it, for it is not going to happen.

Now that we have a clear understanding of how God operates, we will see if He is willing to give **more,** *super abundant, excel, abound, and to spare* than we expect. God blessed Solomon. We know this much. You may have heard someone say or read an article, or maybe even saw a news clip of an incident where something miraculous happened and the only explanation that was given . . . it was God.

With blessings come conditions. So, as we stand in line all excited, waiting our turn for God to abundantly bless us, He says one last thing, "Much more will be **asked,** *required, desired, demanded, something due.*"

It does not take a rocket scientist to figure this out. He says, "You want more? No problem, you got it." If I am going to put a desire in your heart for more, to do good, to help others, I will also give you my requirements. The demands on you and your responsibilities will be many. He wants us to understand something will be due and we will be held to a higher standard.

That something due works two ways. Read Jesus' explanation found in John 14: *"My Father's house has many rooms; if that were not so, would I have told you that I am going there to prepare a place for you? And if I go and prepare a place for you, I will come back and take you to be with me that you also may be where I am. You know the way to the place where I am going."*

We have an earthly responsibility and a heavenly reward. When it comes to God holding up His end of the agreement, the reward will always be greater than we expect or imagine. With rewards, there are usually expectations attached to it.

The problem is not giving the blessing, but how it is handled. They go hand in hand. The requirements God puts on us are really blessings in disguise. We just need to get our heads in the game in order to have a thorough understanding.

Think About It

What is that desire that God has placed in your heart? And, are you ready to accept the responsibility?

_____

_____

HT had been in management for several years. His son was now eight years old. He heard of how the other managers' sons played sports and listened as the fathers bragged about their sons. Since he was taken out of school at age eleven, sports was something he never got to play.

He figured it was time to get his son involved in baseball. It was baseball season and he set out to find the practice times for the local teams. Through work, one of the men told him when and where the tryouts were. He made sure he was free and told his wife he was taking Wayne to baseball tryouts that coming Saturday morning.

When Saturday came, father and son headed to the field a little early. HT spoke with the coach and set everything up. There was only one problem. Wayne had never played baseball and did not know the first thing about the game. This was what HT considered a chance: to spend time with his son and build a relationship.

The coach played Wayne at every position as a courtesy to HT, but unfortunately, Wayne miserably failed at every one. HT was embarrassed and disappointed with the outcome of the little league tryouts that he just gave up on trying to do anything with his son. He had taken Wayne fishing a few times but Wayne showed no interest in it. HT felt there was no use in pursuing any type of bond.

Wayne, like his father, matured early over the next five years. But the relationship with him and his father grew more distant. Wayne rebelled. He started drinking, so his grades suffered, too. By this time, HT had become a pillar in the church—a deacon and Sunday school superintendent. All the talk, rumors, and gossip about Wayne created a greater division between him and his son. This lasted until HT was on his deathbed.

In Luke 16:1-10, we read as Jesus tells his disciples the parable of the shrewd manager.

"There was a rich man whose manager was accused of wasting his possessions. So he called him in and asked him, 'What is this I hear about you? Give an account of your management, because you cannot be manager any longer."

This verse reminds me of the time when HT decided to take on a part time job selling tailor made clothes. Through his connection at work and his standing in the community, he had a very good reputation and was almost an immediate success. The company did not pay him in money, but in top quality tailored dress slacks shirts and jackets. HT had a great wardrobe for a man who made $6000 a year. This led him to make a poor business decision.

One of the church members, a businessman, owned a coalmine. He approached HT about becoming his mine superintendent, which meant a considerable pay raise. HT did not spend any time in prayer or seeking out counsel, nor did he check out the persons' credentials. It would prove to be a big mistake.

While HT does not fall under the same category as the manager in the above parable, the principle still applies. When you first read it, it could easily send a confusing message. The story unfolds and appears to tell us to be a thief, a cheat, and a liar. Knowing the Bible is against these things, let's investigate to see what lesson is being taught.

"The manager said to himself, 'What shall I do now? My master is taking away my job. I'm not strong enough to dig, and I'm ashamed to beg—I know what I'll do so that, when I lose my job here, people will welcome me into their houses. So he called in each one of his master's debtors. He asked the first, 'How much do you owe my master?'

'Nine hundred gallons of olive oil,' he replied. The manager told him, 'Take your bill, sit down quickly, and make it four hundred and fifty.' Then he asked the second, 'And how much do you owe?'

'A thousand bushels of wheat,' he replied. He told him, 'Take your bill and make it eight hundred.'

"The master commended the dishonest manager because he had acted shrewdly. For the people of this world are more shrewd in dealing with their own kind than are the people of the light. I tell you, use worldly wealth to gain friends for yourselves, so that when it is gone, you will be welcomed into eternal dwellings. Whoever can be trusted with very little can also be trusted with much, and whoever is dishonest with very little will also be dishonest with much."

The words that are brought to mind in Luke 16:1-10, are worldly by today's standards. But two thousand years ago, some carried a different meaning or a different set of values when originally spoken. Some words have been reviewed in other verses and may carry the same meaning as before. To get the full understanding of these verses it is necessary to cover them again.

Many times, parables are used as a method of teaching. Every story was a teaching opportunity for the disciples. Since disciple means 'to learn' this message is for all who read the word. We are to become disciples and go throughout the land and spread the Word. This may have been one of the most important lessons Jesus would teach his disciples.

Disciple comes from a Greek word. When translated to Latin, it is 'disciples,' meaning a learner. A disciple was one who followed Jesus as a student during His period on earth. The twelve disciples were the most notable and some say they were the inner circle and were chosen to represent the twelve tribes of Israel.

The word **discipline** is derived from **disciple** *meaning to follow a strict code of conduct.* To many the word discipline carries a negative connotation because it follows an enforcement of order to carry out instructions. Should these instructions not be followed there is usually some form of punishment. God's law is no different than any other law written. There are things that need to be obeyed, and if not, we suffer the consequences. You see it in the news daily. Those who choose not to follow the law and are caught are expected to pay a penalty.

So, as we think back to the parable we just studied, the Master or owner commended his manager for his shrewdness. So how do we apply this to today's marketplace? Put it this way, in order for a Christian business person to function in the business world, he needs to understand how the game is played. He doesn't need to participate in the game, or be part of some of its bad practices, but he does need to know the rules. Therefore, shrewdness is paramount to competing in the marketplace.

HT made a decision that was costly. Within six months that dream job ended, he had created a bad relationship with his previous employer, and was unemployed. Fifty-one years old and starting over is not a good thing.

Think About It

What decisions in life have you made that ended up costing you more than you bargained for? What discipline were you able to apply to it?

_____

_____

In Luke 16:1-10, we note that there was a **rich** man. Rich means *wealthy, abounding with, abundance, possession . . .* In biblical times, just as today, wealth was measured by things. It was your possessions: the wives, land, livestock, and the size of your family that determined your wealth. The big difference between today's and biblical times' wealth is that back then wealth was created specifically to support your family and to pass on to the next generation.

In the beginning of this verse, we see this Master is wealthy and has a manager who has been found to be unworthy continuing in his present position. The Master confronts his manager by **accusing** him of wasting his possessions.

The Master tells his manager, "I have been told you are being dishonest. Come to my office and give me an accounting of all your activities because you are no longer a manager for me." The manager has been put on notice and will be fired unless the records are settled. He's in a tough situation.

Years ago, I was working in retail management for a regional flooring chain growing at a good pace. I had been promoted to management and it was my chance to shine. I took over a new store that had been open a little over a year. The previous manager had run the store in the red since its opening. It took me six months to get the store turned around before it was running in the black. The district manager gave me a salesman that was on his way out the door. Neither he nor I had any knowledge of this being his last chance. Over the next six months we worked like mad men turning the store around and made a profit. The next year was even better. We were among the top five stores in the company and my salesman was number three. I was feeling pretty confident by this time and thinking I was unstoppable. Then I made a management decision that topped all management decisions.

I did a very dumb thing. I purchased a whole trailer load of furniture: bedroom sets, dining room sets, recliners, and a few odds and ends. I had good intentions. Some of the furniture was for personal use, some for the apartments I owned with a partner and the rest we would sell. I was living in a two bedroom, nine hundred square foot apartment so I had nowhere to store that much stuff.

I got this bright idea to leave it at the carpet store for a few days until I figured out what to do. My two or three days turned into a week. One day a customer walked in to buy some carpet and saw the recliners and asked if they were for sale and how much they were. Mr. Entrepreneur makes a sale and thinks this is cool. Two weeks after that I sold two more recliners.

I thought, *As long as my district manager does not come by, I will just leave the furniture here.* My luck lasted two more days. I was out on a call and guess who shows up? As my salesman described it to me it was funny—not at the time—but it was funny.

When I got back from the sales call my salesman told me I needed to call corporate and speak to the VP of Sales ASAP.

Have you ever had that sick feeling in your stomach? You know that this is not good, and the consequence is going to be bad. I made the call and was asked to explain what I thought I was doing. As I proceeded to explain, and actually began to get brave in my response to the questions I was being asked. That was not good. At one point I blurted out, "I did this on my own time, so what is the big harm?"

Not thinking I was using the company store for personal gain I was trying to defend this stupid thing I did. Suddenly, it got really silent on the other end of the phone and the VP's voice calmly said, "Take the rest of the afternoon off, get the furniture out of the store, and if you want to continue your role as manager this will not happen again or I will give you all the time off you want."

It dawned on me that I had been given a second chance and I had better take advantage of it. In my case, the Master made his declaration for an act I had done, but gave me a second chance.

In the Parable of the Shrewd, the Master accused his manager of **wasting** *dissipate, separate, squander, and scatter* his possessions.

One of the signs of a good owner is his ability to control his inventory. Stealing is a huge industry and a top reason for the rise in product cost. I used to live near people who worked in the coal industry and the stories I heard were unbelievable.

As tandem trucks brought in their loads of coal, the guy checking the trucks and issuing the tickets, the coal was received, would issue tickets for empty trucks or give credit for two loads instead of one. The stories I heard were just mind boggling and sometimes for something as simple as a couple of tires.

Everything from double billing to stealing whole truckloads of merchandise, the industry was inundated with pilfering. I had a neighbor who was a retired mine electrician whose garage was stocked with tools from the mine and he did not mind telling you where they came from.

Mine superintendents have a lot of authority. There was a case that made the newspapers in the late 80s involving a mine superintendent who was going to make a very large some of money illegally. The coal, once it is mined, is moved one of two ways: either by rail or by barge. This superintendent had worked a deal with a rail engineer and they had been stacking rail cars on a sidetrack.

I don't remember the number of cars, but the amount of money it brought was over a million dollars. He had all the cars loaded and was ready for shipment before he was caught. Needless to say he was sent away for a while to think about what he did. If you give a man some power, one of two things will usually happen: he will abuse it or eventually lose it.

Eventually, the mismanagement was great enough to cause the Master to dismiss his number one man. When we think so little of the possessions of the one we are managing for we become sloppy and careless and it is just a matter of time until it catches up with us. To squander, scatter, or dissipate is unacceptable to God. He does not tolerate sloppy management.

The Master demanded his manager to **give,** *away, perform, recompense, reward* an account and the manager is required to perform a duty. The manager's reward will be unemployment. This manager made a grave mistake and he is paying the ultimate penalty. The Master is asking for an **account,** *a reason, motive, expression, preaching.*

In my case, when I spoke with the VP of sales he asked for an accounting of my thinking and the reason behind that thinking. In the manager's case, he is already aware of what lies ahead.

It had infuriated his Master to the point of dismissal, but the Master still wants to discern his manager's thinking. *What was the motive behind his thinking?* As any conscious owner would want to know. I am sure the Master wanted to get to the bottom of the situation in order to determine if there were others involved. He probably reasoned, J*ust getting rid of the manager may not resolve the issue.*

The Master next wants to know how **much**, *large, how great* is missing and what magnitude are his losses. Because he is not in touch with the day-to-day operations, he does not know the exact amount and is relying upon the man he has just fired to be honest with him.

The manager knows his job is being **taken**, *remove, smite, cut, separation, departure* away. When you associate the loss of a job with words such as remove, cut, separate, and departure there is no question to the finality of his position.

The manager shifted gears and the spotlight is now on survival. Looking at the word **houses** (family, dwelling) the manager is thinking, *I want to be welcomed into the homes of the men I did business with. What must I do to assure myself of this?*

House also will take on a different meaning for the manager. He is thinking, "I may lose my home—no job—no home."

His thoughts turn to survival. His world has just stopped. How does he react? The men he dealt with daily were **debtors,** *loan owners, transgressors and sinners.* God has never looked favorably upon those who are debtors.

Romans13:8 (NIV) says, *"Let no debt remain outstanding, except the continuing debt to love one another, for whoever loves others has fulfilled the law."*

Debt, back then, just like today was a way of transacting business. It then becomes a question of how the debt was managed. Not having all the information in this parable, we don't know how this debt was being paid. Was it due in full each month or over an extended period?

The Master knew he was **owed**, *under obligation, must, be bound, profit* a considerable amount of goods. Since merchandise was the major source of trade, inventory was a valuable asset and missing inventory that need to be accounted.

Man's reputation was tied directly to his promise; his honor was at stake when an agreement was struck. There was a lot to lose if a man backed out on an agreement. Your word was your bond and a handshake meant more than any document written by an attorney. Word traveled quickly when someone broke their bond in the business community. Reestablishing one's reputation was a difficult task once that occurred.

Those who **owed** were in debt to another. If we owe another, we are bound to that person, an obligation must be met and the other will profit from our debt. But in the case of the parable, the manager is reducing what the debtor owes. He is doing this to create an obligation from the debtor to himself. The manager is being shrewd and using every advantage he has at his disposal.

The Master commended the dishonest manager for acting shrewdly. This brings to realization that the people of this **world**, *messianic period, eternal,* without end deal with each other in a manner that is different than what God expects of us.

This type of business—dealing with God—began with the Jewish people and it is something that will be eternal. We, as Christians, need to learn to deal shrewdly. We need to learn the ways of the world because while we are in the world, we have to interact with the world. For the people of this world are shrewder in dealing with their own kind than are the people of the **Light.**

Light means to manifest, to show, to make known one's thoughts. The Bible often refers to light and darkness and the contrast *"While I am in the world, I am the light of the world"*— John 9-5 (NIV).

The criminal uses the darkness to commit his crime. He conceals himself in the shadow of the night. In contrast, light is considered truth because it exposes everything.

Learning to deal shrewdly only makes one wiser to the ways of man and the way they think. If you take the time to get involved in their lives and expose yourself but remain true to your belief, then you make known your thoughts. In doing this, you are letting your belief shine through in your actions. To Jesus, we give all the honor and glory. It is He who gets the credit.

By understanding this simple principle, we are setting ourselves up for greater riches in this life and the next. I am not talking just money or things—the blessing, the principles, and personal satisfaction are much greater when helping others. There is nothing better than knowing you did the right thing. It all boils down to applying what the Bible teaches and seeing if it plays out in real life. This is where the rubber meets the road.

God's formula sometimes seems complicated. The path He has us take isn't always clear, but if we initiate faith and just follow, it always works out. I emphasize the word "always" and I know many will question and say I can tell you about this time, etc.

This is where self-analyzation and the truth (light) are a must. If we admit to ourselves where we went wrong, made the wrong choice whatever the situation, then we will see why things worked out the way they did.

We are to be **trusted,** *to have faith, spiritual well-being, commit, conviction* with much. We are to learn to deal with worldly wealth: to have faith in ourselves and do it with conviction.

There is so much under handedness in the world. People are working harder to cheat than being fair. It has become an accepted way of life. God wants us to be different, but to also develop friendships through our worldly wealth so we can have the opportunity to share our love with them.

"After a long time the master of those servants returned and settled accounts with them. The man who had received five bags of gold brought the other five. 'Master,' he said, 'you entrusted me with five bags of gold. See, I have gained five more.'

"His master replied, 'Well done, good and faithful servant! You have been faithful with a few things; I will put you in charge of many things. Come and share your master's happiness!'"

As you analyze the above verse, and recognize the blessings in your life, not only do you realize have much you ought to be thankful for, but how **much** you're responsible for. God will open the doors to many opportunities, which can provide an abundant source of blessings to anyone we may encounter. The words associated with much, like many, abundant, and soar tells us, *"He has great things in store for those who are willing to follow his plan."*

The whole learning process behind His plan is about re-tooling our thinking. We must remove from our minds the ways of man, the shortcuts, the *let-me-do-it-my-way* attitude. To grow our minds, we in turn grow our boundaries of vision that He has in store for us.

God can open and create new avenues for us that we never would have considered on our own. Remember, He is the one who made us and He is the one who put the road map of our life together.

As Ross Perot used to say, "Now, here is the deal." If you put a plan together, it is always going to have basic instructions and sound fundamentals. God is not the kind of Master who pulls His leaders into a conference room, close the doors, share with them ideas and concepts that He is not willing to share with anyone. If we expect Him to bless us with **riches,** *money, wealth, fullness, accomplishment, and influence* it is a must that we are able to handle worldly wealth. The expectations He has of us is far greater than we can fathom, and doing it His way takes top priority. What He will permit us to accomplish and the influence we will have on others will prepare us to then be able to handle true riches.

HT was offered an opportunity to increase his income; maybe ten times his salary, but all he saw were dollar signs. He sought no counsel, did no checking up on his employer; instead, he took everything at face value and did not involve God in the process. Thus, the consequences were disastrous. Fear kept him from accepting his first promotion and greed would cause him to make a wrong decision on his second.

We close this lesson with the word **own**, *self, conceit, give, greatly, bestow, minister, power, adventure.* The world has a real problem when it comes to ownership. In most instances, our thoughts and motives are on ourselves, which bare the forbidden fruit of conceit. Man's heart turns inward with pride and his thoughts are all about self: *What toy don't I have? What do I need? What will make me feel better?*

Jesus is all too aware of man's need to feed himself and He knows this has always been a pivotal stumbling block. The philosophy of holding on tight to what one has is just the opposite of what we are taught in the Bible. It teaches us to hold on with an open hand, which when visualized that seems impossible. It really makes no sense.

The vision we have for holding on is like that of a rope climber. He or she must grasp the rope tightly or they will never accomplish their goal. While we are not climbing a rope, we are pulling ourselves out of the doldrums of our thinking and need to understand this principle. If we hoard and don't share, how can we expect someone to share with us? Those who openly share seem to get ahead or advance and we wonder why that can't be us.

In the context of this sentence, Jesus instructs man *'to give greatly and bestow his riches upon others.'* He wants us to use our wealth as a form of ministry. To help others in need and seeing the power this wealth can have when it is properly handled. He also wants us to understand that having wealth can be an adventure. When properly managed, the adventure can be as rewarding for us as the individual receiving the gift.

The next time you say a prayer, focus on your words and listen to what you are asking God to do. I would venture to say that the better portion of your prayer is about self.

The words written in the Bible are not there as a pump me up, make me feel good, or tell me neat stories; they represent a message. It is designed to make us hungry, to learn, to understand, to dig deeper and fall in love with the creator.

God's message will never change. He says, *"Jesus Christ is the same yesterday, today and forever"* Hebrews 13:8 (NIV).

"So I say to you: Ask and it will be given to you; seek and you will find; knock and the door will be opened to you" Matthew 7:7 (NIV).

There is nothing in those words that say, "Sit and wait, cop an attitude, this is all mine, or I am not sharing." The Bible is a two-way street. God will always carry the bulk of the load but we are expected to do our share.

In the second chapter of Proverbs it is titled, "The Moral Benefits of Wisdom." Morals are the principles we live by: the rules that govern our thoughts, the way we function on a day-to-day basis. Morals are so lacking that most people are fence straddlelers when confronted with an issue that requires a decision.

There are those who don't want to be confrontational. Most won't take a stand, but have plenty of opinions once the decision has been made. Having the right morals will give us benefits (rewards). One of those benefits is wisdom. God's Word also says that by having right morals we are given the ability to **teach**, *be skillful, cunning, deal makers, and one who is known to be wise.* Those are benefits I think anyone would like to be known for.

In reference to moral benefits of wisdom, Proverbs 7:1 (NIV) says, *"My son, keep my words and store up my commands within you."* By doing so, we will understand what is right, just, fair, and the good path.

Think About It

In the parable we just finished studying, did God tell us to be dishonest? Was His lesson much deeper? Were we to be cheats, liars, and thieves or were we to be the rose among the thorns? Were we to set the example and do well when faced with adversity or be the one who others know they can trust no matter what the circumstances?

_____

_____

God's lesson is very clear. We are representing Him no matter the surroundings. We have one set of rules and they never change. Yes, we need to be aware of man's carnal ways to be able to understand who we are dealing with and how to serve him to the best of our abilities. The rest is just side benefits for doing the right thing. It is like participating in a sporting event—whatever the game, there are rules.

Dad with employees in font of mine he owned for a short period of time

If you want to play the game, you must follow the rules: three strikes and you are out; you step out of bounds, the ball is down; and if your serve hits the net, it is a fault. These are basic rules of the game. They are not difficult to understand or follow, but must be adhered to for those to want to play.

Learning about prosperity and getting an understanding of God's basic teaching involves much more than just the monetary. HT learned a valuable, but costly lesson when he chose to quit his job and follow the dollar signs. He took one more side road thinking he knew best. He decided to open his own mine.

He negotiated a land lease, bought some used mine equipment and got into business for himself. But, once again he did not consult God or godly counsel. Within a couple of months, the mine was operational. He worked two shifts, five days a week, and while the work was demanding, he seemed to be making headway.

One Saturday, he took his son and drove to the mine to check on his equipment, as he believed someone was stealing from him. The finances were not there to afford a night watchman, so he relied upon those who worked for him to be honest.

That Saturday would prove to be the last straw. He discovered equipment missing, along with tools, cables, and other things of value. He decided to throw in the towel, hang it up, and went crawling back to his old company, asking if they would hire him back. It took some time but eventually they hired him back. Working overtime, he paid the debt he created, built his savings back, and got both feet back on level ground.

HT learned his lesson. He may not have fared all that well working for the Master. He may not have been fired, but he did learn a few lessons. The company had taught him all the experience he'd gained but he'd disregarded it all. Instead, he tossed caution to the wind, and lept without looking. The pain, heartache, tension and lost finances were something he would have to deal with for a long time.

His marriage suffered too. His relationships at his church and his trust in his fellow man was never the same. That experience with a fellow Christian whom HT trusted and held in high respect scared him deeply. His walk became careful, his trust a lot more discerning, and his reasoning led him to seek counsel anytime he had a question.

CHAPTER 10

I CAN DO THIS

Obedience. Now, there's a word that stops us in our tracks. In Deuteronomy 28:1-2, we are told to "fully obey" and "carefully follow." That seems pretty straight forward, doesn't it?

Let's say you have just purchased a new expensive tool.. You're excited, but when you open it you discover it requires some assemblage. So, you try to figure out how to put it together without reading the instructions. Sad to say, but most men would attempt to put it together without looking at the instructions. Even if it was stamped in big red letters "WARNING" warranty invalid if instructions for assemblage are not followed.

Man has this inherent internal clock that says, "I can figure this out—I don't need instructions." As we all know, men are notorious for being 'the leap and then look' individuals. Men are wired to think they can figure this whole thing out about life, relationships, family, marriage, children, work, and God.

You will notice God is last because that is where He is found in most cases in today's busy life. The Book of Deuteronomy, you will soon find, it's more like an instruction manual. It is stamped with big red letters "Warning: read carefully— if you have any questions, call: 1-800-HELP-GOD."

God gives us **commands**, *constitute, appoint, charge, sends a message, and set in order*. These are all rather strong words when tied to the word command. A lot of people have trouble accepting this because many have trouble following orders.

In today's society, where the attitude of doing your own thing is prevalent, marching to the beat of a different drummer is not always popular. When we look at the word 'command,' we see God made it very clear to follow Him and His teachings. When using such words as *constitute*, which means *written law*; *appoint*, meaning *you are responsible*; and *charge*, meaning *I expect you to follow through*—it leaves very little room for misunderstanding.

We have said all along that the Lord is a God of order. In Job 25:2 (NIV), we read: *"Dominion and awe belong to God; he establishes order in the heights of heaven."*

God is not one who leaves any room for error. He's very different from us, who often look for ways to have an excuse, lay blame or point fingers, and walk away from accepting responsibility. God takes responsibility, sends a message, and expects us to set it in order. The beauty of all this is He wants so much to reward us. He loves bestowing gifts upon us, but we rather rebel, sulk, and complain. God is an action person and the sooner we understand that the quicker we will realize His blessings.

We are then told we will be set **high,** above. **High,** all nations, now that is a pretty substantial reward. High meaning supreme, or ascend up, following what the Bible is telling us about our journey through life—it will be different and we will be set apart. It does not mean we will have the easy road, but it is always the better road. We usually want the good life, but not the scrapes and bruises that go along with it.

While Jesus was on earth, He had many joyous times—times with laughter, as well as times of perils. There were times He had to travel by night and stay away from certain areas because there were those who were plotting against Him.

Similarly, we need to experience all life has to offer if we are expected to help others along the way. Not only are we to be set high, but we are to be **above** all the nations.

Above means according to and beyond the time. There is a standard that God functions by which is far superior to what we can even imagine. Does this mean, "I am raising you above, setting you apart and beyond the time," and do we have a designated place, a place already assigned?

We next look at the word **nations.** We will be raised high above all the nations. That means we will be superior to all other nations. You may be wondering, "I thought this meant for the Jewish people," and yes you are correct, it is for them. But let's clarify it a little more. Those who choose to follow and accept Him as their Lord and Savior will be given this right-of-passage along with the gentile, heathen, and the majestic.

Not only are we given this right-of-passage once we make our proclamation, but we have the privilege of being part of the select few. God reminds us that not all will make this journey. It is sad, but nonetheless true. Just as those who scoffed Noah were left behind, some will resist till the bitter end and choose not to accept His offer, and they too shall perish.

The verse continues on to explain that **all** the blessings will come upon you. **All,** meaning the whole, whosoever, complete, and make perfect. Can you understand what is being said here? We can't stop the clock,

"All that's been said will come to pass." God will finish what He started. He will complete and make perfect all He said He would do.

Hey, this is pretty awesome stuff and we are running a special this week. By taking this today it will only cost you, not $100,000, not $50,000, not $25,000 not even $5,000. Today it is only $500. No, wait! My boss just told me today it is $0. It's FREE!

That's right! No money down or monthly payments, you can walk away today with the latest model, all the whistles and bells for just these ten simple words: "Jesus come into my life, be my Lord and savior."

What a great buy you just made. It will never break down, run out of gas, needs a tune up, oil change or new tires. Every time you put the key in the ignition, it will start and it comes with a lifetime warranty. On the coldest night, the loneliest morning, at any crisis, you can depend on this model.

It has never been duplicated. You have one of a kind and it is an original—what a deal you just made! One more thing: we don't want you to keep this a secret—tell as many of your friends as you wish. We will offer them the same deal. Are you excited? We are!

Here it comes. There are **blessings,** prosperity in the present. He promised us from the start we would be blessed if we would fully obey and He now is saying not only will there be blessings, but they will be in the present life as well.

A blessing. What you and I may consider a penalty could very well be a blessing from God. It could save you from financial ruin, the loss of your job, or a marriage gone bad. Blessings from God come in all shapes and sizes. We just need to be acutely attuned to His radar, and the best way to do that is by studying His Word and meditate on it day and night. The wet stone is designed to sharpen the dull knife—just as the Bible is designed to sharpen our knowledge. As we bring these verses to an end he reminds us to **bless,** *to kneel, praise, give thanks* and be very mindful of all that we are blessed with.

In the Book of Genesis, we read as God notices Abram being troubled because he has no heir to whom he can leave all his possessions. God askes Abram to step outside his tent, to look to the heavens, and count all the stars. Then He says, *"This will be how great your descendants will one day be."* Abram loved God and followed Him but like most men still questioned Him.

So, God made a covenant with Abram and swore that Abram would have a son. In the first verse of Genesis 15:1 (NIV), we read: *"After this, the word of the Lord came to Abram in a vision: Do not be afraid, Abram. I am your shield, your very great reward."* How cool is that?

It took some years for this promise to come to pass. Mostly because Abram decided to do his own thing and veer from the path God had chosen for him. God being patient, stayed the course, never changed His mind, and was true to His word. Abram was blessed, so he gave thanks to God, and showed his faith for everyone to see. Abram, who later became Abraham, still to this day is talked about because of the faith he had and demonstrated in the presence of God for the whole world to see.

Moving just a little further, we see where God continues to tell His people how He will bless them. *"The Lord will grant you abundant prosperity—in the fruit of your womb, the young in your livestock and the crops of your ground—in the land he swore to your ancestors to give to you. The Lord will make you the head, not the tail. If you pay attention to the commands of the Lord your God that I give you today and carefully follow them you will always be at the top, and never at the bottom"* Deuteronomy 28: 11-13 (NIV).

Think About It

Think about all the blessings in your life. Then, as you look closer at the last few days, what new blessings can you recognize as a gift from above?

_____

_____

The next word to focus on is **fruit**, and in this context, it carries a meaning of first, bring forth, grow, and increase. God is reminding us that we are to return back to Him a portion of all He gives us when He implies fruit with the word first.

We are told in Malachi 3:10 (NIV) to *"Bring the whole tithe into the storehouse, that there may be food in my house. Test me in this, says the Lord Almighty, and see if I will not throw open the floodgates of heaven and pour out so much blessing that you will not have room enough to store it."*

This is a test of stewardship and management. We, as managers, are asked to watch over what is His and give Him back ten percent. He in turn will give us the rest as a wage.

Think About It

There is more. If we are not greedy and are sure to give Him the very best, He will then give us more than our storehouse will hold. How would you like to have Him as your boss? Well, "hello," think about it!

_____

_____

Just put that thinking cap on and get to know him on a personal basis. All that has been said here can be yours as well. *"For the Lord your God will bless you as he has promised, and you will lend to many nations but will borrow from none. You will rule over many nations but none will rule over you"* Deuteronomy 15:6 (NIV).

We are next told that we will **lend** and not **borrow.** They both carry the same meaning but have very different concepts, of course, depending on which side of the table you sit. To **lend** is *to twine, unite, abide, cleave, and join self.* By just reading those words and taking our modern-day definition we see where as a lender, whatever you lend and to whom it is lent, there will be a very close relationship. So close that the two become one. The one who is doing the borrowing is entwined or bound and must abide by the rules of the one who does the lending. This puts constraints on the borrower until such time that the lender is repaid.

The borrower becomes obligated to the lender and must abide by the rules of the lender, thus losing the freedom of self. The same words that give the lender the power to bind are the same words that take away the freedom of the borrower. As God points out, it is one set of words with two very different end results.

The verse tells us, "We will be the **head,** not the **tail,**" and in the same breath, God reminds us to "obey His commands." To be the head carries with it a lot of responsibility, which some soon discover is more than they bargained for. The **head** lends itself to words like: to shake, place, band, first, ruler, principal, and top.

There are many different views about those who are at the top. They are envied by some and admired by others, yet others work very hard to take the place of those in charge. They even do wrong things to cause themselves to look good while making their rival look bad. Man has this innate desire to achieve and the rules used easily get miscued— enabling one to cheat and lie his way to the top.

We then have the Enron's of the world who at all cost will do anything to be the head. God does want us at the head, to be first but not at any cost. When

Saul became jealous of David, his entire focus changed and everyone suffered. God expects us to maintain order and make sure that all who follow understand. We are to live by the principles that God has laid out and not deviate from them for any reason. Being the head does have a responsibility and it is not all about being the boss, but more about being responsible. God wants us to be truthful, trustworthy and one who will not waiver when decision times become tough. This reminds me of Lee Iacocca—former President of Chrysler—when he took over the company as CEO. The company was in financial trouble so he went to Congress asking to borrow a very large sum of money. After some deliberation, Congress agreed to make the loan.

There was a great deal of talk about that loan in the media. The day Iacocca repaid the loan he made a public announcement on the steps of the White House to millions of TV viewers saying, "We do business the old-fashioned way. We pay back our loans and we do it ahead of time." There was a lot of publicity that surrounded those words: some good and some bad. Yes, Iacocca planned his ten minutes of fame for the whole world to see and it was for the right reason. Those who scoffed at him may have been somewhat like Saul—jealous.

I was proud to be an American that day, and proud to see a man at the top take responsibility and do the right thing. Times have changed. It seems as if that has all been traded in for a different kind of thinking. Our world is in a downward spiral and those in charge don't have very good vision.

Being at the top—the one who is the ruler, principal, owner and the president create a sense of worthiness, a sense of being. Most anyone when asked if they would like to be the one in charge, the boss or the CEO, would jump at the chance; however, not all are qualified to hold that position.

But as we read God's word He says just the opposite, "The Lord will make you the head, not the tail. If you pay attention to the commands of the Lord your God that I give you this day and carefully follow them you will always be at the top, and never at the bottom" Deuteronomy 28:13 (NIV).

The Lord wants us to be rulers and principals but so many of us shy away when put in a place of leadership or responsibility. This is why it is so important to develop that relationship with God. He can and will develop the qualities in us to give us the ability to look to Him and seek the wisdom to be the leader we need to be.

Leaders are not born, they're made. Jesus made Paul a leader. He chose the twelve disciples and their background was varied. They were fishermen, tax collectors, tent makers and doctors, but they all had one thing in common—they chose to follow Jesus.

When they chose to lay down their current profession and make a conscious choice to start a new occupation, they knew they would have some struggles. There would be challenges, and the learning curve would not be easy.

However, they were willing to take the chance and commit to the one who promised to lead them to a better life and a brighter tomorrow that had a much better ending. Over time, they became so committed and their cause so great they even died for it.

We are reminded that "He will never ask us to do or be what He has not already gone through."

We are told we will never be the **tail:** flopping, cut off, rear, or smite. These words indicate the inability to lead. Some will not be capable of leading and are to bring up the rear, having no one to watch their back.

Flopping says we are disconnected, no support, like a loose cannon or someone running aimlessly. A successful CEO makes it very clear you can never be a leader until you learn how to follow. The whole time Jesus was on earth He set the example of servanthood. He led from the position of being a server.

My Father used to say, "You can catch more flies with honey than you can with vinegar," and "If you lead by example more will follow than if you lead by giving orders."

As the verse continues we are, not to turn **aside,** *to turn off, decline, be grievous, leave undone, rebel, revolt.* In a time when direction for the lives of our young people is greatly needed, it is not there. There is more interested in self-satisfaction and personal gratification. Drugs are at an all-time high, teen pregnancy is off the scale and it all seems so out of control. Yet when you sit down and talk with the younger generation and get to the heart of the issue what they tell us is, "we just want to be loved and wanted."

The same thing the Bible teaches us not to do, we are doing to our children. Are we causing them to turn aside, rebel and revolt? It appears that way. It all falls back to the saying, "I can't hear what you are saying because your actions speak louder than your words."

We break God's heart and our children break ours. In closing these verses, God gives one final warning to His people, *"Do not only turn aside, but do not turn to the right or left and follow other gods and serve them."* It is very easy to get distracted in a time when we have so many different opportunities staring us in the face.

Notice in the Bible the term 'right' and 'left' are used a lot and they carry distinct meanings. To the **right** represents strength, south and turn. To the **left** represents wrapping up, dark, north, idol, and image.

To the layperson, these two words simply mean, "Left could be a direction" or "you're left handed," and the right could have the same meaning—just the other side. But to God these two words have a very different and implied meaning which carries a consequence.

Can you imagine having a conversation with a neighbor asking, "Whatever happened to Jerry?" and they replied, "He went by the way of the left," and you understood exactly what they meant. Or the conversation could have gone like this, "He went to the right and became a loner thinking he can do it all by himself." It seems as if Jerry has turned away from all his friends. No one can talk to him for he has all the answers.

God makes a bold statement to His people: *"Be very strong; be careful to obey all that is written in the Book of the Law of Moses, without turning aside to the right or left"* Joshua 23:6 (NIV).

Those words seem so easy, yet for most of us they will fall on deaf ears. There are three ways to learn from mistakes. First, the easy way is to learn from the mistakes of others. Second is to learn from our own mistakes, and third is to not learn from either.

Tragically, for some, they choose the third option and continue ending up at square one— always starting over and wondering why they can never get ahead. The freedom of choice also carries with it the consequence of that decision. In the beauty of following God's path, you are told the end result before you ever begin the journey. It is easy to read the instructions and put something together, but most people like to put it together and then read the instructions.

HT understood consequences. He understood rules. He saw lives changed forever because people did not obey the rules. He believed those same rules applied to what he read in the Bible and he chose to follow them, and it worked out pretty well for him.

King Solomon was one who liked to do things the right way. When he was appointed king at a very early age, he realized he had no real leadership skills. So, what did he do? *"So give your servant a discerning heart to govern your people and to distinguish between right and wrong. For who is able to govern this great people of yours?"* 1 Kings 3:9 (NIV).

That was it, nothing more. No riches, fame or castles: just wisdom and discernment.

Not only was Solomon blessed with wisdom but eventually his knowledge would gain him great wealth as well.

Notoriety fame, fortune, heads turning, people talking. Word gets around you're something special and that's when the tables start to turn. You start to read your own press clippings. This is a pretty good way to start your new occupation—the first day on the job and it's a lot more than the corner office with a view.

Think About It

How would you handle this promotion?

There are some keywords that play a major role in Solomon's young life and guide him into maturity. The first of these is **pleased**, *to yield, mental, weakness, undertake, be foolish.* In looking at the word 'pleased' and associating it with what we have just read, you would not think of the word choice that is given.

God recognized Solomon's weakness, his age, his immaturity, and his mental capacity to undertake such a daunting task. Solomon realized it would be foolish to think he could lead this great nation. He did know one thing for sure: his father David loved God and he was taught to love God. He knew that by relying on Him, he would make it—he just did not realize how good he would have it.

Solomon realized the only way to undertake this task was to yield his personal desires and put God in control. Some scholars say he was twelve years of age, while others argue he was in his early twenties. You may find it hard to understand how anyone that young could undertake such a task. Thinking of our own children who are just starting to mature at twelve, it is difficult to relate.

The custom of the day was to be considered an adult and ready for manhood when you turned twelve. Since Solomon came from royalty and was chosen by God, he was groomed for this position.

God then talks to us about **discernment**, *hear, intelligently, obedience, attentively and call.* One who chooses to have discernment needs to be a good listener, obedient, attentive, make wise decisions and do what is asked of them. Being a great leader requires these skills if you expect people to follow. People need to be given a reason to follow you. Solomon's request was genuine. It was from his heart.

His head, personal gain, or selfish reason was not his motive and God responded accordingly. In granting Solomon wisdom, God expected him to be obedient and attentive to instruction. For the individual who has been given instruction, will they follow it or do they go and do as they please, and can they be trusted?

All good relationships are based on a level of trust and if the trust is broken the relationship will not last. God's promises were straightforward. They required Solomon to hear what God was telling him: to put it into action and the opportunities would be endless.

Almost anyone can see the obvious, but when we are in alignment with God, we have the ability to discern the 'not so obvious' as well. God not only promised Solomon discernment, but a long **life** as well, to be breathed upon and the desire to be greedy. In this context life is first, then you take your first breath, but also a desire, and greed, which was certainly the tone of the day. When someone was appointed king, they usually followed it with lots of proclamations declaring how great they were and everyone would pay taxes, give portions of their harvest to the king and greed would ultimately become their demise.

Solomon would rule for forty years. He would accomplish many things and was considered to be a very wise man. He became the wisest and wealthiest man to ever rule Israel, but what made him wealthy would also take him down.

God warned the Israelites not to intermarry with foreign women. Nevertheless, Solomon's desire for women: 700 wives and 300 concubines led him astray.

"They were from nations about which the Lord had told the Israelites, 'You must not intermarry with them, because they will surely turn your hearts after their gods.' Nevertheless, Solomon held fast to them in love" 1 King 11:2 (NIV).

Solomon, like kings before him and many after him, became his own worst enemy. As God began to give pieces of the kingdom to Solomon's adversaries, it all began to unravel. What was promised by God as a long and prosperous life to Solomon was taken away because of greed and disobedience. What was meant for good would eventually be his demise.

Solomon's request for wisdom was about doing what was right, fair, and wise in the eyes of God. To be **wise** is *to be skillful, cunning, in act and deed, to teach, and deal in a fair manner.* These are skills most men want, but few are willing to pay the price to get. God was so delighted with Solomon's request that he put in Solomon the desire to want to learn.

As you read Solomon's story, you can see his drive to learn and how everything fascinated him. Each task he undertook—small or large—became an opportunity to explore, uncover, and expand his field of knowledge.

He was skillful and his demand for excellence gave him a reputation. His reputation became so well known the Queen of Sheba sought his presence and paid him greatly to sit in his court and talk with him. It seemed the more he acquired the more others wanted to give him. *"And she gave the king 120 talents of gold, large quantities of spices, and precious stones. Never again were so many spices brought in as those the queen of Sheba gave King Solomon"* 1Kings 10:10 (NIV).

The rise to stardom has its perks. You get wealth, attention, recognition, your name in lights, everyone wants to spend time with you. However, all the trappings usually lead to destruction. For those who read their own press clippings and begin to believe what they read will eventually fall from their lofty pedestal.

Solomon was skillful, cunning, and willing to teach and be fair in his dealings. Those never came into question—actually, they are what propelled him to greatness. He was eager to share what he knew, but everything was a challenge to him. The more he knew, the more he wanted to know. In 1 Kings 4:29 (NIV) we read: *"God gave Solomon wisdom, and very great insight with a breadth of understanding as measureless as the sand on the seashore."*

He was wiser than all the men of the east. The drive that God instilled in Solomon was the desire to have a heart of compassion. Solomon's **heart** was full of feeling, intellect and courage he demonstrated daily.

Because of his wisdom he amassed riches that surpassed anyone of his time. Solomon's wealth was so massive that if translated, the zeros were in the thousands. Solomon asked for wisdom and God put in the desire to learn. Solomon took that desire and the promise of God and ran with it.

Think About It

You have a dream, and in it you are given a promise. No one knows of this dream but you. You believe it, and the journey begins. Everything you encounter you question, "why, how, who, and what if?"

_____

_____

You dig for answers, not just any answer, but the right and fair and just answer. You begin to get noticed and you gain respect and now you're an authority. Others start coming to you for advice. You get more knowledge and now people are paying just to spend time with you. They are paying huge sums and it all just continues to grow.

You are now a person everyone looks to with **honor.** They see you with splendor and glory and you carry weight. People now elevate you above others and everyone puts you on a pedestal. Solomon had the weight of the kingdom upon his shoulders and all the perks that went along with it. Keep in mind, God had granted Solomon wisdom and that is what started the ball rolling.

As it happened to Solomon, it happens to many who think they are the reason for all the success. That is exactly the kind of thinking that gets people into trouble—the "I" attitude.

As we will see in the coming verses, God does not take kindly to those who abuse the rewards He has graciously given them. For the next twenty years, Solomon's life was all anyone could expect and more. He built God's temple: a thing of beauty and splendor and upon its completion, it was dedicated to God. Solomon stood before all of Israel offering sacrifices and prayer, giving God the credit and thanking him that he had not forgotten his father David and the people of Israel.

God responded to Solomon's prayer and dedication with words of praise and warning. Those words were a double-edged sword. *"As for you if you walk before me in integrity of heart and uprightness as David your father did and do all I command and observe my decrees and laws. I will establish your royal throne over Israel **forever** as I promised David your father when I said You will never fail to have a man on the throne of Israel"* 1 Kings 9:4-5 (NIV).

That, my friends, is a long time and God is not known to make idle statements. In 1 Kings 9:6-7, God gets very descriptive in his reminder to Solomon by using words that were direct and to the point. *"But if you or your descendants turn away from me and do not observe the commands and decrees I have given you and go off to serve other gods and worship them, then I will cut off Israel from the land I have given them and will reject this temple I have consecrated for my Name. Israel will then become a byword and an object of ridicule among all peoples."*

God is very clear to Solomon. He tells him "to not **turn** away and worship other gods or I will **cut** off Israel and it will become a **byword among all** the **people**."

Let's review each keyword in this passage. We start by God telling Solomon to **not turn** away [to not break, do evil, or lay down his commands]. Would there be any misunderstanding of what was being said? If we just stop and see that God has blessed Solomon with a great life he has had to this point, why would anyone want to turn away or want to mess with that? The short answer is "because he was human."

Man is notorious for doing dumb things. Like, being told not to do something and goes ahead and does it, just because he wants to prove a point that "I can do it on my own."

On my own is one of the most absurd statements we could ever make. Man has the worst track record of messing up because of the attitude 'I can do it on my own and I'll get all the credit.'

There's a long history of fallen men. Those who have fallen from great heights because of the lure of money, fame, glory, and this single mindedness of, *"I can do this on my own."* There are those men who have achieved success and have gained the notion of becoming indestructible with their inflated ego—making it difficult to admit they can do no wrong.

Approaching those men and having a conversation concerning this area of weakness becomes very delicate. Pride is such a destructive thing. Knowing what to say, how to say it, and getting to realize it, can be a real challenge.

God, on the other hand, does not mix words. He kept His Word when He told Solomon, *"If you turn from me I will cut you off. I will destroy you and the covenant we have will be broken and you and all your people will perish"* 1Kings 6-7 (NIV).

In today's society, a promise means very little and people think nothing of breaking it or changing the rules to fit a need without any discussion. God is not like that. By telling Solomon He will **cut** him off carries the implication of perishing—to have pain, misery, and separation forever.

Think About It

Have you ever made a promise to someone and then backed out of the deal?

_____

_____

Solomon's successes caused him to become so confident and self-centered that he thought he could ignore his covenant with God. He never forgot the covenant. He just began to rationalize his wrong doings. If you read the verses again, you will note that this is not a conditional warning God gave Solomon, because as we can observe, he does experience pain, misery, and separation from God.

We all are guilty of breaking promises and changing the rules to fit our needs, or just deciding to change our mind and expecting the other person to go along with it. I can remember when a handshake meant something and when you signed your name you were good for your word. God set those rules in motion many years ago and He still abides by them to this day. His word is good. As the verse continues, a further warning is given to Solomon: "You and your people, the Israelites, will become a **byword**," *taunt, pierce, and prick.*

Think About It

Have you ever had someone taunt you, get in your face, or say things that get back to you through another person?

_____

_____

These conversations trickle to you in bits and pieces like, "Did you hear, or I heard," or "They began to pierce you like a knife and or what I call a thorn in your side." This type of person usually has a motive, an agenda, and they're out to make a statement at the cost of others.

This is exactly what the verse is telling Solomon. If you mess up and break our covenant a lot of people are going down with you, so think long and hard about what you are doing. Isn't it amazing how many chances God gives us? How forgiving He is and how we take advantage of him.

"You will go from being served to being the server. You will no longer be the head—you will be the tail. You will be the center of attention, not for your good, but as a form of profit making for another." What was once good becomes turmoil, and the Israelites will be in the midst of it all. God wants us to be a server to others—but not a slave to others.

The word **all**, *whole, complete* is not a part time thing. We are talking about our disobedience. Our whole life will be immersed into being a slave to others. In closing this verse, the conversation with Solomon *"this nation of people you oversee will become overshadowed—hid in darkness and become obscure if you fail to obey my commands."*

When we allow our ego, life, its pressures, or circumstances to make our choices for us— it is not pleasing to God. First of all, we have not allowed Him to be in the picture, and second, He has given us the ability to reason and stretch our minds to new dimensions, but it all must be in alignment with His Word.

Just as an athlete who has the desire to compete and get better, so God has put in us the desire to do more. Solomon grew in stature and sought to know more. He was not a man who sat on the sidelines and watched. He got in the game and participated.

"At Gibeon the Lord appeared to Solomon during the night in a dream, and God said, 'Ask for whatever you want me to give you" 1 Kings 3:5 (NIV). Solomon, being the son of a king, may have been torn between wanting to do his own thing, hang out, or run a country as great as Israel.

Knowing you are going to be the next king is one thing, but to have the hand of God anoint you is something totally different. God filled Solomon with the desire to learn. He wanted to conquer any subject that caught his attention. This is why he was so brilliant.

He was willing to dig deep into whatever challenge he was presented with to find the root of the cause. He was the Einstein of his day with one exception—God was his mentor. It was God who was running his life and guiding him. It was God who laid out the rules and constantly reminded him to stay on track.

It took seven years to build the temple and up to thirty thousand laborers at times to complete this magnificent work of art. People would stand in awe at the beauty, but it was destroyed when he failed to follow the rules.

Think About It

Why do you suppose God was so adamant about reminding Solomon to stay the course? And, what has God said to you lately about your course?

_____

_____

Just like the athlete who has the discipline to get up every day and spend hours in training, staying away from certain foods, drinks, and activities that are harmful, but then what happens once fame and fortune hit? Many end up in trouble with the law, or worse, dying from a drug overdose. Solomon followed a similar course, as he matured and gained fame.

His natural inclination led him astray, and his great success and fame separated him from God. This is why God was so direct in His warning to Solomon and the words He chose were so poignant.

So how do we relate this to modern day thinking? When someone approaches us and asks if we believe in Jesus, what is the response? Most have some form of skepticism. We want to believe but we question our own thoughts. We can read the Bible, go to church, listen to the minister and when we have a conversation with a non-believer we stumble because of our weak faith.

Our teaching from school begins to creep in. Is it evolution or creation? Does God exist or is it wishful thinking? Even though we can be shown in black and white print, we just don't get it.

Many of us were raised or went to school in the secular community, so we were taught the big bang theory. On Sundays, we were taught that God created the heavens and the earth in seven days. So, from a very young age, we have been given two theories and most of us never really understood either very well. We go through life with two different ways of thinking—one that's prevalent in the workplace and one on Sundays at church.

But today, that is even more confrontational for now we have the atheist who is making an uproar and purposely sending a cloud of confusion into the public arena. So where does one go to get understanding?

The same place Solomon did. He went to God. He had been raised to have a belief system and trust that source. He was instructed to follow some basic rules and could enjoy an abundant life. He was also reminded if he abused his relationship with God, just like when you were a child and did something wrong, you knew you were going to get a spanking.

God acts no differently when we mess up and do our own thing. The actions comes back to bite us—that is our spanking. The problem today is we don't want to accept responsibility for our actions. We want to blame someone else. God's instructions simply tell us to admit our wrong, seek forgiveness, correct our mistakes, and move on. That is way too easy. Instead, we make an excuse, tell a lie, blame another or look for a reason to justify our wrongdoing. Then we have the nerve to go off in the corner and say, "Why me, Lord? What did I do to deserve this mess in my life?"

The answer is in the question. Do you see all those I's in the question? Who is everything centered on? There is no we—no place for God—just me. When we don't involve God in the decision-making process, then we can't blame Him in the answering process. When we are so wrapped up in our wrong doing that we are convinced it is right, no one can tell us otherwise.

As God is having His conversation with Solomon, His reminders are stern and yes, they are warnings of what is to come if he chooses to go off and get in this 'I' mode.

We can see how easy it would be for Solomon to get caught up in the self, with all the fame, riches, and attention he has attracted. Because of a simple honest request at a very young age, God took that request and blessed it beyond anyone's imagination.

Solomon had two jobs. The first was to manage God's people and the second was to manage himself. It would be the second that would cause him trouble. God had instilled in him the desire to seek knowledge and learn everything that intrigued him, and he did.

He became so knowledgeable others sought him out to learn from him. Since there was no television, radio, newspaper, or internet, word traveled by messenger, so it was much slower than today's method. However, over time Solomon's reputation preceded him and being human—this reputation would become his downfall. As Solomon was in his day, so is man today seeking fortune, fame, recognition, and even a simple pat on the back or someone to say good job.

Man hungers for that little bit of recognition. Someone to say, "I am proud of you." That is where we so desperately need to have a relationship with God and understand He loves us unconditionally and He is always ready to say, "I love you and I am proud of you."

This is hard for man to grasp because we are talking about a book that is two thousand years old. A message that is constantly being attacked for credibility as every so-called expert takes their shot at explaining why it is not true. A word of caution to anyone who chooses to read this foolishness: the author has never taken their theory to the experts and to put it to the test; they only go to the unsuspecting public for final approval.

Since man is always on the hunt to find answers, the so-called expert has planted this seed of doubt, making man susceptible to a newfound thought, and a possible solution. It is the age-old problem; the answer is and has always been right under our noses. But man would much rather spend all his energy off on some adventure looking for a new horizon.

There is a story of an angel who was very handsome. They called him beautiful and he wanted to be chosen to lead the world, but it was not God's plan and eventually there would be a parting of the ways. This angels name was Lucifer, which means bright morning star, large capacity, public building, power and suffer.

Lucifer wanted to be God's spokesperson on earth, but God had other plans. This did not set well with Lucifer and so he was kicked out of heaven with his band of followers. God said he would roam the earth and even have rule for a time but will be destroyed in the end.

Lucifer has one goal and that is to win as many as he can to his way of thinking and away from God. You may say this sounds silly, like a big fairy tale. To the unsuspecting, I can see your point of view because I was once there myself.

Even though I was raised in a Christian home, there was a point and time in my life when I chose to ignore what had been taught to me and go in the opposite direction. For years, I strayed and did all the wrong things. I drank, cheated, had affairs, broke hearts, did not care who I stepped on and was greedy. But I had a conscience and it kept haunting me at every turn and every wrong- doing. I was reminded that this was not right. "You were not raised this way, you were not taught to believe this. Why are you continuing to live this way?" My parents asked me continuously.

Finally, one day it got the best of me. I came crawling back broken. I asked God to come back into the life I had wrecked. I had wrecked enough lives and to give me another chance. God is always willing to give us another chance.

I felt a great burden being lifted, a sigh a relief, but that did not correct all the wrong that I had done. I had inflicted pain on many and those were fences I would need to mend and relations I would need to tend to.

People ask, why doesn't God fix our problems, even though we don't listen to His guidance? His words do offer solutions and they can make it better; we just need to submit and follow.

Our messes don't usually happen overnight, so they take time to correct, but the good part is that God has a perfect way, though it's different from the world's. To most, changing direction and going against what everyone else is doing is very difficult. It requires discipline and some set guidelines, which many are not willing to follow, citing that religion does not work.

The truth is, God is not into religion; He is into relationships. His and ours. The principles written in the Bible were never intended to be judgmental, nor a bunch of rules dictated by Him or His angels sent to arrest anyone who chose to disobey them. While Jesus was on earth, He simply stated, *"I came to serve, not to be served."*

Lucifer, on the other hand, wants everyone to bow down and worship him. While God wants us to come to Him freely, and not because He demands it. He desires to have a relationship with each and every one of His children. When we understand that, then we know it is not about religion. God wants to be that friend you've always wanted, the father you never had, or the mother you lost at an early age. *"Keep your lives free from the love of money and be content with what you have, because God has said, Never will I leave you, never will I forsake you"* Hebrews 13:5 (NIV). Never is a very long time.

If you struggle with these statements, if your heart is hard towards God because of what life has dealt you, I can understand rebelling to what is being said. Maybe you are at a crossroad in your life where it has all fallen apart either through choices you have made or circumstances you had no control over.

The only thing I am saying is it does not have to continue, and you do have alternatives. As strange as it may sound, all you have to do is believe and ask God to come into your life. Read the Bible, get involved in a good Bible-based church and associate with Christian people who will give you support and guidance.

God will give you that hunger He instilled in Solomon for His Word and your life will change slowly, but surely. God wants us to be humble and full of wisdom, but to have those two characteristics is not always easy for man.

Man wants to go and hunt, bring it home and tell his wife this is what I did today—I am the provider. He then wants to gather up his buddies and tell them of his adventure. But because his ego needs to be fed, the story always has a little more adventure and flair than what actually happened.

"This is what the Lords says: Let not the wise man boast of his wisdom or the strong man boast of his strength, or the rich man boast of his riches, but let him who boasts boast about this that he understands and knows me that I am the Lord who exercises kindness, justice and righteousness on earth for in these I delight declares the Lord" Jeremiah 9:23-24 (NIV).

He starts out with a word of caution by saying, "Just because you are **wise**, *skillful, cunning,* don't let this go to your head. Use your skills to represent me. Show those who look to you for leadership in your daily actions as you conduct business and deal with others."

We know we need to be cunning and shrewd, but God expects us to display a good heart with good intentions and back those intentions with right actions. In the world of business, it is a rarity to see a businessman who is able to deal with the sharks. Stand toe- to-toe and maintain integrity. He is expected to do dishonest things, pay people under the table and have late night meetings always dealing with someone who wants a favor.

Reading the Bible will teach you how to handle those who think they need special treatment. First things first, stay loyal to God. Being skillful in today's marketplace is a commendable trait in itself. Knowing how to be shrewd, yet honest and fair is a rarity. God then states our hearts need to always be focused on the right thing, having the right intention at all times.

These two qualities are difficult to master while maintaining a good standing. This is why God must be on our side and at the top of our thoughts daily. We will not last long without a direct line to God. We need him on standby constantly.

The next word is **man**, *high degree and worthy.* God created man in His own image, thus He holds us in a high degree and we are worthy to be in His presence. When you follow in the footsteps of one who has a reputation of doing good, being fair, and always doing what is right, it should be a given—the new leader will do the same.

This is what God expects. However, the world has a very different view and the shambles of our economy, our country, and our reputation as a nation shows how little those in power regard doing the right thing. The sad thing is instead of people putting their foot down and demanding the right thing to be done, we are jumping on the bandwagon and being an encourager of corruption.

At every level, be it business or government, it has become a topic of conversation. If we are not directly affected, we just shrug our shoulders and move on.

God is ashamed of anyone who chooses to cheat and lie his or her way to the top and He assures us it will come back to bite us. It did with Enron, the lending institutions and the Wall Street gurus. They all have fallen but many more have suffered.

We are next reminded, "Let not the **rich** man, literally boast, glorify-self, here the word rich has an unpleasant meaning of selfishness." When we look around us today: the advertisements, expectations, and images presented is all about self.

God's whole message centers on taking our eyes off ourselves and being a humble servant to others. American author, Zig Ziglar, often said that if you help enough people get what they want then you can get what you want as well.

Perhaps that statement doesn't sound biblical to you, and you would be correct if your only intent was to help yourself. But if you ever heard Ziglar speak, then you had no doubt where his heart was and whom he served. He loved and served the Lord.

Let's explore the word **Lord** [the eternal Jehovah, the Most High]. The prime root for Jehovah means to exist and come to pass. Those two words should tell us all we would ever need to know about our Lord and Savior.

What that says to me is He does exist and what is written in the pages of His sacred book will come to pass. The most-high—everyone is always looking for a position. I am first, I am at the top, I am number one: these are all positions that say something about where we are. Man has this internal desire to be at the top. God tells us in Matthew 20:16: *"So the last will be first and the first will be last."* Meaning, if we become so consumed with the ride to the top of corporate America, we are on the wrong road and our rewards will be short lived.

This will only work if you have God as your Chief and Commander. If you choose to believe what is written, then you will understand that it is God who **exercises** kindness. It is He who will appoint, govern, bring forth and cause to come to pass. As this is being written we are on the eve of an election as to who will govern the United States for the next four years and history may be written.

Regardless of who is President, there will always be only one, who sits at the head of the table—the Lord our God. Just as God trained and tempered Joseph to eventually be the Pharaoh's second in command. To many who follow the story it seemed cruel and unfair, but as events of his life unfolded the end was right and just.

God brings to pass what is necessary, not what seems good at the time. We all question God—even those who say they don't believe. We are always looking for ways to justify our belief. We question all the illnesses, cancer, or other devastating diseases. Why is this happening, the war, the automobile accident, the little child who suffers . . . the list is endless. There are answers for all of it. Some we will not like and some we won't accept or understand.

Think About It

What does that mean to you?

_____

_____

Information written in the pages of the Bible over two thousand years ago reveals as much today about our life, what is going on and what is to come, but man refuses to accept or see the relevance. God does not set out to deliberately punish anyone, but our choices and actions bring about results that we don't always like. This can be due to lack of planning or just ignoring a situation.

It is not God who sets out to bring about the end result. When we refuse to involve Him in the process, follow His guidelines and seek His wisdom, it can bring unpleasantness. God does not want to run our lives, He just wants to be a part of them.

God not only exercises kindness, but He more importantly exercises **righteousness,** *justice, virtue, and prosperity.* Justice says, "I will always be treated equally, even in punishment, his favor will be with me." This statement may raise an eyebrow because many can site where punishment was or has been unfairly administered.

There is not always a clear and precise answer or one that we can comprehend because of God's insight. He knows the beginning from the end—why and what will come to pass. This plays into His plan even though we humans want immediate retribution. God's action may be in the form of a lesson rather than punishment, a season instead of justice, or what we may perceive as a blessing.

We must understand that He is in charge, accept His reasoning, and be prepared to learn from it. God never makes a move that He is not teaching us something. There is a stark contrast in the word righteousness from justice to virtue, which carries with it a form of humility.

Virtue says, "our good deeds and actions will be recognized by others and we are not to go around tooting our own horn." Virtue also implies we are to be mighty and can do miraculous things with great power. All of this is under the hand of God.

The difficult thing for most, if not all, is we get this big head and want to say, "watch me, I did this" and that is where the downfall begins. God implants within all of us a vision to do good for Him and we get to reap the side benefits, but most want the benefits and ignore the one who empowered them.

In Proverbs 21:21 (NIV) we read: *"Whoever pursues righteousness and love finds life, prosperity, and honor."* We need to get our head on straight, our heart in order. and be in alignment with the almighty God. That is when our soul will prosper.

It is a must that we are right on the inside before we can ever think about being right on the outside. But we look at all who are doing well, some very well that don't follow God's teaching and say, "What about them?"

Malachi 3:18 (NIV) answers that question well: *"And you will again see he distinction between the righteous and the wicked, between those who serve God and those who do not."*

God does take note of these things, we just expect immediate results and He does not work that way. As you read about Joseph, Joshua, or Job, all three are very different examples of God using circumstances to bring about good. There was a side benefit of prosperity because they were all committed to having God first in their heart.

There are many Christians who can testify to God's presence in their lives and answering prayers from simple to miraculous. The church I attend has several different outreach ministries and the other day they previewed a video clip from a true story. It was a true and very powerful example of God working in a young Hindu man's life who converted to Christianity.

Once it was discovered he was a converted Christian, he was put in jail and beaten for several days trying to get him to give up his Christian belief. In one final attempt before they would execute him, he was put in a two-by-two by six-foot cell, sitting down, his knees drawn up to his chest, bound in a rope and blind folded for fifty-three days.

Each morning, the guard opened the cell to discover he had no rope or blindfold. Each night, the guards repeated this and every morning he would be loose. They asked him how he was getting free and he told them, *"It is Jesus Christ who unties the ropes and removes the blindfold."* The Hindus, being a superstitious sec, did not execute him and finally let him go. Every day his life is in jeopardy, but he continues to be a witness for Jesus.

God **delights** in those who exercise justice and righteousness while on earth. To delight is to incline, to be pleased with, desire to, and have pleasure in. Most of us were brought up to do the right thing. We were taught to be fair, treat others with respect, please your elders, your teachers whoever was in charge.

God wants us to have the desire to do well and be of the servant mindset. Be willing to go the extra mile, be thinking of others and their wellbeing. For that reason, we should have pleasure in seeing someone else move ahead or helping another person succeed. While He was on earth, Jesus' greatest asset was His ability to blend in, yet through helping others He always stood out. Just like Zig Zigglar, who says, "if you help enough other people get what they want, you will have what you want." All God wants is for people to trust Him.

Now let's travel back in time to Genesis and see how a coat of many colors gets a young boy in so much turmoil, but turn for God's good in the end. In the verse there are three keywords that we need to pay attention to: **master, found, and blessings.**

In Genesis 39, we catch Joseph's story as he is sold into slavery by his brothers and finds himself in the home of an Egyptian Captain of the guard. *"From the time he (Potiphar) put him (Joseph) in charge of his household and all that he owned the Lord blessed the household of the Egyptian because of Joseph. The blessings of the Lord were on everything Potiphar had both in the house and in the field."*

Joseph answered to Potiphar who became his **master**, *sovereign, owner, adoni.* Joseph was all too well aware of who was his boss and treated the circumstance accordingly, which in turn gave him a greater freedom. Potiphar gave Joseph complete run of his house and concerned himself with none of those duties.

Think About It

Have you ever had someone put that much trust in you? Perhaps the experience was a tremendous honor, but it was probably very humbling.

God wants us to recognize that honor is great, but it is the humility that God is after. When you work from the position of wisdom combined with humility you will exceed far beyond your wildest imagination. When you look at Jesus' life on earth, you can see that He worked from the point of humility.

Joseph was well aware of who his boss was, and more importantly, whom he prayed to. It was because of his allegiance to both, in the proper order, that God showed him favor. When Joseph was instructed by his master, he followed his orders. When Joseph was communicating with the sovereign God he knew where to turn to get his answers because he had the chain of command in order.

Joseph **found** favor in the eyes of Potiphar and was able to come forth, be enough, and suffice. Joseph was able to run Potiphar's house, do all that was necessary and sufficient to be enough to satisfy Potiphar's needs. That is saying a lot because Potiphar was a Roman soldier, and Joseph being Jewish, in those times was not a good mix, but there was something special about Joseph.

Have you ever been in the position of being recognized by someone and you are picked out to come forward, given special assignments or tasks that says to everyone else the boss likes this person? There is something special in you that they like. Perhaps it's your personality, attitude, or your willingness to go the extra mile. This is how Potiphar saw Joseph, who received **blessings,** *to kneel, abundantly, and greatly.*

When a person receives praise, the normal reaction is to gracefully and humbly accept that praise with thanks. In Joseph's day, your point of grace was to bow down and to kneel before the person who was bestowing the honor on you.

By showing respect to the one who bestowed the honor, you actually were turning the spotlight back on them. This is a lesson God continually teaches throughout the Bible of how this humility thing works. Walk in humility and God will bless you abundantly. Read the rest of Joseph's story. You will soon see that there was a season when he was tested, even though he did nothing wrong. He actually did everything right, and still paid a price. Joseph never gave up on God and God never gave up on Joseph. They had a pact that was stronger and a love that was deeper than any circumstance could tear apart.

Before a sword becomes a thing of beauty and strength, it must first go through the fire and be tempered. The fire removes the impurities and makes the steel whole, allowing the master craftsman to mold it to be the best it can be. That, my friend, is what God does with those who are willing to turn their life over to Him.

Likewise, He will run you through the fire to remove your impurities and start a process of being the best that He has in store for you. Just as the tempering process of steel is just the beginning, because it continues to cure for many years, so is man once he turns his life over to God.

When you work at a job and continue to improve over the year's promotions, pay raises and perks are all natural by products of being tempered. God displays throughout the Old Testament how perfection and attention to detail are part of His plan.

The Bible taught HT this very valuable lesson. The more he worked at doing what God's Word said, the more he pleased the company, the more his men respected him and production was always up. Was everything perfect? Did everything always run smoothly? No, but the respect was at such a level even in down times, the shift HT managed did better than the others.

The lesson here is: keep your focus on Jesus and the end will always be better than you expected.

CHAPTER 11

THE TREE

HT decided to shut down his mine and go back to management for a major company, after he realized he had limits and his skills were best being a server for another, which in turn made his reward the greatest.

We read: Exodus 36:1 (NIV): *"So Bezalel, Oholiab and every skilled person to whom the Lord has given a skill and ability to know how to carry out all the work of constructing the sanctuary are to do the work just as the Lord has commanded."*

We start by looking at the word **every**, *the whole, complete, perfect, will do the work.*

If we are called because of our talent and are willing to serve, we must complete the assignment we are given. His expectations are that we complete our work and He accepts no less than our best. He is not one for cutting corners.

If our best is not acceptable to Him we will have to re-do the work. There are usually more re-do's than first time acceptance. But that is ok, because the more we practice, the better we get, and the better we get, the more we are called on because our reputation precedes us.

You get it—the more we are pushed to be better, the more people talk about our work. The more they talk and the more we do, the better we get—pretty cool, right? There is a reason that God has given us this **ability**—also known as a *skill or a learned capacity*—to carry out pre-determined results with minimum time and energy. If God gives us the ability or skill and we use it for His good, our results are pre-determined. Because we are good at it, it actually takes less time and energy to perform. This sounds like work to me.

The definition of **work** from God's perspective. Deputyship, (ministry) property, and we belong to God. If work is a form of ministry and all I have (property) belongs to God, then I had better sharpen my skills and stay on top of my game until He returns or calls me home.

There are two conclusions we can take away from this. One, God does not mention retirement in the Bible. Two, we need to continue to practice the skills that God has equipped us with.

Like the Hindu whose heart was committed to God and prepared to die after the fifty-three days in jail, he could never be convinced that God is not real. Many will argue with that statement and express that they have called on Him several times and He has not answered. So have I. But, I have also found that more times than not it was because He did not give me the answer I wanted. In fact, I was so driven by my own desire, I could not see what He was really pointing out to me.

God is very clear about right and wrong. He is also very clear about doing things His way. In Jeremiah 22:3 (NIV), we read: *"This is what the Lord says: Do what is just and right. Rescue from the hand of the oppressor the one who has been robbed. Do not wrong or violence to the foreigner, the fatherless or the widow, and do not shed innocent blood in this place."*

In the Old Testament, on more than one occasion, you see were the people paid a price because they chose to do their own thing. But once their backs were against the wall and had nowhere else to turn, they came back to God.

The same scenario still plays out today. We choose to do our own thing and when it does not turn out the way we want it to, or there is a tragedy then we go running to God, asking him to make it all better. When God does not respond the way we expect, we in turn become bitter and blame Him for our problems.

In the Book of Psalms, we are given a tremendous amount of insight into our emotions, wisdom, and how God fits into all of this. The very first verse of Psalms tells us what to do and how God will react if we follow that instruction.

"Blessed is the man who does not walk in the **counsel** *of the wicked or stand in the way of sinners or sit in the seat of mockers. But his delight is in the law of the Lord, and on his law he meditates day and night. He is like a tree planted by the streams of water, which yields its fruit in season and whose leaf does not wither. Whatever he does prospers"* Psalms 1:1-3 (NIV).

There are several keywords that will help us to understand God's thinking and how the Psalmist David encourages us to fear God (in a good way). To fear God is to take His teaching seriously, as this is the foundation upon which wisdom is built.

The first word we focus on is **counsel,** which means: *to be prudent, purpose, sit down together, found and ordain.* We are told to seek counsel, get others advice, and be prudent. He is telling us to not just seek anyone's advice, but go to those who are wise in the area with which you need advice.

These are experts who have been down the road you are traveling, who've suffered the bumps and bruises, which may now save you valuable time and heartache. Sit down with these experts and spend as much time as they will allow. Basically, learn from their mistakes (lessons). As your relationship begins to develop, your understanding will grow deeper and your insight will be clearer while developing meaning and purpose.

Finally, you will be ordained, set apart, and be someone others will come and look to for counsel. This is a great and high honor that is not to be taken lightly, nor does it come overnight. This is something that only comes with time and perseverance. So right out of the gate, we are told to ask for help, not just any help but to seek godly men and women.

David tells us to not stand in the **way**. Way is a course of life, journey, high path. Every decision has two options. The one we choose eventually leads down the path of life's journey. If we make the right choice, God will set us on the high path—His path, the way that is right. Our life unfolds according to the choices we make, and those choices are presented to us daily allowing each day to be a new beginning. We don't have to continue with what happened yesterday.

This is the day the Lord has made. Let us rejoice and be glad in it. Yesterday is gone— tomorrow is not here. So, work on today.

HT made a choice to shut down his operation. Once his decision was made, he did not look back. He did what was necessary to close up shop and move forward. He did not lose valuable time with the 'should have' and 'could have' syndrome. It was made clear he was not ownership material, but much more valuable as upper level management.

Blessed is the man who **delights** in the law of the Lord. To delight is to have pleasure, a desire, a valuable thing, to bend, and find favor. David explains that by delighting in God's law we not only find favor in God's eyes, but it is pleasing to Him as well.

Think About It

Have you ever helped someone do something just out of the goodness of your heart that was very pleasing to them and you walked away feeling good in the process?

If we meditate on God's law and follow what it says because we want to, not because we have to, there will be a natural desire that will spring up in us. This will be valuable to us throughout our entire life.

David reminds to **delight**, which means *to bend, be humble, and give honor to others.* Respect the other person's position and acknowledge wherever they are in life, for each person deserves to be recognized. Many feel that once they have attained a certain level of success that everyone should acknowledge them.

David tells us that is not the case. God wants us to learn to be in a mode of service, not a mode of expectation. We don't have to go around expecting God to bless us if we are doing what is being asked of us. The blessings are automatic and come in many unexpected forms.

One of the first things children learn as they begin to understand this world, and how it functions, is if they do something good and someone sees it, they are recognized and given praise for it. Children play that card as many times as they can. When the parents or teachers stop recognizing their efforts, they rebel. They don't understand why their efforts have gone unnoticed. It is unfortunate when this occurs and there are many reasons why it happens. We use everything from being too busy to having a bad day, which by the way is not acceptable in God's eyes, but it happens.

If you want to find favor in God's eyes just meditate on His law. You will never have to worry if someone sees you or if that good deed went unnoticed. He knows and sees it all, and you will be given credit.

According to David, if you want to find favor with God just play by His rules. There is another term for the word 'rule' and David calls it 'the law.' When we hear the word **law** most think of police, judges, courts, dishonest, jail, prison, or people being taking advantage of. These are all things that are not pleasurable. David tells us there is pleasure in abiding in the **law.** Law is a statute, Pentateuch, fig, tree, and fruit. As we look closely we see statue is a written rule, like when the light is red, which means to stop.

While employed for this company there will be no comingling of personal relationships and work relationships. What we see so far is that a statue is a guideline, simply stating what we can or cannot do. We next see the word 'Pentateuch' which is derived from the Old Testament's first five books of the Bible, also known as the Torah.

Pentateuch is a Greek word meaning literally five cases or the first five books of the Old Testament. These five books are what the Jewish people recognize as Moses's writing while he was alive on earth. The books according to Jewish tradition contain 613 commands, 365 restrictions, and 248 positive or good things. It sounds pretty much like what David is telling us. The law also relates to the fig that was first related to us in the book of Genesis as the leaf being used to cover Adam and Eve.

The Fig tree was a very important form of food and also considered a sacred tree. Law also relates to **tree,** which we know has many benefits. It produces fruit to eat, helps clean the air, provides shade on a hot summer's day, and provides lumber for shelter.

We can see how the law can be beneficial in many ways, but when related to fruit it may require some thought. In getting a grasp of how law is related to fruit, look at these familiar statements: *The results of your work are the fruit of your labor. The words you speak have become your fruit. Your children are your fruit.*

They all say basically the same thing but carry a very different and far-reaching end result. What you do at work could get you the raise and promotion you have been wanting or could get you fired.

The conversations you have at work could benefit your co-workers greatly. Your words could move them to a whole new level of thinking. It could also tear them down or impact them negatively and set them on a road to destruction. Your children and how they turn out to a large degree, is what you sow into their life. As they are in your home learning the values you instill in them, seeing the examples you set, and the actions you take—all carry a lot of weight. Those values will go with them long after they have left the nest. These are all fruits or results of decisions we have made. This is the kind of fruit David is referring to when he talks to us about meditating on the law. What are we going to do with the law once we have read it and internalized it? Are we going to obey it and follow its precepts? Choose to just do part of it, all of it or some days do none of it? Even if we don't feel like it, are we going to do whatever it takes to stay on track and obey?

So when we look at the word *law* from this perspective, it takes on a different meaning. We see the tree doing very well because of its location just as our life will do very well if we stay aligned with God.

We are told to **mediate,** *to murmur to study.* To study I know, but to murmur . . . what is that? To murmur is to speak very softly as you utter your words. They are not to be heard by others—it is private between you and God. God expects us to study His word—not just to spend time reading it. He also wants one-on-one time with us. When we spend time in private with Him, that's when we develop a bond, and an understanding begins to flow, for He has our undivided attention.

When you start having these conversations with God, you will discover two things:

1. He opens your heart, and words and thoughts start coming from you that you never expected.
2. You will see thoughts you had in you, and begin to see results as you follow your heart. Deuteronomy 26:16 (NIV) says, *"The Lord your God commands you this day to follow these decrees and laws; carefully observe hem with all your heart and with all your soul."*

Now don't go running rampant with every thought that enters you head. This process will lead you to discover the twelve inches between your head and your heart can be a very long distance when you start doing all the thinking and quit following the instructions. Been there, done that!

When we have a strong desire to want something or have a situation go in a specific direction, we go to God and pray about it. The thing is our mind is already made up as to the outcome and so we say *this is God's will.*

The outcome can be disappointing and even embarrassing, especially if we have broadcast it to others. God is not in the business of showing off His work and He is not fond of those who do. It may go your way for a season but if the plan is not God-centered, eventually it will come to a halt. God does not back things or plans that do not have Him at the head. People are clever at disguising their schemes and can fool almost everyone.

There are always those who see through the scheme. In the mind of the person who is trying to pull the wool over on others, sees this person as a threat. This may result in them being removed or dismissed.

When one persons' thoughts or ideas become obsessive and controlling and begin affecting others, there is usually a parting between the parties involved. In most cases, this is not God-centered. When you pray, your prayer should be in earnest.

The next word David wants us to pay attention to is the **tree,** and with the tree comes *firmness, carpenter, staff, and to close.* The tree is a symbol of strength, firm, and solid— representing God's Word, and taking on many characters in the Bible.

The tree can be a fortress, a firm foundation, shield, and shade on a hot day, to provide a cool summer breeze. These all represent comfort, peace, security and reliability. Throughout the Bible, examples are used to teach us lessons and provide insight requiring us to think.

The tree stands for firmness. It endures the seasons, provides shelter, food, beauty and endurance. Look at the red wood forest, or the Sequoia. Some of those trees are hundreds of years old and are still standing strong just like God's Word.

We had a big oak tree in our front yard and that tree would tell me all the seasons and what was coming next. In the spring, I couldn't wait for the little green leaves to start popping out telling me summer was not far away, as the leaves came to full growth. I enjoyed the coolness of the day from the shade it provided. As a boy, on a light summer's rain, I remember running to the oak tree to provide shelter until the rain stopped. Then the day came when the leaves started to fall and my emotions were mixed with sadness and joy.

The sadness was due to school starting soon and my summer of adventure and fun was coming to an end. I loved the fall. It was my favorite time of the year, with all the beautiful fall colors, cool crisp mornings, and warn fall days. It also reminded me that Thanksgiving and Christmas would soon be here. Then came the winter snow that meant sleigh ridding, building snowmen, having snowball battles and hot chocolate by the fire.

That oak tree meant strength, years of knowledge and endurance. It withstood the years of change and still stands today. God represents the same strength, the test of time, wisdom, and His Word is still here today.

Another word related to tree is **carpenter,** a person who works with wood, a skilled craftsman in great demand. Jesus was a carpenter before He started His ministry.

As we study the Bible, we see God through His various prophets and leaders, sending us messages of what is to come. We next see the word **staff,** which represented a large thick stick used by the sheepherders for protection, as well as keeping the sheep in line. It also carried a symbol of status, meaning leader. Moses always carried his staff with him. God used His staff on many occasions to do miracles, demonstrating power to the Romans, bringing water from the rock to parting the Red Sea. The staff represented trust and leadership.

The final word related to tree is **to close**, *to make firm to shut.* There will be a time when we all need to make a decision for those who choose to follow God. He will close one chapter of his or her life and open another. You will get to join God's team. The beauty of being on God's team is we all get playing time.

There are no runts, no geeks, no super stars for we are all first stringers. We are all starters and everyone gets a chance to shine when you play for Coach God. From the least expected to the suspected, God has a role for everyone and He continues to tell us to pay attention to seek Him through His Word and He will make our path straight.

CHAPTER 12

ALL THE BIG COMPANIES ARE DOING IT. WHY CAN'T I?

O n a dry, dusty, hot day nothing quenches your thirst like a cool clear glass of water. David brings **water** to our attention. Other words that relate to water include juice, urine, semen, wasting, flood, and spring.

These are not necessarily my choice of words for water but remember this is two thousand years ago. Godly men spoke in terms and meaning that carried deep thought and implied consequences to those who chose to read and follow.

That same message holds true today if we intend to follow in God's footsteps. We will be held to a higher and different standard. The fig tree had a place of prominence in those days and it was spoken of often, either as the tree or its fruit. The fig graced the table of Kings and was considered a food for the common man as well.

What does this have to do with water? The tree had to be supplied with water as a main ingredient to create the fruit that would be tasty and sweet from the juice it produced. Juice was a source of nutrition from the fig—a part that actually makes the fruit very tasty. The juice can also be considered the sap of the tree. Sap provides life to the tree. It rises in the spring, recedes in the fall and is the sustainer of life for the tree. If the tree has a proper water supply it will bear a bountiful crop and the fruit will be very good; however, if the water supply to the tree is not good there may be no fruit at all. We can see how important the flow of water is for God to cause the tree to supply nourishment through its fruit.

Just as water is a source of life to the tree, it carries the same implication for man. Our body requires water to survive, but more importantly, it is a cleansing process that causes our body to produce urine. When relieved, it removes impurities to keep us healthy. When we are told to drink eight glasses of water a day it is for a very good reason. The tree was designed to function a certain way in order for it to produce bountiful and tasty fruit water was required.

We are also required to replenish the fluid in our body with water allowing us to be fruitful as well. We are next brought the word **semen,** which is produced to create new life. Semen comes from a natural function that God created to bring new life from a union of man and women. God told his nation to *"go forth and multiply, to settle down, marry, have children, work the fields and prosper. He will bring you to the land that belonged to your ancestors, and you will take possession of it. He will make you more prosperous and numerous than you ancestors."* Deuteronomy 30:5 (NIV).

Just as the tree produces a fruit that has seeds that when planted produces another tree with more fruit, God intended for man to do the same. *"Every commandment which I command you today you must be careful to observe, that you live and multiply, and go in and possess the land of which the Lord swore to your fathers"* Deuteronomy 8:1(NIV).

But in order for the new tree to produce fruit it first must have a season of growth, a time of maturity and a time to take root. The tree must mature before the tree produces an abundant harvest. The tree must be pruned and protected until it is strong enough to stand on its own. Does any of this sound familiar as to how God wants us to be as we grow in his word? In order to be mature enough to stand he must prune us as we go through a growing process. We are looking for help when we first become Christians, thus making our path very similar to what the tree goes through.

We next see the word **waste.** When related to water in modern times such as today, we can easily draw an analogy of being wasteful. There is a passage in the Bible where Jesus and His disciples are leaving a town one morning and as Jesus passes a fig tree, He is hungry and goes to the tree only to discover it has no fruit.

He curses the tree because it was not being productive in the purpose for which it was designed. By evening, as they return from their day's journey, they see the tree has withered and died. *"Peter remembered and said to Jesus, Rabbi, look! The fig tree you cursed has withered"* Mark 11-21 (NIV).

The tree here clearly has no purpose and will be cut for firewood. And just like that tree, we all have a purpose. Unless we apply ourselves to our purpose and make Jesus our focus, our lives will turn out like the tree with no fruit. Jesus had a mission and was always about His Father's business. He knew his time here on earth was limited so He was not wasteful. His love for his fellowman had no boundaries, and everything He did have a purpose and a lesson for His followers.

Jesus set examples, placed responsibilities on certain individuals, raised others up, and forged new paths.

Perhaps after you read the above passage, you don't quite understand why Jesus would curse the tree. That's because the tree was designed with a purpose and it was not fulfilling it, so it was used for firewood.

Use the fertile soil to plant a new one that will bear fruit. It is just like the person who is born with no arms and learns how to use their feet to do the same things their arms were meant to do. They have learned how to compensate and they don't expect special treatment, just a fair shake. It should be no different for us. We have each been given a talent, skills, and ability.

We should use them and not be wasteful or as we are told in Proverbs 21-25, *"Don't be a sluggard. The sluggard's cravings will be the death of him, because his hands refuse to work."* The problem is not with those who have plenty, but how we handle what we have and where God is in our lives.

Our next word is **flood,** which means *a deluge of water, an overflow, or abundance.* How does this apply to our learning? God gave Noah very specific instructions, as we see them unfold in Genesis 6:14: *"So make yourself and ark of cypress wood, make rooms in it and coat it with pitch inside and out."*

All the time the Arc was being built others around him ridiculed him and continued on their merry way. Then came the rain as the waters began to rise there was only one family saved only one. The flood destroyed everything. The slate was wiped clean and nothing was left and everything had a new beginning.

There was an abundance of water that brought an abundance of new life. Being in alignment with God means being prepared and that preparation allows us to be better equipped to handle it.

We end this verse with the word stream. **Stream** can take us in two directions. One is the source of water as a spring. I can remember as a little boy on a hot summer's day, playing in the woods.

When I got thirsty, I knew where I could go and find a spring and get a fresh cool drink of water. I also remember my grandmother's house, where I would be sent to the springhouse to get the milk, butter, or drinking water. It was a cool place where they had built a small building around an area where the water came out of the ground. This became known as the springhouse, a place to get a refreshing drink of cool water and to preserve food.

Spring also relates to a time of year when winter is dissipating and new life is being celebrated. Spring represents newness, a time to start over and to get a new lease on life.

Think About It

If you haven't accepted Jesus into your heart, perhaps today's that day? He will give you a new life and a chance to start over.

When we accept Jesus Christ into our hearts, He forgets our past, wiping the slate clean. It is a new day. Granted, that is difficult for us to grasp because we tend to hang on to the past. We like to remember but we are told to "put our hand to the plow and keep our eyes fixed before us because those who remove their hand and look back are not worthy of the kingdom of God."

If we want to make God first in our life we must believe He is the Creator. We must let Him have control of our lives. Put the things of old away and adorn ourselves with the things of new. Yes, it is great to reminisce and let the good things of the past bring a smile to our face from time to time. God wants us to move on.

Now that we have a good understanding of the tree, let's take a look at its fruit. The fruit is the end result of a tree's labor. It comes to life in the spring and nourished by the summer's sun, gentle breeze, soft rains, warm days, and cool nights. These are all conditioning steps to help the tree prepare to bare its fruit. The word **fruit** carries with it such words as *first, reward, bough, bring forth, and increase.* In the Bible, these are words of power and carry significant meaning to those who bear fruit for God's kingdom.

God tells us time after time to give of our first fruits. Growing up I had to work in the garden. I remember hoeing and wanting to get done before the sun got too hot, but being a kid, I messed around and dragged my feet until the sun was beating down. I had to get finished before my dad got home from work and ended up working in the hottest part of the day to get finished. I did not cherish that job at all. I did enjoy a Sunday dinner with new potatoes, green beans, and corn on the cob just picked from the garden. If you added that to mom's pot roast, boy was it good!

Those were the first fruits. They were the best and had the best flavor. We always looked forward to the first meal we got from the garden. This is what God is asking us to give to Him—the first fruits of our harvest. It is called the tithe—one-tenth off the top, not the leftover. The tithe can represent our money, talent, and our time from the best, not our leftovers.

There is another requirement that goes along with the gift of the first fruit. It must be done with a cheerful heart—not begrudgingly. God knows when the heart is cheerful. It is strange how we send this subliminal message of begrudging to the point of those around you knowing as well.

Think About It

If we give of our first fruits with a cheerful heart there is a reward that will come in many different forms.

_____

_____

The biggest and best reward will be the inner peace and satisfaction you will get from giving money, your time, and your talent. First, God wants this activity to be between you and Him. This is not something you announce to everyone—even if your activity is a group effort. The work you do is for Him—not for others to see or notice what you did to contribute.

This is the training ground for all you do in life. By doing what is right in your personal life for God, it will carry over into your business life and things will only get better.

When I coached middle school football, we started a month before the season began. The kids came in the first day excited, scared, and not knowing what to expect. We practiced twice a day for the first two weeks, and these were designed to see who would stick it out. The rewards for those who stuck it out was playing time, getting prepared for high school, and the discipline of life.

The enjoyment I got out of it was watching them apply what we, as coaches, taught them on a Friday night. These were seventh and eighth graders playing on the high school football field getting a taste of what was to come for those who would excel. Watching these kids (some were chubby, uncoordinated, and slow) compared to those who just had pure raw talent that needed harnessed just made it all worthwhile. Years later, I would bump into some of the boys and they would say, "Hey coach, I remember those hot summer mornings. You made us run the hill. We would get sick, but you would keep pushing us." They thanked me because it made a difference—then and now.

God tells us the benefit we will receive is long-term if we just do it His way.

There will be times when we want to quit, give up and even say, "This does not work." But, God encourages us to hang in there and run the hill one more time because it will be worth it.

How do we know it will be worth it? What or who is there to let us know to keep on keeping on? When Jesus was in the garden praying the evening of His final hours, His prayer was so fervent that the sweat from his brow became drops of blood. *"And being in anguish, he prayed more earnestly, and his sweat was like drops of blood falling to the ground"* Luke 22:44 (NIV).

Think About It

Do you think he was afraid? Do you think He did not want to go through what was about to happen to Him?

_____

_____

There seems to be a time when Jesus wanted things to be different, but as He concluded His prayer, He said, *"Father, if you are willing, take this cup from me; yet not my will, but yours be done"* Luke 22-42 (NIV).

Jesus' life was destined. It was on a certain path. What He did impacted the entire world and we are commissioned to carry it on. Does that mean we are all supposed to be ministers? No. But we all are to act and bare witness when the opportunity presents itself-—this is that part where we bear the fruit.

The reward will come to you in many forms, but the most important one is the peace you will have in your heart. It will be as if you were told *"Well done, good and faithful servant."* If Jesus is first, all the rest will fall into place no matter what your trial is. He will always have your back.

Did HT set an example from all the information? I think he did. He went before his men and set the example. He stood by them when he made a promise. He did not cheat or lie to them or the company.

I heard a man that worked for HT tell of an incident. HT was working the evening shift, which was from 3pm till 11pm, and there was a younger man (his job title the same as HT) working the day shift that had trouble getting his men to follow his orders.

There always seemed to be tension between the men and the boss. The gentleman telling the story said HT could get men to wade through water up to their waist and those same men would not walk through water that covered the soles of their shoes for the other boss.

HT's work ethic preceded and carried over into his home and church life. He was honest, willing to do whatever he could to help the other person and always striving to make a better life for his family.

His time, the money God allowed him to earn and the examples he set were all products of what he read in the Bible, and played out in his life. The Bible was his handbook for how to live his life.

The news is full of companies and CEO's who are breaking the law using other people's hard-earned money for their own pleasure. They developed a trust and a bond then broke it by their deceit. Their actions were similar to a tree. If a branch breaks off, it will die. When the actions caught up with the theft he was separated from society and labeled a crook and imprisoned. For some this would be the final step to destruction, but for others it would be the wake-up call and great change would occur.

The prison is designed to separate the criminal from society—a disconnection that for some is fatal. The psychological impact of being severed from the rest of the world makes a big scar that will always be carried by that individual. Just as a branch must remain attached to the tree to survive, man must have his link to society or he will die.

David reminds us that the tree is the main source of life. It has a support system of limbs, branches, leaves and fruit. But without the bough, those limbs that protrude from the trunk of the tree will not permit life to be carried to the rest of the tree.

I spent a little time reading about the word bough and the modern day meaning ties right in with the biblical perspective. The boughs are the main branches of the tree. They are the big limbs that go out from the trunk; they support all the little branches that bear the fruit that tree produces.

My grandmother had a huge cherry tree right by the side of the old farmhouse. When we visited, my mother parked the pickup truck under the tree and my job was to climb that tree and pick the cherries. I could climb up in the bed of the truck onto the top of the cab and grab one of those big limbs and climb into the tree and pick cherries. I picked two, then eat one and that would go on till my water bucket was full. I did not like picking those cherries, but I sure did like eating the pies and cobblers that came from the effort.

That cherry tree was big and very old, but it produced great tasting cherries year after year. Its branches were big and strong and supported many smaller branches that produced those cherries that we all enjoyed so much. *"Remain in me, and as I also will remain in you. No branch can bear fruit by itself; it must remain in the vine. Neither can you bear fruit unless you remain in me"* John.15-4 (NIV).

The branch cannot survive without the main trunk of the tree and we cannot survive without God in our life. But you say, "Wait a minute. I am doing ok and I see lots of others doing well. Jesus is not in my life or theirs—how do you explain that?

God addresses that very topic on many occasions throughout the Bible and in many different settings. He cites many examples of people He had entrusted responsibility and great wealth, only to see disaster occur or a correction in their life.

It started with Adam and Eve when they chose to listen to the serpent who is to blame for the labor and toil of today. Then Moses who was stubborn and did his own thing and led a stiff neck people and wondered for forty years on what should have been an eleven-day journey.

There is Jonah who refused to follow a simple request and ended up in the belly of a whale before he learned his lesson. "Now the Lord provided a huge fish to swallow Johah, and Jonah was in the belly of the fish for three days and three nights" John 1:17 (NIV). And then, there was Judas, one of Jesus' twelve original disciples. He turned on Him, and ended up committing suicide from his own guilt. *"So Judas threw the money into the temple and left. Then he went away and hanged himself"* Matthew 27:5 (NIV).

This reminds me of the Enron Corporation scandal in 2001. Enron was an American energy, commodities, and services company based in Houston, Texas. Before the scandal which led to the company's bankruptcy, Enron employed nearly 29,000 staff, with revenues of nearly $101 billion during 2000. Reportedly, Enron was "American's Most Innovative Company," for six consecutive years. However, at the end of 2001, it was revealed that Enron's financial condition was sustained by a creatively planned accounting fraud. The saddest part about this scandal is that it brought to light the accounting practices and activities of many corporations in the United States.

They cooked the books, lied to Congress and then one died, probably from all the stress. And one is in prison so how well did they fair? The financial devastation they caused is still rippling its ill effects. I can still picture the face of the couple on the front of Time magazine that lost half a million dollars in the Enron scandal.

As I write this book, look at all the financial chaos and all the CEO's who are lying and think it is ok to stand before Congress and ask them to bail out their debunked company. The uncertainty in the minds of the American people with each passing day brings more and more distrust as we watch our great nation crumble. Our values have disappeared and God is not in the school, as we kicked Him out. He is not in government either because we won't let Him in.

Our corporate leaders are sending the message that it is ok to cheat, lie, and steal. God is not in the work place and yet we are told things are really ok. This country was founded because there was a group of people who wanted to put God first above everything else. They were having trouble finding a town or place that would permit them to just worship. So, they decided to brave a journey and seek a new place that would permit them to do the one thing they wanted to do—have freedom of religion.

This would eventually lead to the founding of America. Did they make mistakes? Yes. Did they do things wrong? Yes. Did they have hardship? Yes, but they did one thing right—they kept God at the center of their lives.

If you study our American history books, you will find that all those who led this country spent time on their knees and studied the Bible. They admitted that the Bible was where they got their strength to continue.

The bough (the branch) will not survive if it not attached to the tree. The only thing it will be good for is firewood. God repeatedly tells us in the Bible to seek Him. *"But seek first his kingdom and his righteousness, and all these things will be given to you as well"* Matthew 6:33 (NIV).

Jesus is the answer to all our concerns. We keep looking everywhere and coming up empty-handed and wondering why it's not working or where we went wrong. The trunk of the tree is the support system for the entire tree. Without good soil and water to develop a solid root system the tree will eventually die. It will suck every bit of life out of the earth that surrounds it and all the nutrients. Once they are gone it will die. Does that sound familiar to anything that is happening in America today?

CHAPTER 13
KEEPING GOD FIRST IN OUR LIVES

As the verse continues, it says to **bring fourth,** which simply means *to appear and to give rise to a plant bringing forth its fruit.* The insight from these two simple words tells us a lot. Literally it means the branch that is joined to the tree will provide the fruit for all to enjoy. That fruit could be the apple, a juicy peach, a wonderful orange, or a bright red cherry. These are delicious fruits that provide nourishment to our bodies.

Hold that thought and let's take it to another level. Let's say God is the tree, the pastors, elders and lay people are his boughs, and they provide His Word through teaching and encouragement. We are taught to read the Bible and study His word—the fruit and our nourishment. If we read and study God's Word, we become nourished in our soul and we are fed spiritual food and now have a balance.

Hold on! There is one more thing. Once we are balanced, we are to go out and spread the seed and plant new trees. Those who are health-conscious eat the right foods, exercise daily, and maintain a good routine. The balance of exercise and physical condition helps maintain a healthy lifestyle. We need to do the same thing to our spiritual body: that our soul and mind needs to be conditioned as well.

Some may say that sounds like brain washing or some kind of a cult, and I am not into that. I can understand how some may think that following God's Word is some kind of religious cult. They may even say all their friends and associates have the same thought process.

Think About It

Does this sound like you?

_____

_____

My life is good. My kids are healthy. My marriage is solid, and I don't bother any-one. I have my friends. I enjoy going out occasionally. I believe there is a higher power, but I don't want constraints on my life. I get along with everyone at work and I am in line for the next promotion so why do I want to go and get involved with some religious thing and complicate my life? Why follow a bunch of rules that for the most part I do anyway? I will check it out later my plate is pretty full right now.

Or maybe this is you, even though you have the trappings of life you feel something is missing in your life and you can't seem to put your finger on it. Maybe your relationships at work seem distant—always a step away from the big promotion—on the outside looking in. The friends you hang with are always chasing one more deal and going to the newest hangout everyone seems to go to.

What are you missing? There needs to be a little clarification. We don't get involved with God to fill a void or complicate our lives. We become involved with God to complete our lives. To get is to have and to become, because you want to. There is a huge difference in having and wanting to. As we seek things to fill a void just to say I have that, it soon loses its appeal and becomes another trinket that ends up sitting in the corner collecting dust.

But if your desire to have something comes from a need to or a want to, then your perspective is all-together different. In your drive to fill that need you develop an understanding of why you have the need.

God is very clear in His teaching: "If you choose to follow me, you and I (God) need to develop a relationship." In John 14:6 (NIV), Jesus said, *"I am the way, the truth, and the life. No one comes to the Father except through me."*

So, how do we know the Bible is for real? Every time I turn around there is another person, a so-called expert claiming the Bible to be false or why Christianity is not the answer. In every aspect of life, we are given choices that require a decision-making process. Those decisions lead to results that we hope will lead to a good or positive outcome. We make our decisions on what we believe to be of sound judgment. We do our research, get answers, and when we are satisfied we make our choice. This is exactly how we should approach God.

The first step is to pick up the Bible and read His Word. The Book of John is a good place to start. Make notes and start your research process. You will have many questions. That is a good thing, as God loves questions.

Ask around and see who has a good reputation as a solid Christian, and see if you can get some time with that individual. Once you have got your questions answered, ask them who they recommend you talk to for a second opinion and go ask your questions again. Do this a couple of more times. By then your heart will be open and you will be inviting Jesus into your life and starting a journey of your own.

Perhaps this sounds like a lot of work. It is. The thing is, would you make a major purchase without researching the matter? The same holds true here. I am not telling you to buy into what is being said, hook line and sinker, without doing your research. If there is one who has your attention and they are strongly for or oppose a view, you need to ask why, get specifics, then see if the specifics hold any water.

The Bible encourages us the search out the truth and that applies to everyday life in all we do. When you get your answers, don't keep them to yourself. Pass them along and make an impact on others along the way. Jesus is all about developing relationships—not about developing a religion.

To bring us back to our thought of **bring fourth**, just as the tree produces a tasty fruit for nourishment for the physical body, the Bible brings fourth nourishment for the mind. We close this section on *fruit* with a word that carries a lot of impact and when used by many ministers, they leave their listening audience with the wrong impression. There is no doubt what the Bible refers to when it speaks of increase about planting a seed and it will multiply. Similarly, when you spread God's Word to just one more person and he in turn shares it with another, and so on—that multiplication fills the heavens with joy.

The tree or vine when properly watered, fertilized, exposed to sunshine and pruned will produce an abundant harvest—an increase. Take a few seeds and put them in the ground and you will see a process starting right away.

The seed has to first die or germinate through this process. When it mixes with the soil and fertilizer, it's reborn and creates a new life. From that life a tiny little tinder shoot burst through the earth. The shoot is protected and with time it grows. As it grows, it becomes strong and then starts to produce branches and those branches produce little flowers or blossoms that are the beginning of a fruit.

With time, the flower drops off and the fruit continues to grow until it is ripe and ready to harvest. This process goes from life to death, to new life and produces more life or an increase.

Everything on this earth works the exact same way. They may take on a different look or be called by a different name, but it is the same. A new baby is born today. I just got my first job. I got that promotion. We just got married. We just purchased our first home. My divorce was final today . . . these are just starting points. A journey that leads us down a new road that has a beginning and an end will bring an increase when handled properly. This is why when handled God's way not only will there be increase to those who choose to follow God's law, but they will be fruitful and multiply.

This thing we call 'multiplying' gets everyone excited because for most, self-included, when first heard, our mind shuts down to all the qualifications that follows. We are not interested in all the grunt work. We want to get in the fast lane and go for the gusto. You just read all the plant "must" go through in order to produce its fruit, well we "must" go through the same process.

The minister who chooses to wet its congregation's appetite but does not finish the story, only sets someone up for failure. One bad apple can spoil the whole bunch. You do a good job and maybe a few people will hear about it, but one mistake and everyone knows. Increase is a very important part in God's plan. Many who are non-Christian have grasped this concept and become successful but do not understand the dying to self-part which is the key to God's plan for success.

It is my hope you let these words grab your heart, and drink them as one who has walked a dry and dusty road for a long time and longs for a cool drink of clear water to satisfy your parched throat. God not only will supply the water that refreshes your thirst, but He can refresh your soul as well. He calls it "the renewing of your mind."

It is like taking an engine that has two hundred fifty thousand miles and completely taking it apart and rebuilding it. When the engine is put back together it is as good as new or in most cases better. The down time you spend rebuilding the engine is the time God works on renewing your mind—rebuilding you as a godly person. It's amazing how much similarity there is in the way all things work that we do.

"Blessed is the man who does not walk in the counsel of the wicked or stand in the way of sinners or sit in the seat of mockers. But his delight is in the law of the Lord, and on his law he meditates day and night. He is like a tree planted by the streams of water, which yields its fruit in season and whose leaf does not wither. Whatever he does prospers" Psalm 1:1-3 (NIV).

David next reminds us that we need to be aware of the **season.** Season, in this context means *time, eternity and without end.* This paints a pretty clear picture, so let's explore these words.

Season is a time of year, but in the church setting you hear ministers use the term 'season' for a period of someone's life, when they may be going through a particular struggle or a season when everything is going great. There could be a season when life has you busy with your kids, whose lives are very active.

It could be baseball or soccer for one, or dance classes for another. It could be your job that has your focus because of the upcoming promotion. These are times in our lives that our focus is on things—not on God, even though He may be part of our lives, but not necessarily in our lives.

So how does this tie into what David is saying? The first word, 'reflecting season' is time that in itself can be specific or vague. In defining time and its use in relating to this segment of the verse, we see it can be as specific as the time we have for our lunch break to eternity everlasting.

From a specific point of view, we see that in a certain span of time the tree will bare its fruit. There will be a harvest for the fruit will be ripe for picking. My mind always goes back to when the garden was ready to pick the corn, dig up the potatoes, and pick the green beans. All these vegetables not only could provide immediate nourishment, but we could store them and they would continue to provide food for a longer period of time. In essence, we could extend the season because of our planning.

'Time' also means in this context *eternity, everlasting, and without end*. We know that the fruit a tree produces will have an end. If not used it will perish. But here we are reminded if we follow God's law we can have eternity, an everlasting relationship that has no end.

You may say, "Wait a minute, this is a little far-fetched. You are really stretching your thought." Well, let's look at it from this perspective. A person is born and lives 70 to 80 years, and then they die. Since this is a given, we are all in agreement to this point, right? During our life span on earth, we go through many seasons: birth, childhood, teenager, adult, marriage, new life, senior years to death. These are all seasons. They all carry a great deal of significance, but if you find God and develop a relationship with Him, you get to add one more season to your calendar, and that is eternity.

This is why when looking at the word 'season,' David reminds us we will yield our fruit in season and it can have a long-term effect. Not knowing what season you will be in when God comes into your life—assuming He does—that's when you begin to yield His fruit.

That long-term effect is tied to our relationship with Him. He is the only one who can provide eternity. Not only can you prosper in your present life, but you can have an eternal life of prosperity as well.

Finally, David tells us, "It is also without end," meaning it will continually produce fruit. The tree has a season to bear its fruit and then it is gone till the next year. Like the tree, our relationship with Jesus will grow and continually get better. Will there be periods of struggle? Yes. Will it always be easy? No!

Will He abandon you? You can call on Jesus whenever, wherever, and know He will respond. Yes, yes indeed. That is the beauty of developing a relationship with Jesus. He is always just a prayer or a page away.

But you may argue, "I can't see Him or hear His response." My reply to that is, "Oh, yes you can, once you get Him in your heart you will hear from Him quite often."

David next tells us that not only will the tree yield its fruit in season, but the **leaf** will not **wither.** Let us first look at **leaf**, *coming up, cause to rise, ascend and fall.* What a power packed group of words. Just for a moment, let's look back at the previous words, which are 'yields its fruit in season.'

We have covered the fruit part, so where does the leaf fit in? If you know anything about the process of a fruit-bearing tree, there is a cycle as the seasons change. Let's start with spring.

In the spring, the winter's harsh weather has passed and the snow has melted as the cold water seeps into the ground and temperature begins to rise. The ground starts to warm up and new life springs fourth.

The sap in the tree begins to rise and over a period of a few weeks the sap rises throughout the entire tree to tip off every branch. This is the life of the tree. The sap provides nourishment and once the sap rises little buds will start to come out and on the end to the branches tiny tender little buds. Those buds are the beginning of a leaf.

Here you have this giant tree with a massive trunk. Big limbs are protruding with many branches, but it is simply useless unless those tiny little buds appear. It is not long before those little buds grow into a bright shiny leaf that covers the entire tree.

The leaf provides oxygen to clean the air and a giant air conditioner on a hot summer's day that lets the summer's rainfall gently fall to the ground. These actions are all precursors to the tree bearing its fruit and will not happen without the leaf. We see this tiny green thing on the massive tree that plays a vital role in its existence.

Even God, who sent His only son to earth to die for our sins, realized if He goes there for others just to worship Him, then it will be no different than all the pagan gods they have been worshiping.

"For God so loved the world that he gave his one and only Son, that whosoever believes in him shall not perish but have eternal life" John 3:16 (NIV).

Just as the tree represents strength, leaves are a vital part of the process of survival. If the tree stays bare and has no leaf, it is only a matter of time until its only use will be firewood. Those who choose to believe in Jesus and follow Him are the leaves that continue to breathe new life into their fellow beings.

God planted the tree and it is up to us to prune it, harvest the fruit, and protect it. God knows the tree needs water to survive. David planted his tree by the stream to ensure an abundant source of water. *"Now if the foot should say, Because I am not the hand, I do not belong to the body, it would not for that reason stop being part of the body"* 1Co 12-15 (NIV). Jesus knew His role was to provide eternal life for all who wanted to come and associate with Him. He is the tree and we are the branches.

The leaf will not **wither** or *fall away, be foolish, vile, or dishonor.* Have you ever examined a leaf and its texture as the season progresses and changes? When it first appears it is very tender, soft, and supple as it matures to its full size. The texture becomes more rigid. This allows the leaf to withstand the wind, the rain, and summer's hot days.

All these conditions are essential to the cycle of the tree in preparation of the bearing of its fruit. David is reminding us if conditions are not right the leaf will fall away and serve no useful purpose.

Wither also carries with it the thought of being foolish. How does this apply to a tree? We are reminded in the Scriptures the foolish son dishonors his father, just as our actions many times daily dishonor God.

The tongue slips so easily that we find ourselves in trouble by the words we speak. The foolishness that comes from our mouth is a pathway that leads to dishonor. Staying connected to God provides us with the lifeline: not to fall to the pressures of daily living. They are rigorous enough and we need all the help we can get. God is always just a prayer away.

Wither also means *vile, wicked, crime, punishment.* These are pretty harsh words and carry a strong sentence with them. If we become so hardened, we turn to crime and our ways become wicked. It is just a matter of time till our actions catch up with us. Even those who do not become a criminal let their motives drive them to become self-centered.

Sometimes your closest friends don't want anything to do with you and in essence you have written your own sentence. David, in reminding us that the leaf will not wither is telling us not to dishonor God.

To **dishonor** means *to be naked, be put to shame, there will be confusion, you will be despised and found guilty.* These are all paths of destruction if we allow ourselves to disconnect from God. As the seasons change and the sap returns to the ground for winter, the leaf falls, the bark begins to turn grey, and the beauty of the tree is gone.

This grey color represents death from whence it came, to where it shall return. "Even though you still have life, if you disconnect from me and become worldly in your ways, it will not be the same."

But the beauty of it all as David reminds us that his tree was planted by the stream, and its leaves did not wither. Who is our stream? Who is our lifeline that continues to supply us the inner nourishment? As we close these verses David tells us whatever we do shall prosper.

The word **whatever** covers a lot of possibilities. According to the Hebrew, *whatever* means to *complete, any, all, and whole.* David is very explicit in his explanation of these verses. He tells us where to walk, where not to sit, what to focus on, who to align ourselves with, and what will occur when we obey. This is a complete package. You don't need any more.

To 'complete' also indicates life's cycle. Just as the tree goes through its cycle of four seasons, we too have our seasons. As God provides for the tree, He is ready and willing to do the same for us. If we put forth the energy to dig into His instruction as David refers to it in the book of the law, any situation, and I mean any, is covered in God's book.

This book, let's call it a study manual, is just like any other book you read and study when you prepare for a test. When you read some of the questions on the exam you scratch your head and think, *Did I read the right book?*

You have no idea where this question was taken from, but then you re-read the question and with a little closer examination you remember reading something similar. You then realize you are not ready for the exam, so you go and study some more. Upon reviewing it a second time, you find the answer plus much more than you did not grasp the first time.

Each time you go to God's Word, He will reveal more and different information than the time before. Isn't that the way life presents itself? The problem that is plaguing us today usually can be solved if we just back away and get a fresh perspective. We may need to ask for a little help, do a little more research, and then find the answer. We suddenly realize that it was right there all along, we just needed a little more time to dig and find the answer.

David makes it very clear that if you want the complete package with all the upgrades to cover any situation, you need to buy into the whole thing. You can't stick your toe in, test the water, and try it for a season. No, you must adhere to all the rules if you want to be on God's team.

I loved Friday nights in high school. It was game night and was time for me to suit up, put on the pads, and go knock heads with the opponent. Some nights I got beat up and other nights I did the beating. When I shined, it felt good, but when I got knocked around I had to go back to the basics and practice. I needed to study the film, ask the coach for guidance, see where I messed up, what skills I needed to work on, and see how I could improve. "Son, you are a good player, but if you work with your teammates and become a team player you will be a great player," my coach said to me.

David reminds us of all the different components that are needed for a tree to bear fruit, and as a reminder for us to have all of our components in order as well. As a fruit tree has to grow and mature before it can bear fruit, we need God, His Word, prayer time, study time, and counsel time in order to mature into His fold.

There is a process that we must endure just as the seasons strengthen the tree. Over time, our fruit will be sweeter and our rewards greater by following David's formula for planting the tree. The Scriptures continually remind us "it is not about me." God needs to be our pilot.

If you are traveling and have got turned around in an unfamiliar area, you stop and ask directions to get back on track. It does no good to get back in your vehicle and say, "That guy does not know what he is talking about, I will figure this out on my own."

Now that we have GPS, we think we don't have a need to ask directions. When we read God's Word it is exactly the same way as if we say, "I don't need this. I am capable of handling this on my own and you may be right for a season."

There will be a time and there will be a situation when you will cry out and as we read in Romans 1:28, *"Furthermore, since they did not think it worthwhile to retain the knowledge of God, So God gave them over to a depraved mind, to do what ought not to be done."*

In short, God will be the one who does the walking away. This may not sound like the loving God you have probably heard about. But it is. It is all about choice. If you choose to keep breaking the law and pushing your luck, eventually you will get caught and have to pay the fine. Or, you can turn on God's GPS!

All the odds are in God's favor. He holds all the cards. He knows the beginning from the end. As we keep resisting and saying, "I'll check into this later or I am way too busy for this God thing now, let me get my life a little better situated." "I am really focused. I need this promotion. This affair is not hurting anyone, nobody knows. I'll check it out tomorrow."

We are told in the Bible to focus on today for each day has enough worry of its own. As you read the word *tomorrow,* listen for an "echo" because there will be a point when tomorrow will no longer be an option.

In the movie, *Dirty Harry,* Clint Eastwood says as his victim is staring down the barrel of Clint's 44 revolver, "I know what you're thinking. Did I fire five rounds or six? Well punk, do you feel lucky today?"

God may not call you a punk, but one day the devil will be leaning and whispering in one ear and an angel tugging at your heart and it will be decision time. You make the call. What will it be? The one thing I have come to grips with is I don't have as much control I as would like to think.

So, as David informs us that whatever we do will prosper it will be complete, it will be whole, and it will encompass any and all situations. Don't isolate the word prosper and forget the rest. This is an all or nothing deal—as much as we dislike ultimatums, this is one of those occasions. What we don't see is all the good because we are conditioned to think negatively when given an ultimatum. I am going to be bold and step out on a limb and say, man can really be stupid sometimes, as we let our pride blind the truth. Or, as my mother would say, "You are being bull headed."

Once we understand how fruitful the tree can be when properly planted it only makes sense. There are no catches, no 'gotcha's, no one changing the rules, or saying it is my game."

He is the same yesterday, today, and forever. David has given us a tremendous insight into where to walk, who to associate with, and what to study. He also informed us on where to plant and who to align ourselves with. He has given us some additional verses in Psalms.

CHAPTER 14

WALKING LIKE DAVID

In looking at Psalm 128 1-4 (NIV), we are told: *"Blessed are all who fear the Lord, who walk in his ways. You will eat the fruit or your labor; blessings and prosperity will be yours. Your wife will be like a fruitful vine within your house; your sons will be like olive shoots around your table. Thus is the man blessed who fears the Lord,"*

Does this mean I am to be afraid of God? That He is going to constantly be looking over my shoulder and every time I mess up He is going to be on me like flies on rice? Life throws us enough curves in a day; we don't need one more. Let's see what David is saying.

We are informed at the beginning of the verse, "**blessed** are **all** who **fear** the Lord." Blessed, meaning *straight forward, happiness, honest, go forward, prosper.* These all sound like character building words with a bonus thrown in at the end. There's this popular expression that says, "be straight with me" or "he was a very straight forward person."

Both carry the same meaning: Someone who is not only honest but in their communication and doesn't mix words. This kind of an individual can rub some people the wrong way, especially someone who is a little sensitive.

In his communication, Jesus spoke two ways. One was in parables using story form or example, the other was very direct or straight forward. He knew there would be times when we needed to hear nothing but the facts.

We are taught to be honest and then we get caught up in what is known as 'a little white lie' in trying not to hurt others' feelings. What we consider a minor cover up can end up being a major catastrophe because of not thinking. This is why Jesus spent so much time developing relationships with His disciples. Once He had a strong bond, if it required Him to speak in tough love they might not have liked what they heard, but they knew it was for their own good.

You develop happiness and peace of mind when your bond is based on truth. Then we are told we can prosper. The type of prospering that David is referring to is the developing of a strong family bond. This permits the family to move forward as a unit and because of the atmosphere, success is more likely to happen. In the very first word we discuss there is a complete formula for success in the family unit.

David next points to the word **all,** which means *whole and complete.* This is great. This is awesome, right? Out of the gate David says we as a family will prosper and go forward being complete, lacking nothing.

What is being said is nothing less than mind-boggling. If families will take to heart what is being said and apply it, God will be their guiding light and beacon in the night. Whatever life throws at them they will be able to handle. This information is not only character building but provides you with the armor to withstand any test you may encounter.

Here comes a word that I, as a little boy, remember so vividly—*fear.* It could be Sunday morning or a revival but every time the church doors opened my parents were there. I can picture the preacher in my mind as clearly today as when I was 10. The longer he preached, the redder his face got, and the sweat would pop out on his forehead. He would loosen his tie, start pounding the pulpit pointing his finger (which I thought was at me) and say, "If you don't repent and give your life to Jesus, you are going somewhere not very pleasant." I was scared to death because I didn't want to go to an unpleasant place.

The picture he painted put so much fear in me that I thought, *Where do I find this Jesus guy?* Well, when I was 12, I accepted the Lord as my Savior and it was in part because of fear and in part because I truly wanted to have a relationship with Him. God wants us to have a reverence and respect for him. He wants it to be a desire to be associated with Him, not out of fear of Him.

A friend of mine described a time he got caught stealing a handball. It just so happened the store manager saw it take place, pulled my friend aside and said, "I am going to make you a deal. You promise me you will never steal again, and I will not tell your father."

For my friend's father to know was worse than death. This resulted in my friend developing a healthy fear that he still holds to this day. According to him, two things occurred that day. First, he never attempted to steal again and second, he feels that by being caught, it turned his life in a totally different direction.

Just as the preacher made a lasting impression on me, the store manager made a lasting impression on my friend and in both cases, they turned out for the better. By the way, my friend is Jewish and a very strong Christian. I feel doubly blessed to know him for he has a great heart and a strong desire for God.

In both cases fear played a good role in directing our decision-making process and we both went on to be followers of God. My friend and I were not acquainted as childhood friends or even as young adults; we met later in life. We have developed a great bond of commonality and through conversation it is amazing how much our lives traveled similar paths.

God is noted for orchestrating paths of people in His timing for His good. We want things to happen on our schedule or our plan. There are times and circumstances that God will dictate when He is ready, because simply put, He knows better.

Think About It

Do you think HT was able to comprehend what David says in this verse and in any others?

Remember, he only had a fifth grade education, and so, his reading skills were limited. Still, he dug into God's Word, asked questions, listened to the preacher, did more research, and prayed for discernment. In his simplistic way, HT did exactly what God instructs us to do. *"Seek me and you will find me. Knock and the door will be open, and ask and you shall receive"* Matthew 7:7 (NIV). God was right there with HT guiding and giving him wisdom because he was hungry for His Word.

In Psalm 128:1 (NIV), we are told, *"Blessed are those who fear the Lord and **walk** in his ways."* To **walk** is to *exercise, prosper, and be weak.* In the Old Testament time, travel for most meant walking, so conditioning was an everyday occurrence. If you planned to go somewhere, you figured how many days the journey would be and how long it would take you to walk there and back.

This required strength and endurance, which came only by doing. It is like the athlete who wants to train for the Olympics. The days are long, routines are tough, and you give up all your bad habits. No junk food, staying up late, sleeping in . . . It's all about discipline. Well, guess what? If we want to follow God, we have to give some things up as well. We may have to give up some of our friends, our old hang outs, the language we use, the movies we choose to watch, and the sites we visit on the internet.

Perhaps this sounds pretty restrictive. Ask the Olympic Gold Medalist who trained four years or maybe eight years or even longer, if it was worth it. Ask them what it meant to stand on that podium, raise the American flag and have millions of people from all over the world see them receive that honor.

Some made the front cover of Wheaties, the breakfast of champions cereal box, not to mention the opportunity to share that experience with all those who want to follow in their footsteps. Everything in life has a price. You can pay now, or you can pay later.

By following Jesus, you may think that you will not get that kind of notoriety, and you may be right.

But, here we are, some two thousand years later talking about some pretty great men. They have made the front pages, front covers, television, magazines and radio—they have done it all. When Mary Magdalene poured the Alabaster jar of perfume on Jesus, He said, *"They will be telling this for years to come"* Mark 14:3,9 (NIV).

"While he was in Bethany reclining at the table in the home of Simon the Leper, a woman came with an alabaster jar of very expensive perfume made of pure nard. She broke the jar and poured the perfume on his head. I tell you the truth, wherever the gospel is preached throughout the world what she has done will be told in memory of her."

Those who go into strict training to win a prize that will not last, but he who endures much more to spread the gospel will endure in the end. We are reminded to not only exercise the body, but to prepare our inner soul as well. We need to strengthen our relationship with Jesus, continue to study His Word and continue to grow in our faith or we will slip back into our old ways.

To walk is also *to prosper.* Have you ever been troubled and thought, *I just need to get away, be alone, take a walk, and clear my head?* Jesus was a great encourager of taking time to be alone with His Father.

I am a person who exercises daily and for many years I was an avid runner. I became very selfish with my running time. At 5:30 every morning, I hit the road—winter or summer—no matter what the weather.

Part of my routine was memorizing Scriptures and prayer time as I ran. I would plan my day and when I returned from my run, I felt refreshed and ready to tackle my day. What does that have to do with prospering? We need Jesus on the inside as we go about our day. We can call on Him constantly to help make decisions and to remind us what and who is first. His presence will keep us from doing wrong, being tempted or following the crowd.

By keeping Him first in our life we increase our chances greatly of success in every area of life. It is like tuning your car. If you only change half the plugs and the oil, but don't check the air filter, belts, wires, tires etc., the car may perform worse.

Through reading and memorizing Scripture, you are tuning up your mind. When you are in a tight spot and about to lose it, call on a verse. When it's deadline time and you are a little tense, call on a verse. The words we speak, the actions we take, the counsel we seek will have a far greater impact with those we come in contact with daily because Jesus is on the inside.

Not only have we prepared ourselves outwardly with physical exercise, but we have developed a mental toughness backed by biblical soundness. To walk also means to be weak. If we want to be on Jesus' team, we must understand there are rules we need to follow. Rules cause resistance. I know this and will be the first to admit it. I have on more than one occasion been rebellious when told I had to do it a certain way and ended up messing up.

From a biblical point of view, it is not about restraining or binding us to some regiment. He is showing us real freedom, once we understand His ways. Being weak also means admitting we don't have all the answers. We can't do it all on our own and maybe the people we have been seeking advice from are not helping, so where do we turn?

If you have tried everything else, why not give it a shot. You know the definition of insanity, don't you? It is continuously doing the same thing, but expecting a different result.

Would you consider an alternative path? I felt like a huge load had been lifted from my shoulders the day I recommitted my life to Jesus. It was humbling. As I walked forward for the first 10 or 15 seconds, I felt as if every eye in the building was on me. I was moving so quickly I don't remember the walk from my seat to the front. Then, it was just me and Jesus, even though there were many standing with me.

It has been a journey of learning since that day 35 years ago. Maybe it's time to humble yourselves, turn to Jesus, submit your life to Him and ask Him to become your mentor. I can attest you won't regret it and your world will change. Being weak is a good thing. When we are weak in ourselves we find strength in Him.

As we learn to walk with Jesus, we develop character and learn to develop an inner strength. Our journey teaches us that prosperity takes on many different faces and that being weak and admitting we can't do it all, then seeking Jesus for guidance is a good thing.

Nehemiah reminds us in our next word we will **eat** the fruit of our labor and that is to be taken literally and figuratively. To **eat** means *to burn up, consume, devour and be wise.* We look forward to when the garden will be ready for harvest, so we can taste the fresh fruits and vegetables we have labored over. This looks at both sides of the figurative and the literal. So, how could that be? We labored and worked the field and now we get to enjoy our efforts? This is the ideal scenario, for God always loves to see that our works produce an enjoyable end result. The same applies to our work place—you are given an assignment that you have a month to complete.

You have worked hard, put together a great presentation, your boss loves the idea and you get the promotion. Now how do you respond to those on the second floor you left behind? They were an integral part of your daily life before the promotion. This is the real test.

Yes, your new position will require you to travel in different circles, meet new people and your lunches will now be appointments. There will be time away from the family. Will Jesus still be your number one mentor? Will you forget all who helped you get to that corner office?

We must be cautioned for our work can devour us. Many forget those who helped them climb the corporate ladder or even worse, spend so much time at work that we neglect our family and create marital problems.

CHAPTER 15
BALANCING YOUR LIFE

I f we don't balance our life and keep Jesus first, family second, and work third, destruction is imminent. Countless executives lay victims along the highway to success because they made wrong choices, sold out the company causing broken families, bought into the idea of "I did it," and "it was me."

This is how the downward spiral begins. We start thinking that we don't need Jesus anymore. That we're on a roll and nothing can stop us now. As the spiral begins to gather momentum, by the time we realize we are heading for disaster, it is too late.

A friend of mine came home from work one night, walked in the house and saw his wife waiting for him. As he looked into her face, he got this feeling inside something was about to happen. She looked at him. There was dead silence, and then she said, "Sit down we need to talk." There was a sick feeling in his stomach, a cold sweat coming to his forehead, because he knew what was coming next. Within a month, he was out of the house, and his whole life changed. In just four months, he was divorced.

Living alone, losing connection with the children, being by himself and wondering, *What are all my married friends saying?* The children were confused for they didn't know what to tell their friends. My friend was lonely and wondering, *How did all this happen?* Though our work consumes and eventually destroy us, our words, choices, and actions can carry an underlying tone to our demise as well.

Nehemiah has some interesting words on this subject. To 'eat' means to burn up. That seems simple enough for when we consume food it becomes energy that we burn as fuel to get us through the day. But here is an interesting twist. To '**burn up**' also carries the connotation of being foolish. This implication can take us in two directions.

On the one hand, we should not be foolish and over eat, gain excess weight, and destroy our health. Nor should we run at such a pace that we eat poorly, not taking care of the body our gracious Father has given us.

In either case, we are not being wise or thoughtful of others when we abuse ourselves in this manner. This is a good example of the fruit of our labor turning against us. If we choose to ignore our health, it will come back to haunt us.

The other direction that 'burn up' is the food we consume in proper portions to be fuel for our bodies and don't eat in excess or lots of junk food. We are reminded to do things in moderation, be wise in our choices and there will be rewards while here on earth. Not only do we need to replenish the fuel for our bodies, but our minds need replenished as well. The continual study of God's Word is the fuel source that will provide the necessary growth.

There are reasons for everything since we don't always understand the inner workings. We want proof. Having faith and knowing others who have gone before us provides courage. If we will put the effort and do what it says the results can be amazing. All this insight has come from such a simple word as 'eat.' This is not about God looking down on us, pointing His finger and saying you must do it my way or else. It is allowing God to empower us to be the people we were meant to be.

In continuing our study, we see the word **devour**. In the English dictionary devour is to *eat fast, greedily, gorge without chewing.* If you are a picture person like me, I imagine someone sitting before their food, kind of bent over it, pushing their food in as fast as they can with this wild look on their face. You can take that same person and put them in a position where their focus devours them, and they become so obsessed that they will not permit anything to get in their way.

That can be good, or it can work against us. If we let our desires devour us and become consumed with passion to the point of sin, our wrong now becomes right. That which drives us to great heights will be that which causes us to fall. The fall will be great and painful as reality sets in. But guess what! God is right there ready to bend down, extend a hand, be forgiving, never judging, and reminding us his way is better.

Picking up the pieces can be painful—even devastating. I have been there and the climb from those depths is difficult. It does not happen overnight. We are going to need help and that may be our most difficult challenge. To someone who has been on top and taken the fall—whether self-induced or caused by outside conditions—finding the courage to seek guidance and ask for help sometimes is found to be our biggest stumbling block.

As you sit there among the rubble of shattered dreams and broken promises wondering what to do, God is patiently waiting on standby, ready for you to call on Him.

Man has this thing called an ego and it has a tendency to get in the way of common sense. If this occurs while we are young, we feel we have the stamina to get right back in the mix of things and we don't need help. We can do this on our own.

But get a little older and a tragedy like this can be devastating and destroy our confidence. We feel like crawling in a hole and pulling it in after us. In either instance if we are grounded in godly principles and firmly entrenched in His Word, the struggle still has to be dealt with, but His strength makes it sufficient.

Jesus should be the first name in your contact manager system or speed dial on your smart phone. He always welcomes your call. We can never wear out our welcome by calling on Jesus for help. He is on call 24/7. He does not want to run our lives—He just wants to show us how to run it better.

When HT struck his deal with God, he also gave up drinking. In the beginning, there was little change, but as time went on he began to see a big difference in his family. They became more loving and wanted to be around him. They were proud to be called his children. He could remember a time when that was not the case and he knew who to give the credit to. I want my family to be like that.

To eat the fruit of your labor also means to be wise, to teach wisdom, be skillful, cunning, artful, and deal wisely. If we are going to eat the fruit of our labor, it will certainly pay us big dividends to be wise in our work.

How we raise our children and the way we manage our finances are all things that come from the fruit of our labor. This is part of God's lesson plan. Being good stewards goes beyond tithing and involves managing every aspect of our life. If we can just grasp this one concept, everything we do will turn out better.

Think About It

Here is a novel idea. The next meal you have with your family at home, turn off everything to get everyone's attention and have a real conversation. Write here what happens!

Nehemiah tells us blessing and prosperity start here. I remember growing up and all that took place at the kitchen table. The food was great, good conversation, always instruction and fond memories. Some may say those were simpler times, but I felt secure because my parents were always there, and a sense of security was grounded around that kitchen table. My father blessed the food, he set the example of leadership in our home and we did many things as a family. Attending church was a regular part of our life. He was the Sunday school superintendent and God was present in our house on a daily basis.

It is true what is said in Pro 22:6 (NIV): *"Train up a child in the way he should go and when he is old he will not turn from it."*

I strayed for a period of time, did some very foolish things, made many bad choices which brought about broken hearts, shattered dreams, and plans left undone. All that occurred during a period of my life that could have been much different had I applied what I was taught.

Being raised in the sixties was a time to spread your wings, be independent, do your own thing and rebel against the establishment. That is exactly what I did. I can't undo the past and dwelling on it will just bring me down but what I can do in going forward is to make sure God is the center of my life, seek His word, and help my family and others not to make the same mistakes.

Nehemiah encourages parents to be godly examples. It all starts at home and the kitchen table is a great place to start. When you have a bank president come to you as you enter his bank and tell you he had the privilege of meeting your son and was very impressed, you should be proud of him, as he represents you well. When you are paid a compliment like that about one of your children and it has nothing to do with how big your bank account is or which side of town you live on, you know that kind of upbringing started at the kitchen table. Just look up and say thank you, Jesus, and be sure and share the compliment with your child. There is so much to be said about what goes on in the home and the bulk of it can and should take place at the kitchen table.

Nehemiah shares with us how our next word **labor** is our best friend when we truly understand its real meaning. Labor in the Hebrew has some of the same meaning as today. I expect it goes beyond what we call the job and carries much more implication. To labor means *to toil, produce, property, gasp, and exhausted.*

As we read in Genesis, when Adam and Eve ate of the forbidden fruit in the garden two things occurred. God told Adam, *"To Adam he said, "Because you listened to your wife and ate fruit from the tree about which I commanded you, 'You must not eat from it,' Cursed is the ground because of you; through painful toil you will eat food from it all the days of your life. It will produce thorns and thistles for you, and you will eat the plants of the field. By the sweat of your brow you will eat your food until you return to the ground, since from it you were taken; for dust you are and to dust you will return"'* Genesis 3:17-19 (NIV).

In spite of God's anger, He sent His son to earth to die for our sins and paved the way for us to have a good life. All He asks is that we follow him.

In every aspect of our lives, where there is labor there is also some type of reward. We plant the garden, we get to enjoy the food, we go to work and earn a paycheck. We learn to plan and save so that one day we can retire. We plant the flowers and enjoy their beauty. The list is endless.

Think About It

Do you think things through before you make a decision? What is your thought process?

_____

_____

In making choices in business or at home, being wise and taking the time to think through the end result is crucial. The thought that may come to mind is sometimes the situation requires an answer now. Meaning, no time to think. God makes it a point to tell us there is no crisis that we can't take a little time, be still, pray, and think it through. We are talking 60 seconds just to focus on God and the problem. You will be amazed at the result.

Choosing not to consult God is when labor becomes toil. Your solution backfires and these words come out of your mouth, "I don't understand what happened." Seeking godly wisdom may not be a prayer, it might be a phone call to a Christian mentor or a well-grounded business man. We are told we will never be a good leader until we learn how to become a great follower.

Nehemiah reminds us of all that occurs inside the walls of our home. We as parents have control over our family, with very few exceptions. Even the exceptions when we call on Jesus to provide an answer.

To **toil** means to *work hard, break a sweat,* maybe stay up at night, even burn a little midnight oil. It may require study, research, figure out all your options, stretch yourself, increase your awareness . . . all of this helps you grow. God provides the tools and expects us to use them. Do you want to spend the day in your backyard making mud pies, or accept an offer to spend a day at the beach and see how others live?

When I step outside my comfort zone and into an unknown, I tread very cautiously for fear of looking foolish or making a blunder. The Bible has taught me that God is not much on how others view His opinion, since He wrote the book.

He is, however, greatly concerned as to how we live our lives and the direction we are headed.

In the Bible, which may as well have been called the *Basic Instructions Before Leaving Earth*, God outlines the true path and if you decide to walk it, that's your choice. He expects the same from us as we labor. He expects us to do our job the best we can, not to take short cuts, not to find ways to make the work easier, but to find ways to make the work better.

I remember sitting in church one morning, listening to the minister give his message, which he titled "Money Madness." His message was very insightful. I found myself paying close attention as to how he would approach the subject of wealth and the church. He based his story on 1 Timothy 6:3-20 (NIV), which says: *"Timothy guard what has been entrusted to your care. Turn away from godless chatter and the opposing ideas of what is falsely called knowledge."*

He wanted to make sure everyone was aware that financial gain without God in the picture is like putting a new set of tires on your car without balancing them. The minister reminded his congregation to not be so concerned with finances, because they could consume us, as we pursue our dreams. He also pointed out it was the love of money, not money that is the root of all evil.

He reminded the congregation to put it in the proper prospective, making the most of what one has. Understanding to put God first, be generous, and willing to share is when you will lay up treasures in heaven for yourself. In doing so, you create a firm foundation while here and you are able to take hold of what life truly is about.

As I listened to the message, I found myself being critical, waiting to see if he would begin to back-peddle as the message became more sensitive. Especially for those who were wealthy or had acquired wealth. Sure enough, he apologized more than once when referencing those who had the ability to earn a greater income than others. This is one of the reasons I wanted to do this study, because I too felt uncomfortable when talking about the Bible and money in the same breath. But as we can see, as we study the Bible, God has no problem talking about wealth, financial gain, prosperity, abundance or anything remotely related.

God makes it very clear there is an order of things. And, if we want the maximum benefit we must follow His plan. The toil is hard and it has not changed since Adam messed up. Just as economic times challenge us to be creative and to be ready to shift gears at any given time, we are to be productive and produce results. When you are on an assignment and it is crunch time, homework is a must. Your presentation needs to be polished and preparation is the key.

You're next, and you are sitting in the outer office waiting for your name to be called. Your mind begins to race as you run your mental checklist one more time. Did I do everything I could have? That is a key question we should always ask, "did I do all I could?" All the other questions, "Did I leave anything out, am I going to say the right thing?"

The pressure, the little beads of sweat begin to pop out on your forehead. This is not a good sign. I have been in this spot so many times, what I remember saying is, "Stop, you can't prepare any more. If you are not ready now you will never be." Then I say a silent prayer to God asking for this presentation to be put in His hands, to let it be His words that guide my thoughts and let His will be done, not my wishes, or polished presentation.

I ask for honesty and integrity in my words, in Jesus' name. Amen. In every instance, a peace would come over me. A calm that gave me the confidence to walk in the room and face the people. Give my presentation, answer the questions and have that peace as I left that I had done my best.

Did I land every job? No. Did I beat myself up because I didn't? No. Did I follow up to see what I could have done differently? Follow-up is part of the process of being productive.

Labor next leads us to the word **property**. In Psalm 50:10 (NIV), we are told:

"For every animal of the forest is mine, and the cattle on a thousand hills."

Think About It

Well, what about that deed of the house that has your name on it, or the ground, the house and all that sits on it? What are your thoughts about this statement?

_____

_____

Most of us defy this statement, if not outwardly, possibly inwardly. Our chest puffs up, our head goes back and we look at the land, the house, the stuff and say "I" own this *property*, forgetting the pecking order and taking all the credit. In Malachi, we are told that even those who challenge God, prosper. Malachi 3:15 (NIV). *"But now we call the arrogant blessed. Certainly the evildoers prosper, and even those who challenge God escape."* However, unless they change their ways the reward they have is here and now and that's all they will receive.

In the Old Testament, the word property was used mainly to refer to land. It could also be referred to as the things that possessed the land. The cattle, the sheep, the vineyards and the people. God used Joshua, David, and many others to take over certain lands as inheritance to give to His chosen people. They were to be the stewards of that land, manage it, make it productive and use it for the good of all of God's people.

In many instances, we read how God's people misused His land and He would turn it into waste, clearly stating, "this land will no longer be productive, even though it was once green lush and fertile."

What happened two thousand years ago is very much relatable to our world today. This is when decision time requires choosing a side and stating where you stand. You either believe in God's Word or you don't. This a black and white issue. There is no room for a grey area.

I volunteer at my church to work one night a week at their radio station. I answer the phone, screen calls, for a program called CR Tonight (Christ Redemption). It deals with those who have addictions. From week to week, the calls vary from addiction, sexual abuse, to broken homes and even anger issues. Some callers want to be anonymous, others openly share their name, but the point of the show is to get those people on the road to change and help them to understand God is a forgiving God full of love.

I have witnessed several young men who now volunteer alongside me, and the stories they have told me of what they did and the danger they lived in is unimaginable to me. There's a story of an 18-year old who had ninety thousand dollars in his pocket on some dead end, dark street. Somebody hit him over the head with a blunt object, took all his money, and left him for dead. This young man survived and continued his lifestyle for another six months or so before he was so broken and out of control that he finally checked himself into a place called Calvary House. Life today is amazing and his zeal for God is over the top.

He works beside me at the station and I let him answer the phones. I see and hear the compassion in his voice. So many of these guys who come there have changed and you ask any one of them if God has made a difference in their lives and they will answer you with a resounding "Yes." Ask a reformed alcoholic if he permits a grey area in his life and he will tell you no, because one drink is all it takes. God is the same way. We are either on His team or not.

The choice is actually real easy. Yes, I believe, or no, I don't. There is one other option, which is, "I hear what you are saying. So, can I get more information before I say yes?" At some point, you will need to come to a decision. These young men discovered at an early age that possessions caused and cost them much more than they bargained for.

CHAPTER 16
DOES WORK HAVE TO BE THIS HARD?

The last two words that labor relate to are 'gasp' and 'exhausted.' These words go together appropriately and are fitting to close out how God looks at labor. Ever since Adam sinned in the garden, God did not pull any punches as He cursed the ground.

The Bible also speaks of the ground as being good for man, as he lies down at day's end after having done a full day's work. To **gasp** means *to fight for, to crave, or desire* and this is how God looks at our relationship. Jesus died for our sins. So, we should be willing to die and fight for Him, as well as have a desire and a longing for Him because this is exactly how He pursues us.

To **exhaust** or be exhausted carries the same commitment. We have either given it our best effort, or we have labored hard, using all our energy. The Bible teaches us to pursue, to pray without ceasing, to uncover His Word like digging for gold, to ask questions, seek counsel, and exhaust every avenue.

When we have a desire to be close to our Creator and through all the toil we learn discipline, we learn the principals of prosperity. We will have an unshakable relationship with our Lord and Savior Jesus Christ. Amen! Through each word we study, we are uncovering more of an understanding of how God wants us to function and how we can align ourselves with Him in our everyday lives. By laboring diligently, daily blessings and prosperity will be yours.

Blessing means *happiness, straight, level, honest, go forward, and prosper.* These words all indicate a movement in our lives of the good that God has to offer. Keeping in mind that prosperity comes in many forms and is not always or only related to the almighty dollar.

By choosing to structure our life from a biblical point of view we can enrich our lives beyond what we could ever imagine. This journey is as exciting for me as I hope it is for you as we travel this path. I picture walking along a trail where I am not sure of my footing, and as I place one foot in front of the other, carefully testing my steps to make sure I will not slip. My confidence grows as I put the weight of my body on that foot and feel comfortable that I am on solid ground.

I spent a lot of my summer time as a boy playing in the woods being adventurous climbing trees and cliffs, and finding caves, and swinging from vines. It all required a certain amount of bravery; stepping out in faith and trusting the unknown. With each adventure my faith would increase, which in turn gave me more courage to take on the next challenge. My adventures as a little boy were on blind faith for I did not have a manual of instructions. Resistance comes into play immediately to those who respond to an invitation of having a relationship with Jesus. Many immediately say, "You are asking me to give up my sight and go on blind faith." My response is, "If it were blind faith you would have no instruction manual."

When you purchase something that requires assembling there is an instruction sheet that comes with it. In some cases, we are shown what the parts look like before and after it is assembled. All we have to do is follow the steps and *voila!* It's done.

The same applies here if we read the instruction manual (The Bible) and come upon something we don't understand. We ask questions, follow the manual, and our lives will turn out much better than making our own way. I can hear the uproar from the naysayers who tell me of countless people who have done ok without God in their life.

"Explain that!" you say.

First of all, I am not a CS Lewis, or a DL Moody. I am just an ordinary guy with an extraordinary desire to help others have a better understanding of God's Word from a layman's perspective.

I read an article about the Smithsonian Institute needing $300,000 dollars to preserve Thomas Jefferson's 189-year-old Bible. The Bible has great historical value for many reasons, most importantly, is that Jefferson made notes in the margin throughout the Bible. As he read and studied, it became one of his main sources for his decision-making process.

His Bible is 189 years old and those who speak from a position of authority say God's Word is over two thousand years old.

Think About It

If the Smithsonian is willing to spend $300,000 to preserve Thomas Jefferson's Bible, what do you think God's written word is worth to you and me?

_____

_____

Scholars have proven the approximate age of the Bible. And even though it still generates controversy, it has sold more copies than any book ever published. The words written in both The Old Testament and New Testament are as applicable today as when they were first penned. Is that a stroke a luck or is the Bible full of those 'just luck' examples?

If you are willing to pick up the Bible and sincerely read it as instructed, there is no doubt you will come away a changed person. The only question left is, are you up for the challenge?

It is the third quarter with two minutes left. Your team is on the fifty-yard line and it's fourth and one, and your down ten points. What do you do? If you win, your team is in a major bowl. Oh, did I mention if you lose you will be looking for a new team to coach? The team you are playing has one of the best defenses in the country. One yard and four more downs, what do you do? All you need is about fifteen yards and you have the best kicker in the nation. But it's only the third quarter—should you chance it?

Psychologically, getting the first down will boost your team's confidence tremendously, as well as tear down the defenses moral. So what do you want to do, coach? Risk it, or play safe? Do the unexpected or the expected?

Think About It

If you were on God's team what do you think He would do?

_____

_____

As I said before, HT's formal education was very limited, but so was Thomas Edison's. HT knew he would have to perform better than the guy who finished school or maybe had a college degree. He knew he had to learn to read beyond a 5th grade level. So, he learned to read, study, and even how to pronounce the words in the Bible. HT listened to the minister closely and learned how to pronounce those words he had problems with.

HT's brother sold magazines and he gave him subscriptions to Field and Stream, Saturday Evening Post, Life, and his favorite Hunting and Fishing. These all became resources for him to increase his reading skills and be a better communicator.

He knew upper management was looking at him and also knew they were questioning his ability to comprehend. He understood that climbing the ladder meant a pay raise, so he did whatever it took to educate himself.

Think About It

Does any of what we have read to this point relate to what HT was willing to do to move forward?

You may think that is all just common sense. But, if that were the case, why aren't more people doing it? HT's lessons came from the sweat of his brow. He was not afraid to get in the trenches, to roll up his sleeves, stand alongside his men and follow through on his promise. I believe when HT went home, I believe he heard, "Well done, good and faithful servant."

The truth is, HT didn't have it easy. There were days when he questioned God. And there were many others when he embarrassed himself during a conversation, as he failed to pronounce a particular word. And yet, he stepped out in blind faith and did it anyway. HT pronounced the word 'article,' 'ar-tic-el,' and very few corrected him.

We will never grow unless we are willing step out of the boat and ask God to take our hand and help us. Call it intuition or call it street smarts, but HT called it "God leading me to be a better person." And God blessed him accordingly.

Think About It

How would describe blessing?

"You will eat the fruit of your labor, blessings and prosperity will be yours" Psalms 128:2 (NIV). It's good to be blessed, and as we see here, one of its meaning is happiness.

There are some parts of the Bible, like in the Old Testament, with all the killing, incest, punishment and hard work—when you think, *Where is the joy in this?* But once we get deep into the study we soon realize the flip side to the lesson is peace, joy, and happiness.

The road is not always going to be smooth and life is not going to be wonderful every day. Still, there can be happiness even in times of trial once you are in alignment with God.

Happiness presents itself in many different ways, but many times we don't recognize it because we tend to be centered on the end result. We are reminded to stop and smell the roses along the way for you may never pass this way again. Take a little time and enjoy the scenery, drink in the beauty, enjoy the sunshine and take advantage of the rainy day or the winter's storm. When life stops us in our tracks there is usually a reason, so take a moment and enjoy the breather and move on.

Our next word is **straight** and in many verses in the Bible God tells us our path will be straight if we follow His instructions. *"But small is the gate and narrow the road that leads to life and only a few find it"* Matthew 7:14 (NIV).

Straight in this context means the choice we make by following His instructions will be much better than the alternative.

The adage, *"You need to follow the straight and narrow,"* means the path are traveling does not give you options. I discovered that options provided excuses and made it seemingly easy to walk away if the task became difficult. If we are looking for quicker ways to get ahead or get to the finish line, the shortcuts we choose may come back to haunt us at a later date. Keeping our feet on level ground is the best route.

As a youngster, I spent many days in the woods climbing, running, playing, and being adventurous. I can still remember placing myself in dangerous situations where sure footing was required. It seemed the more dangerous it was, the more I was drawn to the adventure.

One day, I scaled along a cliff's edge carefully, placing one foot in front of the other as my body hugged the rock. I occasionally looked down to see if there was a way for me to shortcut my adventure. Being seventy-five or eighty feet in the air and walking a narrow ledge was not adventurous enough for me. I wanted to increase the adrenalin. My eyes began to scan the surroundings. I looked out and found a tree just out of arms' length and thought, *If I could just reach that tree and climb down that would really be neat.* Sure enough, the next thing I found myself hugging was the tree. *Now what?* I thought as I hung on for dear life.

There was no way to get back to the cliff's edge so I began to slowly descend down the tree until I finally reached the ground. Boy was I happy! I made my mind up that it was pretty cool, but I would never do that again.

"Give careful thought to the paths for your feet and be steadfast in all your ways" Proverbs 4:26 (NIV). In other words, God won't let us do those things that put our lives in jeopardy. The great thing about being a follower of Jesus Christ is His encouragement of seeking counsel when we are in a tight spot, need another opinion, or just someone to bounce an idea off of. He is always there or He will direct us to an open door to get the answer.

CHAPTER 17

DIFFERENT MEANINGS OF BLESSING

Blessing is a word with many meanings. One is honesty. And when you are on God's team there is nothing that has a greater impact on your daily life than being honest. If we make a promise and don't follow through there are usually consequences. Tell the boss at work that you can get it done, tell the children you will be there, tell your spouse you love them . . . and don't follow through . . . the damage done can take a long time to repair.

You can make excuses, but in the end, it's no use.

In Proverbs 12:14 (NIV), we are told, *"From the fruit of his lips people are filled with good things and the work of their hands bring them reward."* There are days where it seems nothing goes right—from the moment our feet hit the floor until the light goes out that night. It would have been easier to have stayed in bed that day, surely. But, how we deal with challenges set the tone and the outcome of that day.

When I was younger, the way I dealt with things like that was to ignore it, put my head down and bull my way through it, not caring who I ran over or stepped on in the process. I am sure there were people who would like to have taken me out back and beat me to a pulp. I was so busy being on the move they weren't able to corner me, thus saving my life on many occasions, I am sure.

Nehemiah says part of the blessing is to go forward. The example I just gave is not the going forward he wants us to do, by the way. Blessings come in many forms and is not always recognizable to the human mind, as we would like to think. However, at day's end or at some obscure moment as we find ourselves reflecting about our day. We find ourselves catching a glimpse of a thought or a picture flashes across our mind and we realize that God was at work in our life that day.

Sometimes that catches you off guard and as that thought or picture passes, a tear may fall from your eye or a little lump comes to your throat, and you are humbled. It is then you realize He has been by your side all day and you have not slowed down enough to recognize His presence. All He wants is for us to take a moment and thank him.

We are reminded yesterday is gone, tomorrow is not here, all we have is the present, so use it wisely. *"Jesus replied, No one who puts a hand to the plow and looks back is fit for service in the Kingdom of God."* Luke 9:62 (NIV).

Think About It

Have you ever tried to walk forward while looking back? What would you say about your direction?

Just as in the movie, *Paying it Forward*, the message is continuing to do a good deed for another with nothing expected in return. God expects the same from us. As we are blessed, He expects us to share our blessing and that requires a forward motion—not one of selfishness or keeping it a secret.

As we read in 3 John 1:2 (NIV), as John is writing to Gaius to give him encouragement he says, *"Beloved, I pray that you may prosper in all things and be in good health, just as your soul prospers."* Here, the reference of the soul prospering has nothing to do with financial gain, but everything to do with honesty. John is pleased that his brother in Christ is walking in truth. This truth and inner piece gives Gaius the comfort of knowing as he journeys, his life will have purpose and his walk will represent the one who's message he is sharing.

This gives John no greater joy than to know he has equipped a brother in Christ who is walking in truth. Knowing we are doing what is right gives us an inner satisfaction, and according to the Bible this is where our prosperity begins.

If we go to bed at night knowing we did our best—were fair in our dealings, even to those we are not fond of, and gave God the honor—for the day, we have won more than half the battle. God needs to be present all day, not just a little time in the morning before we head out the door or a quick blessing under our breath at lunch.

By doing that, we are treating Him like a pal, not someone whose guidance we need or are committed to follow. He can't honor us when we give Him our second best.

In the movie, *Facing the Giants*, the story takes place in a small southern Georgia town, where a Christian high school has made it to the state playoffs. This is a team that should not have had a winning season, let alone facing a team that was bigger, faster, stronger and looking for their fourth state title. The coach saw the look on his players' faces as they watched their opponent come onto the field, in pre-game warm ups, the intimidation and the fear as they saw the size of these players. The coach knew his battle was not on the field but in the hearts of his players.

As they headed back to the locker room for last minute preparations, the coach reminded his team how proud he was of them and how far they had come. He then reminded them of the commitment they had made on the practice field after their third loss in a row at the beginning of the season.

What occurred over the next seven games was nothing short of a miracle—leading them to be in that locker room on that evening. The transformation that took place is because of one person deciding to change, to recommit and put God back at the head instead of the tale. The prospering that took place was far reaching and went beyond winning games on the field.

The power behind committing to God and what will be transformed in your life is difficult to put into words. Most people are so skeptical and unbelieving, but it is real, not just in the movies but in everyday life. Just be willing to give it a shot.

"Your wife will be like a fruitful vine within your house; your children will be like olive shoots around your table" Psalm 128:3 (NIV).

To be **fruitful** means to *bear fruit, bring forth, cause, and increase.* These all seem logical in sequence to the wife's roll in the Bible. The wife was looked upon to make sure the linage of the family name was carried on. In Proverbs, we are reminded in many different verses that the woman can be a blessing or she can be a curse. The cause of which a wife will be, is set in motion by how she is treated, how much she is respected and loved by her family.

God is all about relationships and not just the one with Him. He expects the home front to be the same. If we expect the wife to be fruitful in the home then the climate has to be right and the conditions need to be acceptable. This all takes place when man has his alignment in order. The wife has such an influence over the children, how they progress and learn, and being godly means all the difference in their eventual outcome.

The wife's impact on the home goes beyond just being able to have children and preserve the lineage. The wheels were set in motion when the child was born, but the cause of the final product will be greatly influenced by the mother's presence in their life.

Increase was expected from the child as well. One day they would be expected to marry and have children to carry on the family name. Family carried a much greater meaning to the people of those times. So much of this attitude was orchestrated by the wife and what she did, which in turn was set by the tone of the husband and his submission to God. I know that the use of the word 'mother' would be more appropriate, but these are God's sacred words and I am not qualified to change his work.

Men, you can see there is a pecking order, and this does not take a rocket scientist to figure this out. *"Love me as I loved the church and love your wives the same."* Nowhere in that short, straight-forward sentence given its due in our society. It will not be seen of TV or read about in your magazine while waiting in line at the grocery store. It is something the man has to step up and follow Gods' instruction.

I was reminded in a conversation by a lady who stated, "I don't remember seeing an asterisk by the word 'worse' in my marriage vows that would give me an out if things got too difficult." As I listened to her express her concern as to how easily married couples today just quit. Then have the nerve to jump right in and start another relationship thinking that will solve everything.

The reason God goes to such great lengths is to get our attention. He explains to us in so many different ways throughout the entire Bible the *world* wants us to think it is a quick fix society. If God was explaining this 2,000 years ago and it's still applicable today, don't you think that maybe, just maybe, He was on to something.

The Bible often mentions 'wine' which comes from the fruit of the vine. The Bible also mentions the vine and the vine dresser, He is the vine we are the branch, the mention of the use of the word vine or inference to it is numerous again God wants our attention and He wants us to be an extension of Him.

John 15:5 (NIV) says. *"I am the vine; you are the branches. If you remain in me and I in you, you will bear much fruit; apart from me you can do nothing."* This brings us to our next word **vine,** *to bend, grape, bear fruit blossom to coil or wrap around and the base.*

Nehemiah reminds us that the wife is the real glue that holds the family together, as he has reminded us that man is the glue that holds the marriage together. These words cannot be said often enough, nor can we be reminded frequently enough of their importance in our daily walk. As we dig for 'meaning of life,' these four verses we are looking at now may be some of the most impactful words a man and his wife need to put on the walls of their hearts, their refrigerator, frame them by their bed and then promise to live by them until death do they part.

Just as Jesus is willing to do whatever it takes to comfort those who commit to Him, the wife will do the same in a home where she is given that same respect. "Being the vine" says we are to bend, to sacrifice, give, and show strength through our love to our family just as Jesus does for us. This love will bear fruit, a sweet fruit that will blossom and a bond that will develop in which the children will want to wrap themselves around their mother and she will be their base, their safe haven.

Job 15:33-34 (NIV) says, *"He will be like a vine stripped of its unripe grapes, like an olive tree shedding its blossoms. For the company of the godless will be barren, and fire will consume the tents of those who love bribes."* Here, we are reminded of what happens when you choose not to involve God in your life. Your vine will be stripped of its fruit or the fruit will be lost while it is still immature and the house will be full of strife.

What does that mean and how do we keep God first in our busy lives? We have all these pressures, demands, and what we think should be at the top of our priority list. In our daily surroundings, the message we receive is "Me first." Our church on Sunday tells us it is God first. If we are more heavily influenced by society, who do you think will win? The Bible states many times there needs to be a clear-cut decision, you need to get on one side of the fence or the other. God does not like the lukewarm.

Just as the wife will be like a fruitful vine within your house; your children will be like olive shoots around your table. The olive was a fruit that graced everyone's table from the poor to the King. It was a fruit that was plentiful and the tree was even recognized as special.

The word **olive** means *illuminating, oil, tree, and branch.* Your sons will be like olive shoots around your table. An olive shoot is the young tender branch for it needs care, nurturing, and attention to enable it to grow and be productive. Our children when young need our attention, our guidance, and they need our love. What occurs at the table and the lessons we teach our children will reflect back to us in the future. We get oil from the olive, and in early biblical times it was used to anoint, and fragrance was added to give it a pleasant aroma. Just as our children are our offspring, their actions as they mature bring an aroma back to us. The word oil also comes from a Hebrew word aphar (aw-far), *to be gray, dust, pulverize, earth, clay, and rubbish.* The Scriptures have subtle ways of reminding us that all we do is a reflection of ourselves. As we are reminded when we point a finger at someone else, there are three pointing back at us.

Taking into account the oil could be an anointing, a blessing, and a disgrace or it could turn back to earth. As I sit here and think, to my knowledge everything is a derivative of the earth in some form or fashion. Whether our children leave us with an aroma or rubbish it will be a reflection on us. Nehemiah warns us to take the time to be with and nurture our children while they are young. Provide the proper atmosphere of love, example setting, time, and making sure that God is the center of your families' life.

The olive shoot is an extension of the branch that receives its life from the tree. God is the tree, and we are the branches. He is constantly pruning us to be more productive in all areas of our life.

In the home, the parents are the tree and the children are the branches. Parents have to constantly prune them while they are under our tutelage, preparing them for the day when they leave and face the world on their own.

God has one way of doing things and it has and always will be the same. He is the head and as long as we get our direction from Him, even in difficult times, we can count on Him not to abandon us. Just as we gather at the table to replenish our body with food, God's word is just as important.

The table is where so much of life is taught. As parents, we have the opportunity to teach and share with our children and we should not to miss this chance. The **table** in this verse speaks volumes. It refers *to spread out, send away, wise, appoint, forsake, and stretch forth.* We, as parents, have to seize the moment when our children are young and impressionable. They grow so quickly. There is no better time than at meal time to tell stories, set examples, discipline with love and to plant the seeds of God.

One day your children may be spread out as mine are in Connecticut, Pittsburgh, and Houston. Without good seed planting, you don't know how it will end. There will come a time as you are sitting at your table that it will dawn on you the conversation you are having is about them moving away for they are ready to fly solo.

There will be a joy and sadness in your heart as the realization of this moment appears. As your children leave the nest, you will have the opportunity to reflect over the time you spent with them around the table. Children who have been raised under the watchful eye of godly parents and have a solid foundation of right and wrong understand God is not one who forsakes or gives up on them. They know life will deal them blows and there will be many valleys and life will not always be a ride on the peaks. But because of the lessons learned at the table of putting God first they are prepared to stretch forth and put faith to their action, knowing He is not a God of disappointment.

Is this to say it is always going to work out in their favor or they are going to come out on top every time? No. What it does say is God is in control and the end will always be better than the beginning. By spending table time with our children planting seeds and sharing our feelings for God we set a precedent and develop a belief system that is firm.

When times of trouble come, our children are anchored and decisions will be made that follow Christian principles. On the other hand, you can look at some of those same words and they can carry a completely different end result.

If we choose not to spend time at the table, Nehemiah reminds us our children will be spread out, (cast away) choose to leave, and have little or no communication, or worse run away. There may have to be decisions on your part to ask them to leave, breaking your heart and forsaking all you had hoped for. The blessings we have talked about in these verses far outweigh any amount of money one could have in the bank and the impact is much longer lasting.

As we continue our study, what we have learned to this point reminds us that obeying the Scriptures can cause an abundance to come to our life. These same Scriptures also caution us as to how we should handle it.

CHAPTER 18
THE TEACHINGS OF SOLOMON

The Book of Proverbs is mostly credited to Solomon who was granted wisdom, a wise and discerning heart, stating there will never be one as wise as Solomon, before or after him. Quite a lofty grant, wouldn't you say?

Solomon proved during his reign as king to be wise and discerning, eager to learn, and pen much of his knowledge for others to garner. In Proverbs 3:1-2 (NIV), we see some of Solomon's basic principles and the benefits of wisdom as he tells us, *"My son, do not forget my teaching. But keep my commands in your heart, for they will prolong your life many years and bring you prosperity."*

I can hear it now. Here we go—someone telling us we can get rich or have abundance by reading a book and following someone's philosophy. Those who promote this type of teaching usually want you to either purchase something or make a donation mostly for personal gain and this becomes a turn off. Then you get typical response of "No thanks."

Solomon reminds us to not **forget,** which means *to mislay, be oblivious, and from want of memory.* I am notorious for laying down my keys, forgetting where I put them and spending countless time retracing my steps. I have been in many homes and seen by the kitchen door some sort of board designed to hang keys, thus eliminating this regiment. Just as someone had the idea to design a board to eliminate the hassle of looking for the keys, Solomon says it is necessary we put into practice God's teachings.

Years ago, as a carpet salesman, I made a big mistake. When I was measuring a job early in my career I was just excited to get the sales call. Being new, before I left to go to the customers home, I made sure I had my tape measure, my pad, a couple of contracts, my calculator, and directions to where I was going.

There are many things to know when measuring carpet in making sure you figure the job properly. This being my first solo job, I was enamored by the size of the house. It had a stairway with beautiful woodwork and all the things you don't want to encounter on your first measuring job. The home was located in a part of town where most of the wealthy people lived. This couple had just purchased it and wanted to replace some carpet. I began to sketch the area to be carpeted that included the living room, the dining room, a hallway, a beautiful stairway, and an upstairs hall as well.

There were several offsets, closets, cut outs, and of course the stairway itself. For my first assignment it was a difficult job to measure. Carpet mechanics do not like to do a lot of piecing so making sure there was enough carpet to do the job properly and not have bunches left over was a concern. Once the customer decided on the color we next had to decide on how she wanted the steps covered. Did she want a waterfall or each step tailored? She wanted each step tailored. The stairway was long, each step had what we called a bull nose or overhang and the exposed side had two spindles per step. One mechanic spent as much time installing the carpet on the steps as the rest of the crew did in completing the remainder of the job.

I needed the lead mechanic to do the steps because there was an art to doing it the way she had requested. The floors were beautiful hard wood and the staircase had some hand carved woodwork as well. It was a shame to cover it with carpet. I spent a good two hours measuring and figuring, erasing, re-measuring, refiguring before coming up with a price installed.

We discussed where the seams in the carpet would go and how it would look completed. She was happy with what I had quoted and how she envisioned the completed job. I called the store to make sure we could have the carpet installed before Thanksgiving and the store manager assured me we could, so she wrote me a deposit check, signed the contract, and off I went.

I was excited! This was my first job and it was a big job. Quality pad and quality carpet. I would make a nice commission, and all was well, or so I thought. The day finally came for the job to be installed. I wanted to make sure I got the best crew to do the job, and I did. I came to work early that day to meet the crew and explained how I measured where the seams were to go and how the steps were to be installed. The mechanics arrived at her home about 8:30 that Thursday morning and it was about 10am when the store called and my nightmare began. I had a customer and was called to speak to the mechanic at the job. I excused myself and the words that no carpet salesman ever wants to hear came through the phone: "You measured the job incorrectly."

We are short on carpet, we need another five yards and I don't have enough to do all the stairs. My heart sank! This was a special-order carpet. The customer was upset for her plans for Thanksgiving were going up in smoke, the mechanic was upset for this was holding up his crew and I am standing there with my mouth open, not knowing what to do. I forgot to add a measurement which I had taken. In all my figuring and refiguring, I left out a measurement. Getting the carpet was not the issue, but getting it from the same roll could be.

In a panic, I got the store manager to call the manufacture and luckily we were able to get the additional carpet from the same roll and it all ended well. We made it in time for her Thanksgiving party, but my commission was zero and it took a couple of more jobs to make up for my mistake.

From that point on, I had a checklist and each time I measured a house I went through the checklist. I never quoted a price or put pen to paper to tell someone how many yards of carpet it would take to do a job without my checklist.

Forgetting also indicates we are not paying attention or choose to ignore the instructions, thinking we are better equipped and do not need to listen. My mother would say, "You are being bull headed." Knowing full well because I chose to ignore her instruction it was going to backfire or take me twice as long to complete.

When we get wise, counsel or pray and ask God for help, we get an answer, but then do the dumbest thing. We don't do what we were instructed to do. Then the deal goes south or things fall apart and we have the audacity to look up and say, "God, why did you do this to me?"

If we are in God's Word, he tells in Deuteronomy 6:8 (NIV): "Tie them as symbols on your hands and bind them on your foreheads." If we take the time to study, He tells us to not to mislay or be oblivious to His Word. Don't play dumb or stand there and look like a deer staring at headlights getting ready to be hit by a semi- truck.

By constantly seeking His Word and putting it into practice we are ready when challenged. It is ingrained in us, giving us the ability to help ourselves or someone in need, anytime, anywhere.

I am sure you have encountered a person who seems to be walking around in a daze and you have tried to have a conversation with them and find yourself saying they don't have a clue. That same person may have made an obvious choice and have the attitude of 'I don't care; I am not concerned of the outcome.' They don't want to be bothered with the details or the explanation and feel 'let someone else sweat the small stuff.'

God calls this person lazy and foolish and Solomon warns us that a little sleep, a little slumber and poverty will come over you like a bandit. Solomon reminds us to keep God's commands in your heart.

To **keep** means *to guard, obey, maintain, and movement.* In keeping God's commands, we need to be on guard at all times. Sin is always lurking and looking for openings and we can never be too cautious. To **keep** also means to obey or maintain.

We are told to obey the laws God has given us and our path will be straight. By taking the time to choose the path you travel, you will be able to determine where you will eventually end up. This allows us to maintain a direction and those who look to us for guidance can see we have made the right choice. God expects words and actions to be line so the questions we should be asking ourselves are "whose words are we following?"

Keep my commands, meaning to collect the law, ordinance, and precepts. Throughout the Bible, the commands are referred to as laws. The Bible is a constant reminder of God's rules. We have the option to take them as valuable instruction as we use as a map, or they will become a burden.

The news as of late has been a constant reminder of the CEO's of various companies who have decided to operate outside the law, or think it applies to everyone except them. Take a moment and see how this relates to the Roman Empire. The Sadducees and Pharoses' sat in the seats of government and created the laws for everyone else, but did not apply to them.

Greed, misguided direction and desire for power at any cost in biblical times is just as it is today. Without regard for the law it eventually will catch up with you.There will be a time when, there will be no more second chances. For the individual who is not familiar with God's Word, I understand your thinking or feeling of disbelief when reading this.

It's hard to understand why God would bring harm to anyone, as He is is supposed to be a loving God. He is a loving God, and it is not Him who brings the harm; it is the choices we make that bring the consequences we have to bare.

I live in the Sunshine State and the winter months bring what is commonly known as snowbirds. They come in great numbers, populate the towns and are welcomed by local business owners. Those who live in Florida year around don't always share the same sentiment. For the next four to six months, the working people's schedule will change, tempers will flare, and you will be late more times than you can count.

It is an adjustment you have to make because the snowbirds are a driving force to the economy. They will drive you nuts in traffic, it seems they are oblivious to the surroundings and do pretty much as they please. I have a good friend who is a police officer and from time to time, he shares with me a portion of his day. He is amazed at what a person will say to his face after they have committed a blatant violation of the law. He patrols the beach, where there are lots of new construction areas that have just been completed or being completed, which in itself creates some congestion. One day, he was observing a traffic light. As it turned red, he watched a person makes an illegal U-turn. Seconds later, a lady decided she doesn't want to wait for the light to turn green so she pulled on through. She did this against oncoming traffic. As horns blew and breaks screeched, she pulled into a shopping plaza oblivious to what has just occurred. My friend observed all this in amazement and proceeded to pull out to go after the lady. Just as he went, he got a call to be a back-up so he had to respond. He couldn't just let this lady go unnoticed, so with lights flashing he pulled into the parking lot behind the lady, got out and went to her car to ask her what she was thinking for she could have caused a major accident.

In broken English, she replied, "I did not know it was wrong to do this for I am not from here." Not having much time to deal with this drama, my friend quickly went to the rear of the car to see where the license plate was from. It was a Florida plate. He walked back to her and asked if this was her car. She responded yes. He then asked how long she had owned the car? She said five years.

He had to hold his tongue because he wanted to give her a lashing but said as politely as his anger would permit, "Lady, consider this your lucky day. If I did not have to get to this emergency call I would write you a very big ticket. One for running the red light and posing danger to oncoming traffic and an additional cost for being such a terrible liar."

The lady did not care what was going on around her or who was affected by her actions for she was on a mission and that was all that mattered. There are times when focus is good, but that moment and time was not one of them.

My friend is a strong Christian and the testing ground God has him in proves to be an environment that calls for a higher level of patience, quick thinking, and God's hand in his work throughout each day. He said that he could have taken down her plate number and told her that would call her later to take care of the ticket, but he chose to let her go.

God constantly reminds us to be on guard, obey the law, be knowledgeable and maintain a level of awareness because there is always going to be a movement that is trying to get us off track and move us in another direction away from God.

Solomon reminds us the **commands** are ordinances and precepts, and we need to collect them. It has been a long time since I sat in a high school classroom and taken an exam. Years ago, in the class room the teacher gave an assignment and told us there will be a test tomorrow on the following material. We had fair warning to come to class the next day prepared. Even if I aced the exam, I couldn't repeat that score again today. This is why Solomon is so adamant in telling us again and again to collect the laws, lock them into your brain, let them be a way of life and be a doer not just a hearer of the word.

One final reminder! We are not to elevate ourselves because we are familiar with God's law. We should not go around pointing our finger, have wagging tongues and be hypocrites. No, actually by being in tune to God's Word, we become very humble. These are the same laws that our country was founded on, the same premise that Harvard University was founded on, and in today's news that university made a decision to denounce that foundation as its corner stone for existence.

Those who came to this country to have a fresh start would be sad for it was their dream to set a standard and teach their principles to generations to come. Those who embark on our great shores do so for the freedoms they were not allowed to exercise. That is supposed to be the beauty of America for we can express our differences, share our ideals and be heard. What once made us great has taken a back seat—not voluntarily, but with very little resistance.

The time for Christians to stand up and say, "enough" is now. We have been pushed to the back of the line, asked not to speak and not to share our belief while those who choose to have a different belief march forward and demand equal time. Our display of faith has become hidden behind the walls of the church and we have become the modern-day Jekyll and Hyde of religion. We need to be bold and confident in him who we represent. Let our light shine speaking in truth and giving God the glory. Be a doer of the Word and God will take care of the rest.

CHAPTER 19

THE CHALLENGES OF BEING A CHRISTIAN

Being a Christian presents challenges in the decisions we make, the thoughts we think, and how we respond. When driving the highways and someone crosses three lanes and cut you off this is when your true Christian colors shine. How we react in the heat of the moment is what people remember. The impression we leave someone with is when they witnessed our ugly response to an incident. That is the real you or me.

For some, that becomes a lasting vision never to be erased and as time goes on they share the incident causing it to take a life of its own. Solomon reminds us to *"Trust in the Lord with all our heart and lean not on our own understanding."* The more we think we know, the more we discover we don't know.

In high school and college during football camp, we did what was called "two a day practices." One was early in the morning and the second was late afternoon. The heat took its toll on our bodies and we couldn't get enough fluid.

In high school, my sister used to tell me I was eating for three people. In college, we had meal tickets and the cafeteria people would load us up with food. After our evening meal most of us would head to a local drive in a restaurant where we ordered a burger called "a poor boy." It was huge and had everything on it. We would also get a large order of fries and a drink. Man, what a burger that was and there was always snacks in the room for us to munch on before lights out. The desire to replenish the calories and fluid during football season seemed to be never ending.

God wants us to have that same desire as we read and study His Word. He wants our craving to be real and never ending. Solomon uses the word 'command' for a specific reason. It is an order and the same rule applies here as anywhere that word would be used.

If you want to get along in the military, you listen to the drill sergeant. When the coach told me to do a particular drill again, I did what he told me or I would find myself on the bench. The same rules apply when we play for God. This is the drill: He wants us to know what to do when we get in the game.

Once we read and study we must then become a follower of His word, "a doer." He wants us to exercise our disciple muscles. Don't panic, He did not say you had to be a preacher or go stand on a street corner where people will jeer you. But there will be times when you will feel a little tug on your heart while in a conversation or a certain situation when God will call on you to share your testimony.

He is not asking you to get on a soapbox, make a scene or be a Bible thumper; but He does expect us to be bold and seize the opportunity. That is where the command part applies. The commands are to be kept in our heart. The heart we most commonly think of is the main control panel of our being where everything evolves. It is the command center, blood pumping, valves opening and shutting, oxygen flowing, cleansing, signals being sent, raise this arm, look to the right, don't respond to that statement, think, all this evolves around or is in conjunction with the heart.

When Solomon talks about the **heart,** he refers to the center of our being, our intellect, and our courage. There will be a time in almost everyone's life when we will experience an emotional hurt. It will come from a tragedy. It could be a death, a divorce, an illness, loss of friendship, or your best and dearest friend turning on you for whatever reason. The pain will pierce your heart and for some that pain will last a lifetime. Regardless of how we deal with the pain, it will leave a lasting scar as a reminder.

In order for this to make sense, we should have God first in our life, make Him our center, our source of strength. So, when a horrible incident occurs, we are better prepared to weather the storm. When our heart stops, so do we, and life is over as we know it in this world.

If the heart is the center, intellect and the place we get our courage then we need to take good care of it. Just as we need to eat properly, exercise regularly, and get the necessary rest to insure as good of a life as possible, we need to feed our spiritual command center as well. The spiritual food we need is God's Word and we need to exercise our intellect.

This can be done by attending church, Bible studies, small groups, being a disciple, and learning to help others. This will give you a peace because of your alignment with God, which is more wonderful than the best night's sleep you've ever had.

Think About It

Everyone wants the good life! What do you think is the good life?

Well, if you listen to the world they will tell you all you need to get is the good life. The houses, the cars, the vacations, jet setting—all those things that are just out of reach for most of us, so we become wannabe's.

We are told the commands will prolong our **life**. In this context life means *raw, fresh, promise and revive*. The Bible tells us God made us wonderfully, but there is a process we must all go through that is called "going from the raw to being mature." There are two types of maturity. One is physical in stature and the other is mental or mature in our emotions.

Regardless of where we are in our physical and emotional state, once we become a man or a woman of God we are raw and He will make us anew. He will give us a clean slate and a fresh start. He devises a game plan with us and makes us a promise that He will never leave or forsake us.

During the process of maturing in our walk with God, He revives us and breathes a new life into us. This may sound a little far-fetched to a non-believing person or even a little weird, but to any Christian who has walked this path they will tell you that having God in your corner is far better than going it alone.

God saves and prolongs everything that happens in our life because it happens for a reason. We as humans make some real blunders that can have a devastating impact on us as well as family members. Rest assured, God does have a method and will use it to our good.

I was in my second year of college and four of us guys were taking summer classes together, so we would commute daily, taking turns driving. It was a hundred miles round trip and we usually arrived back home each evening around 4:30pm. On this particular day, after getting home, my mother said dinner would be a little late and should be ready by six. I told her I was going into town and would be back in time for dinner.

I worked at a service station on weekends for extra money so I thought I would hang out a while, plus I was dating the owner's daughter. A good friend was just leaving work when I arrived and after exchanging hellos, we began to talk about whose car was the fastest. One comment led to another and the next thing you knew we were challenging each other to a race off Swell Mountain.

Well, the challenge was on and now it was time to lay down the ground rules. The two cars were a rear engine four-cylinder Corvair and a four door six-cylinder Chevy Nova. We're not exactly talking Mario Andretti or Big Daddy Don Garlitz types racing here and the course we chose was just plain crazy. We drove to the top of Swell Mountain, which was a three lane, very curvy dangerous highway.

I proposed that Mario Andretti (me) got a two-car spot, figuring Parnell Jones (my buddy) having the six cylinder should give me a break. The rules were set and when I took my foot off the brake and hit the gas the race was on. I was in the lead. Adrenalin was pumping, tires were squealing and engines screaming. We were two-thirds of the way down the mountain and coming into the last curve and I was still in the lead. I came into that last curve in the outside lane of traffic coming up the hill. I met a car head on, so I cut and swerved to the right to avoid the oncoming car. I then had to cut back to the left to keep from going over the hill and that is when it happened.

Having all the weight in the rear of my Corvair, when I cut back, the car started to skid. I was going sideways through the curve and the momentum was pushing me across the road toward the hill. Once my front end hit the bank, the speed was such that I continued to skid down the road.

I had no control. I looked out the passenger window and could see a mound of what appeared to be dirt and gravel at the end of a driveway I was rapidly approaching and then wham. The car was propelled into the air and flipped a couple of times. I remember seeing the passenger side floor mat suspended in midair from the force of the flip. Next, I felt this thug as my body hit the ground. I blacked out but immediately came to. Lying on my back I saw the car go over my head then heard this loud slam of metal and gravel and passed out again. I came to a second time, trying to gain my composure and get to my feet. The dust was thick in the air and I could hear tires screeching as my buddy was trying to get his car to stop.

By the time he got turned around and back to me, I was standing on the side of the road in a daze in the midst of the smell of rubber, a cloud of dust, broken glass, and an unrecognizable Corvair. The car was a complete total.

I was having trouble standing, my clothes were torn, blood running down my face, but I was alive. My injuries were not that serious—I had some scrapes, minor cuts and a lot of bruises. The next day my body was very sore but within a few days I was as good as new. God had a plan for me because if you would have seen the car, I should not have walked away and been here to write this story today. There were many people at the little Baptist Church, including my Aunt and Uncle, who continually prayed for this old boy. I was a pretty unsavory character when I was young. We all have our stories and many can say God had His hand in our lives.

As Solomon wrote Proverbs, his words were inspired by God. Solomon in all his wisdom and wealth was subject to his downfalls as well. This tells us, we never get beyond seeking the counsel of God and continually including Him in our decision-making process. It has been said "we are only one choice, one decision away from devastation or complete freedom." When you look at life through this set of glasses, the Bible is—your choice for freedom—will open doors and lead you down halls. It will put you with and in front of people you never expected to see or meet. Understanding and accepting God is in control is difficult. At best it goes against everything we have been taught.

Yet, you read the Bible and see the many lives and examples of people who put one hundred per cent faith in God. In return they were rewarded in ways they expected and ways they did not expect. There is a plan. We have to agree, to submit, and follow, and for so many of us that is much easier said than done.

HT spent 48 years in the coalmine industry and did not get as much as a hang nail. Why was that? He became a study of his work environment, conditions and dangers and knew that you must obey the rules or they could come and get you in a body bag. He became so good at low incidents on his shift, the company wanted to know why his shift was more productive, had less accidents, and less down time than any of the other shifts. That was one of the many reasons the company would seek him for management.

HT attributed a lot of his success to reading the Bible. He did what Solomon recommended, followed Joshua's lead and worked hard following the footsteps of Jesus. He never considered himself anyone special, was always willing to do a little extra, go the extra mile, lend a helping hand and be there for his fellow man. Those all seem to be basic principles that God lays out for us. Learn to do your skills well and they will serve you well.

"Trouble pursues the sinner, but the righteous are rewarded with good things" Proverbs 13:21 (NIV). When we look at the word **misfortune** it is broken down in two parts: mis and fortune. To **mis** means something we overlooked and something we passed by. We are warned by our parents and others in authority to slow down, ask questions before committing, think and get a second opinion. But for those of us who don't, we miss out. We never know where we could have gone

had we taken the other road. The closest we will ever get is saying, "That could have been me."

The second part is **fortune.** To most people they think of large sums of money or a lot of stuff. There can be abundance in this life as well as the next, but that abundance is at His direction. This does not sit well with a lot of people.

In Malichi 3:15 (NIV), we read: *"But now we call the arrogant blessed. Certainly evildoers prosper, and even when they put God to the test, they get away with it."*

Just a verses to the right, in Malichi 3:18, we read: *"And you will again see the distinction between the righteous and the wicked, between those who serve God and those who do not."* Rather than consume ourselves with the should ofs, could ofs, and would ofs, which is called living in the past, we should keep our eyes on Jesus — always looking forward, never looking back; always looking up, not looking down; always looking outward, and not looking inward. Jesus tells us to live in the "now' as tomorrow has enough worries of its own.

CHAPTER 20

WE ARE ALL SINNERS

The fortune you and I seek is right under our nose, but we will never recognize it until we have our priorities straight: God, family, and then our jobs. In Proverbs 13:21 (NIV) we read: *"Trouble pursues the sinner, but the righteous are rewarded with good things."*

It seems misfortune pursues the sinner and seeks him out like the hunter seeking his prey.

Think About It

Who is a sinner, or more explicit, what is a sinner?

_____

_____

According to the Hebrew, a **sinner** is a criminal and someone guilty who is condemned and forfeits his rights. Our prisons are full of hardened criminals who have committed crimes that have cost them their freedom and place in society.

The news media is full of acts of violence that occurs daily from spouses hiring someone to kill their wife or husband, children shooting their parents, teenagers beating homeless people and the list continues to grow. It seems as if the American people are numb to all the crime that is going on around them. As long as the crime does not directly affect them most will just turn a deaf ear.

In Ecclesiastes 8:11(NIV) it is written:*"When the sentence for a crime is not quickly carried out, the hearts of the people are filled with schemes to do wrong."* Our judicial system has tied its own hands. By creating laws that counteract other laws the attorney who figures out a way to create a loophole to get his client off by leaving that slightest hint of doubt just opens Pandora's box. Now others will commit the same crime and walk.

Crimes are categorized in different levels, such as white color, blue color. Just as the person who chooses to commit the crime knowing full well they stand a chance of getting caught but in their mind, they think the reward is greater than the risk. They are willing to take the chance of being found guilty, condemned to possibly life in prison and forfeit all their freedom for this one act.

It is like the policeman who worked with the K9 unit. His German Shepard was his partner and they were inseparable. He was married with two sons and never for a minute thought his boys were into drugs. The dog lived in their home and was trained to sniff out drugs. The father had regular talks with his boys about drug use and he and his wife felt sure their sons were not into anything.

The policeman had a hobby. He liked to rebuild computers and always kept some of the pressurized spray to blow the dust out as he worked on them. He had just purchased two cans a couple days earlier and went to get one, only to discover they were both empty. He was upset and asked who had used them. His sons said they were messing around and had used them. He told them not to waste his cleaner anymore and went to purchase another can. The next morning, his wife was fixing breakfast. She went to each boy's room to tell them breakfast was ready and she didn't want them to miss the bus. She knocked on their bedroom door, but there was no response. She pushed open the door and found one of her sons sitting on the bed.

She said, "Come on now, you are going to be late," but he didn't respond. Knowing he was a prankster, she walked over to the bed and lightly pushed him on the shoulder. When he fell over, she saw a tiny red straw in his hand and an empty cleaner can on the floor.

Lives would be changed forever that day, a void where once a young boy lived, played, brought sunshine into others' lives and whose parents had hopes and aspirations all vanished. Just like the hardened criminal, the son made a choice to do something out of selfishness and the consequence affected others for the rest of their lives.

The parents questioned themselves, "Where did we go wrong, what could we have done differently, how will we fill this void?" The guilt they felt was unbearable as if the sentence had been pronounced on them. Recreational drug abuse among teens is off the chart and spiraling out of control and seems as if we don't know how to stop it.

As we continue we see that prosperity is the reward of the **righteous,** which *brings forth, spring, grow, just, cleans, and make right.* Righteousness is not something you earn;it is a gift from God—a result of following God and allowing Him to be the ruler of your life. That sounds simple enough, but we all know the challenges we can encounter in a day's times that test our faith, our patience, our temper and anything else that can be tested.

As God gives us the gift of righteousness, we are cleansed, our past is forgiven, and more importantly forgotten. He brings us forth out of the darkness. Those thoughts, activities and places we used to hang out no longer seem to be the places we want to go. We look at our old buddies differently. The language they use sounds foreign to us—all of a sudden we have lost this desire to communicate using those words.

God has given us a new mindset. The old ways must change and a desire to do the right thing and make right what we could have cared less about in the past now makes a difference. We now have a desire to grow in His word. A new well springs in our hearts and we want to share what we know with others. This will cause a separation and our old will pass away.

This is a natural process for a new person in Christ. This is all part of God's plan as it unfolds in our life and He welcomes us into His family. The prosperity of righteousness is a life long journey that continually produces rewards.

These rewards may appear in the form of challenges that help us grow. Some we won't understand, others bring joy and some just a peace that passes all understanding. Paul reminds us in the Book of Romans 3:21 (NIV): *"But now apart from the law the righteousness of God has been made known, to which the Law and the Prophets testify."*

The prosperity that Solomon mentions comes in many forms. Just in knowing it is Solomon speaking the words indicates there is some form of wealth associated with it. There are those who have studied Solomon extensively to see how he did it and what made him tick. They have tried to duplicate him, and those who think they have figured him out may have had different degrees of success, thus fooling themselves and others into thinking they have got it.

Man comes to the conclusion he does not need God because he has a winning formula. The world is full of those who have fallen into that trap believing they don't need God. They have succeeded even beyond what they expected. When life presented them with twist and turns, there were fortunes made and fortunes lost and they took what life gave them and moved on never bringing God into the picture.

The Christian who has God at the center of his life may encounter the exact same scenario, but the difference is God is in on every decision-making process and always gets the credit. What happens in the case of tragedy? The Christian has God as his comforter, bringing a supernatural peace and clarity.

Each day's challenge provides the believer and the non-believer the same decision-making choices. It is how each chooses to get their desired results that will become the proving ground for the on-looker.

The apostle Paul says in 1 Corinthians 9:24 (NIV), *"Do you not know that in a race all the runners run, but only one gets the prize? Run in such a way as to get the prize."* Go into strict training just like the world-class athlete. Run to finish the race and to get the crown of glory that lasts forever so you will not be disqualified.

To those who choose to make God an integral part of every aspect of their life, they have an inner peace and an ability to withstand the storms, understanding that one much greater than they are in control.

God tells us in Malichi 3:10 (NIV), *"Bring the whole tithe into the storehouse, that there may be food in my house. Test me in this says the Lord Almighty, and see if I will not throw open the floodgates of heaven and pour out such a blessing that there will not be room enough to store it."* He is clear to never state what the blessing may be since He knows our real needs and will supply accordingly.

Solomon says in Proverbs 21:21 (NIV), *"Whoever pursues righteousness and love finds life, prosperity and honor."* The word **righteousness** takes us from criminal and condemned to justice, morally right and prosperity—the opposite of what we just covered. God wants justice for us, which is the quality of being morally right and not to be one who demands justice to condemn others. Those who pursue righteousness through the eyes of God, live with a code of conduct that conforms to the principles that God has set for us. Your moral standards are high and you love and respect others the way God loves you. We all know this is a tall order but as we have been reminded in the past, God never mentioned life's journey being easy. Instead, He said, *"It will be worth your effort. You will be morally right."*

This breaks down to be just a simple concept of doing what is right, not from a legalistic, but rather, from a moral point of view. Righteousness also suggests prosperity, meaning if you choose to do the right thing and are consistent in your example setting, your reputation will precede you and people will want to do business with you, use your services and employ you because you are some one of character and others know they will be treated fairly by you.

He who pursues righteousness and love **finds,** which means: *come forth, attain, acquir.*

Can you imagine finding love, true love and how wonderful and exciting that would be? Two people deeply committed to each other following God's plan for their life.

Perhaps true love or the thought of marriage doesn't thrill you. But consider the meaning of *come forth*. Other words to define 'come forth' are arrive, emerge and break through. All are all actions words that carry a positive impact on our lives, and even more so when applied to God's principles.

Solomon was a man of action. He asked for wisdom and God responded kindly. Solomon was paid millions if translated into today's economy by people who just sought to set in his presence and listen to him speak.

When Solomon asked for knowledge, he knew he would have to study, seek, and ask questions. When God gave Solomon knowledge it was in the form of a desire to learn. He wanted to have an understanding of everything that crossed his path. He is a prime example of what each of us can obtain simply by applying ourselves. We too can come forth, attain, acquire, and take hold of much more than we could ever imagine—all we have to do is ask.

Just remember that we as humans in our carnal thinking want things and God does not think in things. Solomon realized that by asking for wisdom his responsibilities were going to be great, and to whom much is given much more is required.

As we pursue righteousness and love, we find **life**, *raw (flesh), plant, water appetite*. God loved His son so much He gave him up to suffer for our sins, then He died and rose again. The first word related to life is 'raw' or *in the natural*. God is not one who likes deception or phony images. He never puts on a false front. What you see is what you get. Paul tells us in Philippians 4:13 (NIV): *"I can do all this through him who gives me strength."*

CHAPTER 21
GOD'S RETIREMENT PLAN FOR US

"Whoever pursues righteousness and love finds life,
prosperity and honor."— *Proverbs 21:21 (NIV)*

God takes us in the raw. He molds and shapes us just as He did with Solomon. if we let Him. We are like a cornel of corn that is put in the earth. It needs water to grow; it takes nourishment from the soil, but with no water it will not survive. God is that valuable source of water. His words are the water we need to grow strong, be wise, and do the right thing. Our appetite will grow stronger as we read and understand His Word.

God calls His word the living water. *"Whoever believes in me, as Scripture has said, rivers of living water will flow from within them"* John 7:38 (NIV). That which does more than quench our thirst, it is the sustainer of our life and we must develop an appetite for the living water.

The word **honor** means *weight, splendor, and glorious.* In closing this verse, we find by pursuing righteousness and love we find life, prosperity and honor. When someone is elevated to a position of honor the responsibility that comes with it can be very heavy and must be taken seriously. The weight that is put on the shoulders of the person in charge is tremendous. We are encouraged to go to Jesus, as He wants to carry our burden. When a person and their position are raised many will come to them for advice and look for guidance. This is where many a man has met his demise.

Rich Devos spoke to a group of graduating seniors at a local high school. As he sat on a stool, he reminded them the higher you elevate yourself the further and the harder the fall. The only thing that can prevent the fall is not forgetting from where you came and who gets the credit.

If you go into a partnership with God, it is a full partnership. So, don't call on Him just when the problems are insurmountable or you are in a jam. God is in this deal 24/7, and expects you to do the same.

With the weight comes the splendor, the good stuff, and the understanding. He will never give you more than you can carry. By the way, He does not have a problem pulling the rug out from in under you to get your attention.

The prosperity that we are offered through God comes in something as simple as a peaceful night's rest, having good health, good friendships, talents, and specific skill.

The Bible is full of examples of hardship, trials, successes, and tribulations and is not there just for reading pleasure. It is full of lessons on how God in His divine glory has a plan.

If we are willing to study, turn our lives over to Him and commit to a lifelong program, things will always work to and for the glory of God. God will always have our backs and He will teach us how to manage the highs and lows, the bountiful years, and the dry seasons.

We are reminded by Paul in Philippians 4-12 (NIV): *"I know what it is to be in need, and I know what it is to have plenty. I have learned the secret of being content in any and every situation, whether well fed or hungry, whether living in plenty or in want."* It all comes down to this: God does not care what title we give ourselves. Whether you are a CEO, CFO, or president, the pecking order is what He wants to be clearly understood. God is the owner of it all and we are his managers.

He has given each of us a job description and an operation manual with everything we need to succeed. He says, "I own it, you manage it and keep 90% of the profit." We need to think long and hard on that statement. It covers life, family, work and self. It covers any problem we will ever encounter.

His instructions clearly state that when you are in a jam all you need to do is call on him, day or night, and He will be there. Just remember—what you think is a jam may only be a bump in the road and what you would like the answer to be may not be the answer you need. Just a note: When you are in management on God's team, there is no discrimination. You are never too old, your skin is never the wrong color, the wrong gender, or ethnicity. He does however promote according to ability. Keep in mind, He knows what you are capable of and when you have reached your maximum.

As Paul wrote in 2 Corinthians 12:7-10 (NIV), *"Therefore, in order to keep me from becoming conceited, I was given a thorn in my flesh, a messenger of Satan, to torment me. Three times I pleaded with the Lord to take it away from me. But he said to me, 'My grace is sufficient for you, for my power is made perfect in weakness.' Therefore I will* boast all the more gladly about my weaknesses, so that Christ's power may rest on me. *That is why, for Christ's sake, I delight in weaknesses, in insults, in hardships, in persecutions, in difficulties. For when I am weak, then I am strong."*

Joshua is one of my favorite books of the Bible. My sons all have biblical names. One of them was named Joshua Caleb, two of many heroes in the Bible. They were under the leadership of Moses for forty years and had plenty of time to learn the right thing to do and heed God's warning. They were the only men to come back with a positive report after being sent to spy on the Promised Land.

The thing about Moses is that his temper got him disqualified to enter the Promised Land, along with all the acts of idolatry from those he was leading. God is a stickler for rules. He makes them plain and very elementary with no grey areas.

Think About It

Do you suppose this is why we make life so difficult and create gray areas?

Look at our court system and the lawyers who spend vast amounts of time to create gray areas to justify why a crime was committed, or to make it less wrong and more acceptable. God sits on His throne looking upon this country. A country He blessed richly as mankind makes a mockery. Twisting simple truths, tuning lies into maybes, creating doubt and confusion. Do you think that God has pulled His hand back on blessing America? Those on the outside looking in seem to think so.

They see our system as easy prey and have taken advantage of it. When Jesus returns, He will right this wrong. He will eliminate the grey areas. He says in Matthew 5:37 (NIV), *"But let your Yes be Yes and your No, No. For whatever is more than these is from the evil one."*

Before Moses' death he stood on top of Mount Nebo and spoke these words: *"The Lord was angry with me because of you, and he solemnly swore that I would not cross the Jordan and enter the good land the Lord your God is giving you as your inheritance"* Deuteronomy 4:21 (NIV).

Moses died in Moab as the Lord had said but no one knows where his grave is. The Israelites grieved for thirty days for the death of Moses and then their time of mourning was over. Now Joshua, who Moses had laid hands on was filled with wisdom and eager to do God's will, so the Israelites listened to him as they prepared to enter into Canaan.

In business, it would be great to have a partner who was right there every time you messed up, caught your mistake and watch your back making it so you were constantly covered.

We do have that in Jesus, our silent business partner. He is the majority owner but we don't treat Him that way. More and more, we find out the true colors of men in business who have convinced themselves it's ok to steal and blatantly rob others. They boast in their arrogance of their accomplishments in thinking they are invincible and will never be caught. When they are found out and exposed they continue to lie and try to figure ways to soften the punishment they will receive.

In chapter seven of the Book of Joshua, God shows us how He deals with the theft. He shows us two things that will occur. First, when you have a person of bad character it will eventually bring division and destruction to the whole organization. Secondly, God will not tolerate that person on His team who is more devoted to his own agenda than the team. He will banish them in no uncertain terms. This person has violated God's covenant and become a disgrace, so he will be destroyed. God set an example that was unforgettable, and He did it in the presence of the others by having them be the executioners. There will be those who jump to their feet and cry foul and say, "You are being too harsh and the punishment you are doing is despicable."

Man's law has become so distorted that we are better protected after committing the crime. God has warned us by lessening or prolonging the punishment we encourage the crime. If we could have had the privilege of having a one-on-one with Joshua for some wise council I think it would go something like this.

You need to stay on your toes and be on guard for there is always going to be an enemy in your camp. Have strong moral convictions and set examples for those who will follow. Do more, not less, be better, not average, reach higher, don't settle for, move forward for time waits for no one and let God decide what your reward will be. It's His team.

Our next verses take us to the book of Joshua where we will look at Joshua 1:9 (NIV). *"Have I not commanded you? Be strong and courageous. Do not be afraid; do not be discouraged, for the Lord your God will be with you wherever you go."*

Joshua is one of very few that God chose to lead that did not mess up. So many of God's chosen somewhere in their life got the idea that they were invincible, so God had to rebuke them and in some cases, remove or destroy them.

But Joshua after having the privilege of being under Moses for forty years and being a witness of God's hand, both when things were going right and when He was angered, had learned his lessons well.

As we enter the Book of Joshua, in the first few verses it is as if the general is going over his final instructions with his key leaders before battle, except in this scene the general has chosen one man to lead the charge. God shows us through Joshua that leaders are tested by opposition and must be more committed to courage than taking the easy way.

God set the stage for Joshua for approximately the next eight years his leadership role would be to lead men against a more formable opponent and do battle. God tells Joshua, "Be strong and courageous. Do not be afraid or terrified because of them, for the Lord your God goes with you; he will never leave you nor forsake you" Deuteronomy 31:6 (NIV).

To **forsake** means *to loosen, relinquish, be destitute, and refuse.* In the book of Deuteronomy 7:9-10 (NIV), we read: "Know therefore that the Lord your God is God, he is the faithful God—keeping his covenant of love to a thousand generations of those who love him and keep his commandments." But to those who hate him, He will repay by destruction. Meaning, God is not the perpetrator. It is man who chooses to loosen himself from God.

The final straw came for Moses when his temper got the best of him. "Then Moses raised his arm and struck the rock twice with his staff. Water gushed out, and the community and their livestock drank" Numbers 20:11 (NIV). In Moses' case he could claim temporary insanity, but by allowing his temper to take control, he relinquished a lifelong dream that was promised.

Think About It
What does it take for God to get our attention?

You may be thinking those verses quoted were from the Old Testament and after God sent his son to die for our sins He is no longer a God of vengeance. While this is true, we must also keep in mind that God's rule book did not change and it is never God who rejects us; we are the ones who refuse Him. We have no idea of the impact that a decision of not maintaining a relationship with God can have on our life in the immediate and long-term.

The long-term effect of lying in bed on Sunday mornings . . . not taking your family to church . . . not taking time to expose your children to God and godly principles can be devastating.

I've read countless stories of people whose parents failed them, and yet there was someone in their lives who led them to Christ. Like the athlete who never knew his father and his mother was on drugs, it was his grandmother who was his rock. Even though he resented her at times and hated when she took him to church, she was the one who prayed over him, and somehow he made it out. He got through college, made it into the pros. Today, there is no question that having God in his life is what saved him.

Once God knows He has our heart, He watches over us day and night, our families, our work, and everything is under His watchful eye.

Most people who are skeptical will immediately begin to raise a ruckus and state, "What about all the disaster, the disease, and needless deaths? My husband leaving me for the other woman, our son dying from a drug overdose and my neighbor is dying from cancer? It all seems so unfair."

Some of these questions are easily answered, while others are not. The weatherman can give a logical explanation as to why the raging storm came and destroyed a certain area. It is easy to figure out why the man left his wife for the younger women. Lust, blindness and God were not the center of his life.

The son or daughter who takes an overdose because they think it is cool and are influenced by the wrong people. Maybe the family is not grounded in God. Maybe you can say 'that is not true' because so and so was in church and every time the doors opened their children were involved in all the church activities and it still happened.

Even when we as parents think we have all the bases covered, kids still make unwise choices—usually because they don't think beyond the moment. They just don't think.

I can site so many examples of young boy and girls who in the heat of the moment did very foolish things and we as bystanders say, "What were they thinking?" And the answer is, *they weren't thinking.*

When we look at the words **loosen, relinquish, destitute** or **refuse,** from this prospective these things occurred because of choices we have made—God had no say in it.

When God spoke to Joshua it never entered his mind to question or doubt if God would be there for him.

Joshua learned well by watching Moses and he understood that you will always come out on the short end of the stick when you challenge God. If

God is to forsake us He will loosen us, meaning He will relinquish us. So, let's say you are having a struggle and you come to God and ask for guidance, but then you choose to go your own way and do your own thing, ignoring what God has laid on your heart. God will gracefully back away and release you.

To be **forsaken** also means 'to be destitute'—losing sight of God, family, friends and wandering aimlessly. In this down and out broken state, we turn inward and refuse to accept the circumstance. We refuse those who want to help and take God out of the picture and then the downward spiral begins.

Refusing to accept responsibility, to acknowledge, you have abandoned God. Those who love you endure a hardened state of bitterness and blindness that can take years to overcome. The sad part is when this occurs we are the culprit, and our pride becomes our enemy. Even though we feel He has abandoned us He is always there.

CHAPTER 22
THE EMOTION OF GUILT

Guilt can make us feel abandoned, loneliness can leave us feeling empty, and anger can miscue our thinking. All of these are feelings that can rule over our emotions. Once our thoughts turn inward, unless we have a good biblical base of support and study habits, we can go in a downward spiral that is difficult to stop. All that happens from being forsaken. And it is not because God has given up on us; it's just the opposite. We either give up or chose another path.

Joshua is encouraged to be strong and have faith and do what he has been instructed. To be **strong** is *to seize, fortify, bind, conquer, prevail, and withstand.* All these are action words that say, *with God in our corner, we will be standing.*

From Genesis to Revelation, there numerous examples where God used His chosen people to be strong and they won the battle. It is like the body builder that has strength in all the muscle groups, which is necessary to have balance. God is that balance in man's life that makes him well rounded.

In God's final instructions before sending Joshua into Canaan, Joshua didn't have any doubt as to God's ability. "Then Caleb silenced the people before Moses and said, 'We should go up and take possession of the land, for we can certainly do it'" Numbers 13:30,

Joshua was aware of how much territory he had to conquer and all the different clans he needed to destroy. His confidence came in knowing God was with him, and so when God told him to seize the lands and fortify them, he believed God's words. And he conquered, prevailed, and nothing was able to withstand him, just like God said.

The hearts of the people who were going to be attacked were melting with fear. The reputation of all God had done for Moses had preceded them and it was Joshua's duty to carry out God's orders.

In the context of which **strong** is used, it leaves no room for clarity. God has covered all the bases right down to "just follow his instructions." It doesn't get any better than that. The key to Joshua's success was not that his army was superior. Actually, he and his band of fighters were out matched in every way, except God had promised him victory.

Joshua was following God's instruction, and the rest is a done deal. It was not about military strategy; it was about faithfulness to God.

Think About It

How many times have you wanted to take on a new task, knowing it would require every ounce of commitment you had?

Joshua had forty years to prepare. He had every example shown to him during that time, but all that didn't matter. All God wanted from him was to obey His word. It does not matter how hard we work in the gym if we are not going to obey the instructor, so why should he commit his time to us?

If we eat the right things we should not drink alcohol, smoke cigarettes, abuse ourselves and not rest properly. If we do why should we expect the instructor to stick with us?

He would probably say, "When you get serious, come back and see me."

There is a training program for everything: your work, workout, learning a new skill . . . the list is endless. Becoming a student of God is no different. The training program consists of: reading God's word daily, digesting it, binding it around your heart, developing a relationship with Him, and getting to know Him."

God's next encouragement for Joshua is to be courageous because great numbers of people are looking to him to be their leader. In being **courageous** you will be *alert, confirm, prevail, steadfast, and with speed.* Being the leader from God's perspective means that you will be on the frontline and alert to what your men are doing. You are to confirm the plan of attack with the ones you have put in charge. You will be steadfast and your plan will prevail.

Keep in mind, Joshua is eighty-five years old and he is excited to take on this daunting task. Most people I know who are eighty-five, either have severe heath issues or are figuring out ways to pass the time of their days until life ends.

Not Joshua or Caleb. No sir. They were ready to do battle. They had waited forty years for this and now God was giving His final instructions to Joshua. Within approximately seventy-two hours, he would be put to the test. I can imagine the pressure beginning to mount and hearing the rumblings in the camp as the men tried to figure out the point of attack. None would have a clue as to how God would use His chosen leader to do battle. The tactics God employs are so different than we could ever imagine.

This is no different than today in our jobs when we are given an assignment and expected to carry it out. The one in charge expects us to pay attention to the instructions, report on our progress, stick to the game plan, do not give up or give in for there is a deadline. This is the same courageousness with which God employed Joshua. Even though you have a daunting task, the commander of all commanders has said, *"I will be by your side. I will not let you falter. Always obey my laws."*

The beauty of what Joshua discovered when he sent out two men to spy happened upon their return, as the people's hearts were melting with fear. They knew the Lord their God of the heaven and the earth was with them.

If one opponent is planning a strategy of defense and one of offense, one is planning to win, and one is planning NOT to lose. It is not about talent or size, but it does have to do with the leader, the optimist, and the team planning to win and prevail. The success is in the planning.

Years ago, I recall sitting in the football stadium of WVU on a beautiful fall day and watched Penn State and WVU grind it out. I saw a master out smart his opponent with a really simple mind game that worked to perfection. Joe Paterno was a legend in the major college arena and his reputation was far reaching.

That Saturday was no different. WVU was the underdog, but they had the home field advantage. You can say, they were holding their own. WVU was rated in pre-season to finish well and this Saturday showed promise of pulling an upset over the highly favored Nineney Lions.

WVU was ahead and it was late in the game. The fans were into the game, creating high momentum, and then it happened. A fumble. And then, Penn State recovers. The clock was in WVU's favor, but the wind had been taken out of their sails, their shoulders slumped, heads dropped, and you could read their body language. With time running out, coach Paterno called time out recognizing the moral of WVU's defense and told his team they were going to play, not to lose. Perhaps, you know the rest of the story. WVU went on to have a winning season and was invited to play in a bowl game, but Penn State was not added to their win column.

The same principles that God applied to Joshua can be applied to us as well. By following God's instruction, Joshua will inherit the land, and we will as well.

To **inherit** is *to distribute, cause, divide, and to have.* God is very clear in His instruction to Joshua in telling him that will lead these people to inherit the land. Joshua knew his duty at hand was to do battle with the various tribes and kingdoms that God would assign to him.

Think About It

Wouldn't it be awesome to start your day having a conversation with God? Sitting at the breakfast table, planning your next move, and listening to Him telling you how it will unfold as He again insures you He has your back. What would you say to Him?

We may not have the privilege of the same conversation with God as Joshua did. Still, He reminds us that we can come to Him anytime. We don't need an appointment. He will listen and respond. We just have to be ready to receive his instruction.

Joshua knew to be prepared to distribute the spoils of victory for those who were to inherit this land. The victories that were to come in the days that lay ahead caused a divide, possessions were taken from those who currently occupied the land and given to those God had promised.

You may be reading these words as a non-Christian and say that it is not fair for these people did nothing wrong and have worked hard, so why was God doing this? When Moses had started this journey many years earlier he knew those who had been mistreated would be repaid.

Now Joshua is preparing to conquer the land that was promised to his people and divide the spoils of someone else's labor.

"Do not take revenge, my dear friends, but leave room for God's wrath, for it is written: It is mine to avenge; I will repay, says the Lord" Romans 12:19 (NIV).

As God continues to prepare Joshua for battle, he reminds him again to obey the **law**, the statute, the Pentateuch, fig, tree, fruit . . . these words all ring with familiarity.

Let us go forward in time and look at our Congress and the laws they have created over time. These laws are so numerous that large law firms employ law students who have just graduated to spend countless hours in the congressional libraries researching these laws in preparation to do battle in the courtrooms.

They're looking for loopholes and ambiguous wording that can indicate 'duel' meaning or create reasonable doubt. Guess what? When one of those lawyers wins a case and sets a precedent, a new law is created and put on the books. It becomes a never-ending cycle.

All of this congressional and political hoopla started with God's Ten Commandments. Many try and argue today that this is not the case, but if Thomas Jefferson, Benjamin Franklin, John Hancock or any of those who signed that famous document were here today they would set us all straight.

God's foundational principles are everywhere. They are represented by laws in business plans and in the smallest of settings to the largest of corporations. We as a people have the nerve to say, "Remove God from our business, our schools, our government, he does not belong there."

Let me go on the record as one who believes the biggest reason our country is in this mess it is today is because we have removed the one thing that kept us together. We now see the effects of trying to operate the ship without its captain.

CHAPTER 23
THE PENTATEUCH

The law as God puts it, it's a must for Joshua to adhere to. These were written words a statute and a set of guidelines were to be followed. They were no different than a set of instructions that come with a new toy or a piece of furniture that requires assembly. The paper gives instructions for a reason. They don't want you to spend needless time putting it together only to discover you left a piece out and have to take it apart and do it all over.

The same exact thing is being told to Joshua and to us: "Please follow my instructions and get it right the first time. The laws that Moses wrote down are for a reason use them as your road map for life."

It amazes me that for a people who are so dependent upon others how quickly we want to become independent once someone starts giving us orders. That is one of those oxymoron things, I guess.

Not only does the law refer to **statute** it was also referred to as the Pentateuch. The Pentateuch was the five books that Moses wrote at God's direction on the Mountain where he spent forty days. Those five books became the Arc of the Covenant—the most treasured possession that Moses had.

The law is next related to the **fig**. The fig is a fruit that was plentiful and part of the diet for the lowliest of man to gracing the table of kings. This fruit was thought to be holy, and even though plentiful, it was not to be wasted.

Everything that God designed has a purpose and when that purpose is not being fulfilled one of two things will occur: it is corrected or destroyed. You say that is ridiculous. What kind of a God would do that to his people? We are told He is a caring God.

As we have covered to this point and will do so throughout the remainder of the book, I will demonstrate God's love through mercy and rebuke. In

Deuteronomy 8:2 (NIV), God is explicit in telling His people, "Remember how he Lord your God led you all the way in the wilderness these forty years, to humble and test you in order to know what was in your heart, whether or not you would keep his commands."

Remember, it is only an eleven-day trip on foot. God brings up Moses on the mountain for a reason—to set the rules in place. His laws would govern his people because they were an unruly people who needed guidelines. Those five books of the law—The Pentateuch—later became the Arc of The Covenant.

When the laws are obeyed, they produce the fruit of prosperity. The evidence is a green and lush tree that provides multiple benefits. However, if we fail to obey the laws, the tree is fruitless. Even when the tree is full, and its leaves are green, providing shade and producing oxygen that helps clean the air, it's main function is to produce fruit. The farmer sees that tree as doing more harm than good. Because it takes nutrients from the soil that can be used for productive trees, it will be taken down. This seems cruel to us because we want our cake and eat it too. We want the best of both. We want the good life, but we want to take the short cut to get it. We are even willing to compromise, to cheat, even step on others—but when God steps in and disciplines we think how cruel He is and is not a loving God.

God is just like the wise farmer who recognizes the tree that is not productive and needs to be replaced. Not a lesson we like to hear, but one that needs to be said. One of the lessons I have found that is difficult to comprehend is how open-minded God is. How quickly He drops his thoughts of what you or I did that upset him and continues to love us without skipping a beat. What an awesome God He is!

As we have been reminded so often he does not let the wrong we do go unnoticed or unpunished; but He does not let it loom over us as a constant reminder either. Our own consciousness will take care of the guilt feeling. We carry the guilt way too long afterwards and God has even told us, *"To come and lay that burden at His feet and He will carry it."*

The reason I bring this to your attention is in verse 7 God is telling Joshua that Moses his servant gave him these laws. God referred to Moses as his servant—his most loyal of servants. Let's explore what God meant when he used the word servant.

To be a **servant** meant *you were in bondage, it meant work, and you would labor.* To me all this sounds like hard work and this automatically creates a barrier in the relationship between the worker and the Master—thus we have a problem.

People, myself included, are the ones responsible for this barrier. We draw this distinction, make ourselves inferior and elevate the Master (boss) to be untouchable and the line is permitted to widen.

But as we read the Bible, there are countless examples of where Jesus came alongside the common man and sat down with, ate with, healed and spent the night in his home to close that gap. He realized there would be different social, economic, and personal development levels, but that didn't mean we could not come together as equals in the eyes of God.

Being a servant from God's point of view simply meant you had a job to do. The bondage you were in was a good thing and your employer was one who wanted to continually praise your efforts. The assignments you would be given were very rewarding and a hard day's work meant a good night's sleep and your labor would not go unnoticed.

To say that God was always going to be there and encourage you with a pat on the back would be incorrect. He will give you the ability to see the good that you are doing and it will bring a smile to your face and peace in your heart.

When you get to that place in your walk with God, let's say you have arrived. There will be days that you will have that feeling and days everything you touch, do, or say will turn to rubbish. Those days you will feel like a failure and you will go crawling to God asking, "What is wrong? Why can't I get it right?"

Well, that too is part of this labor process called learning. Its knowing how to stay humble. Amidst this brokenness, frustration, anger and feeling alone God reminds us He is always there—just a prayer away. God has this twisted sense of humor—or so we think. In our imagination, we see Him sitting at this huge table watching us go through our daily battles with self and we imagine Him maybe saying something like this, "I told him not to do that and now he is going to go around the rest of the day beating himself up or making more mistakes because he won't come to me for help. How far do you suppose he will go before he finally gets it?" Of course, this is all in our mind since we don't really know what God is really thinking.

Once we understand how much more one can receive from being a person of servitude, it becomes a labor of love. This is the desire of God's heart for each of us. Isaiah 55:11 (NIV) says, *"So is my word that goes out from my mouth: It will not return to me empty, but will accomplish what I desire and achieve the purpose for which I sent it."*

It is amazing how much more we could accomplish if we would just grasp this one simple concept. I am reading the book *Multiple Blessings* and I am at the point where the protagonist by the name of Kate is starting to have some depression issues and her thoughts are very inward. She realizes what is occurring, but the desire to let it take control of her life is still there. When life begins to challenge us, and we are thrown many curve balls, one after the other, it is very easy to become consumed with self, and that's when the 'woe is me pity party' begins.

Joshua's best friend's name is Caleb, and he too is eighty-five-years old. In chapter fourteen Caleb has just been told what land he will be given. Actually, given is not a good word. Caleb will have to go to war to get the land. Not only will he go to war, but his worthy opponent will be the Anakites.

Their cities are large and fortified and if that is not enough the battle will take place in the hill country. You may be saying who could go to battle at eighty-five? Here is what Caleb had to say in Joshua 14:11-12 (NIV): *"I am still as strong today as the day Moses sent me out, I'm just as vigorous to go out to battle now as I was then. Now give me this hill country that the Lord promised me that day. You yourself heard then that the Anakites were there and their cities were large and fortified, but, the Lord helping me, I will drive them out just as he said."*

Caleb was eighty-five when he undertook this assignment. That does not sound like an attitude of self-pity, woe is me, does it? He was assigned to do a job; his life had a purpose and age was not in the equation.

It says the land had rest after the war. Does that mean God kept His promise to Caleb and let him live out his life in peace? It sounds that way to me. Do you think these leaders felt their lives were in bondage in a bad way? As we read about the rest of Joshua's life up to his death there was only one time you read of him complaining and that was due to his own mistake.

When he fell on his knees God was quick to rebuke, then provide resolution, and bam! The problem was solved and life went on. God is not one to linger over yesterday nor is He one to dwell on a problem. He immediately goes about to discover a solution and implements it and moves on. Choices have consequences. It's how we deal with them that make the difference.

Think About It

Why would you turn away from a blessing or a blessed life?

_____

_____

God told Joshua not to **turn** from it, to the right or the left. To turn meant to decline, leave undone or rebel. Joshua had forty years of good training and watching the people that Moses was leading as they acted like a weather vane. A weather vane reacts to the wind. It turns to the direction the wind is blowing and if the wind shifts its direction, so does the vane. This was how the people were reacting and their actions spoke much louder than their words.

Each day brought a different set of complaints. One day they were for God and the next day they were against Him. Since God was always on a mission and everything He did was designed with a purpose, the Israelites were constantly complaining and driving Moses up the wall.

The Israelites wanted to take shortcuts. They questioned everything Moses was doing. They rebelled and didn't follow through on their commitment, leaving things undone.

None of these were characteristics God honored. Quite a contrast to Jesus, who left His position next to the Father to come down to earth. He said, "I came to serve, not to be served," and He stuck by his words.

Many people want to be a Christian of convenience—when it fits their schedule. That could be on a Sunday or when things are going their way. When I was first learning to be a carpenter, I knew nothing about construction, building material, remodeling, or repair. I was willing to jump in and learn as I went. Some lessons were funny, some were expensive, and some were hard.

Our first house was only fifteen thousand dollars and between the realtor and my father-in-law we were able to purchase it. Coming from a small apartment, the house seemed huge. It was a two story, three bedrooms, one bath, and a full basement with a big fenced back yard.

We only had the one son at the time, Christopher, and his German Sheppard. They loved the back yard. We had big plans for the house, but very little money and even less knowledge on how to repair, fix or replace any of the projects we wanted to do.

Our first project was to take a little room over the porch and turn it into a playroom for our son. The room was small and the project seemed simple enough, or so I thought. Talk about starting out on a shoestring budget! But when you are young and full of life, nothing is impossible. The lessons I learned in fixing that little room has since been told hundreds of times and still brings laughter and good memories of long ago.

I was made fun of for all the effort I put into fixing up our son's first playroom. Money was tight so the materials I used were not expensive, but the finished result looked good. My work for a beginner stood out, not because I was a good carpenter, but because I didn't know they made something called a corner molding.

Designed to cover mistakes, I had no idea that such a thing existed. You can imagine the hours I spent holding cheap paneling and my dad's hand-me-down antique planner making those corners fit perfectly.

One day, a neighbor came by to inspect my handy work and said, "Why didn't you just use corner molding?" I said, "What's that?" After his laughter subsided, he explained. Needless to say, I felt a little foolish. The neighbor did comment on how good the work was but ended by saying I'd spent way too much time on such a small project when I didn't need to be so meticulous.

As our family grew and our needs changed, we sold that home and moved on to other projects—larger and newer homes and my mastery of carpentry became much better. I became a better carpenter because I did not give up. I asked questions, read books, bought tools and practiced a lot, learning how to use them.

Being a Christian is no different. You ask questions, seek counsel, read God's book and get other tools so you can better understand His word. That's how you grow.

Just as God told Joshua not to turn, which was in a sense rebelling, or leave an assignment undone, He is telling us the same. This journey called 'being a Christian' is not an on again, off again project. It is something we must maintain, be true to our cause and steady the course. It is called being diligent.

CHAPTER 24
NOBODY IS PERFECT BUT GOD

As my knowledge grew and I moved on to do bigger projects, and perfection became less important, I focused more on what I could use to cover my mistakes, whenever I made one.

Isn't that how most of us approach life? Let's just do what is needed to get the job done and if there is a problem let the next person take care of it. Or you hear someone in the background mumble, "This guy is Mr. Perfectionist. He needs to lighten up!"

Well, God is the ultimate perfectionist. He pays real close attention to details. So why should we be any less? In this fast-paced world, we have a tendency to frown at the person who takes what we consider to be too long to get something done. We poke fun at them and call them names when in fact they take pride in what they do. To them, it is a labor of love, but we see them as obsessive.

Think About It

What do you think has happened to perfection? And, why should we strive to be perfect?

While God is the only perfect One, doing things well is a high standard He expects us to follow. The truth is, the world has run amuck and the evidence is everywhere. We have found things and ways to cover up the miss cut, the column of numbers that don't add up, the promise not kept, the alibi we invent, the reason we won't be home till late—all to our own justification.

These were the very things God was warning Joshua not to do. When God spoke, every word had meaning and carried impact and were expected to be followed. Yet, as we read His words, we immediately begin to pick and choose what we want to digest and what we will discard.

Thus, the term 'perfectionist' comes on the scene and it immediately takes on a negative connotation or a hint of difference. God knew what He was up against. This is why He spoke to Joshua. He kept reassuring him not to turn to right or the left for He wanted his complete attention. To turn to the **right** meant stronger or south. The last thing Joshua needed was a head trip an attitude that he knew better than his instructor.

I have always had a desire to help others through teaching and have had the privilege of doing so on many occasions. Since my background is real estate, I wrote a curriculum and it was approved for the State of Florida Board of Realtors. It was a seven-hour continuing education course. I was teaching a class of about thirty people who were renewing their license. About halfway through one of my classes, I noticed a young lady who seemed to be very disturbed and annoyed. I wanted to speak to her after class, but as usual there was always someone or a few people who took up my time with questions. I never had the chance to see if I could help this particular person. At the end of the course, I asked for comments to be written as to how I could improve the class.

This is where I discovered what bothered this particular person. She was annoyed with me because I had a little bit of an accent and thought my country demeanor was beneath her. She proceeded to tell me how I was not qualified to instruct her. She was so preoccupied with my style of communicating that she got very little from the class and her comments were so negative that it caused me to re-evaluate my method of delivery. Had I not received several good responses from the questionnaire, I would have considered not continuing teaching the course.

This is why God was so adamant with Joshua in reminding him to stay in His Word, be strong, and not to turn from His teaching. Joshua, having had plenty of time as an understudy of Moses,' witnessed all the leaders who thought they had a better plan. In previous leaders' lives that Joshua knew about, he knew God had to present a stark reality. It was God who set them on the path to greatness.

We need to understand that God is the leader and we are the follower. God also told Joshua not to turn to the **left.** That meant *wrapping up, dark, idol, image,* all which carries a meaning to worshiping someone other than God. This is another lesson Joshua learned while mentoring under Moses. God is a forgiving god and has ways of getting our attention when we choose not to obey. If we get wrapped up into thinking that it is all about us, everything else becomes miscued. Then our eyes are so inward that all is dark and we become an idol to ourselves. God knows man's faults and that is why He is so patient with us. But, there are limitations.

God next mentions to Joshua that he will be **successful**, which means *intelligent, instruct, prosper, prudent, and wise.* Four of the five words indicates success, which has to do with being intelligent. The other word deals with prosperity.

But when you research prosper you find it leads you back to *intelligent, teach, expert, guide wittingly.* So everything tells Joshua he will be successful and God is preparing him for the next generation.

Success is not about the toys, the houses, the cars, the perks, the fancy clothes—it's about the relationship. God had already promised them a land. They did not cultivate the land, build the house, or own livestock. Success was already theirs; they just had to demonstrate the faith.

The most important reminder of all was what the verse would tell Joshua next. *"Do not let this book of the law depart from your **mouth**."* Mouth meant *blowing, edge, two-edged, scatter into four corners.* I am sure you have heard the term, "I blew him off." In other words, "I knew better than my instructor."

When you look at the words related to mouth, *two-edged scatter into four corners* they may seem harsh, but this was a warning from God. Joshua understood that it was wise to continually go to the Book of the Law for it will give courage, strength, and it was there God would be found. Joshua knew that by reading God's words in the Book of the Law it would also provide him guidance and victory, which is the *two-edged sword.*

"Keep this Book of the Law always on your lips; meditate on it day and night, so that you may be careful to do everything written in it. Then you will be prosperous and successful" Joshua 1:8 (NIV).

The only way to prepare for battle is to not let the book of the law depart from your mouth. You must **meditate** on it, God tells Joshua. To meditate is to ponder the word, study it, and talk about it. And by doing these things God will be on your mind.

When we ponder something, we spend time on it and give it attention. Once you internalize what you have read, you can see how they apply to you and affect you in the now. God is telling Joshua, and us, to think about what we read and don't just gloss over the words for they have a deeper meaning.

The impact that is evidenced by others who see the change in you, as you witness to them, will only grow stronger as they see your life change and the peace you possess. This inner strength is what you are to talk about and share with others. *"Go unto all the world and share the good news."*

Not only does God tell Joshua to mediate on His Word, but to do it **day** and night. Day means *daily, time, sunrise to sunset, and perpetually.* First, it is clear what God's instruction mean.

Think About It

Some may speculate this is a little bit obsessive. What do you think? You probably have a job, family and lots of responsibilities. You give God time on Sunday, and even perhaps on Wednesday nights. How are you supposed to fit it all in?

_____

_____

The truth is, if we want a sense of order in our lives and calm in the midst of the storm, then He is our answer. He can provide calm, direction, and most of all a sense of peace. He told Joshua to 'meditate.' He meant daily, and to perpetually have Him on his mind all the time. *"I will guard you, protect you, and provide a way for you,"* God told Joshua.

When darkness appears, it presents a whole new set of problems and God reminds Joshua to meditate at **night** on His Word as well. The night brings adversity with twist and turns. Evil lurks in the night, man's thoughts turn to subversive ideas seeking and doing wrong: cheating, lying, stealing . . .

In Proverbs 4:23 (NIV), we read: *"Above all else, guard your heart, for everything you do flows from it."* Joshua understands he has two purposes while here on earth. First, to obey God, and second was to set that example for his household. His past experiences had given him the ability to understand that he would encounter struggles along the way. These are called lessons. Joshua was told that as long as he placed God first in his life, He would always provide the answers and the understanding to cope with the answer.

Joshua also knew he needed a mentor and what better mentor to have than the author and creator of the universe? There is much to be said for a long-term apprenticeship. By being exposed to the good and the bad we have many chances to observe. This supplies us with the innate ability to adjust to most any circumstance because of our training.

But here is the beauty of where all this is leading. This is why faith plays such an important role in a Christian's life. God asks Joshua to follow His lead, read His rule book and He would do the work. He just needed to be present. Joshua was a good leader because he was a good follower.

Think About It

Now, how can you know an outcome just by reading a book and believing it will come true?

The difference in reading a book written by a successful person who says, "If you do 1-2-3, you will get 4," and following God's Word is the expectation. The expectation is not in the outcome, but in God. Faith was the lifeline between God and Joshua. He knew that being a good leader first started by being a good follower.

If you had the privilege of speaking to Joshua and ask what his job description was it would not be a seven-page document. It would simply consist of the following: Read the book of the law, meditate on it day and night, be the leader of your house, show your family and followers God is first, and the fruit you bare will be all the evidence you need to successfully witness to others.

The night can be dangerous. Which is why Jesus says in John 10:10 (NIV): *"The thief comes only to steal and kill and destroy, I have come that they may have life, and have it to the full."*

God goes on to remind Joshua to meditate on the **written** word. Moses had written God's word on the stone tablets that became the Ark of the Covenant. These were the words.

God wanted Joshua to study and mediate on. This was not someone's interpretation or what someone had read and then put in their own words. This statement I am sure will bring to your mind the question of exactly what has occurred with the Bible and this is what you are doing with this book.

My only defense is this: when I quote something from the Bible, whether in part or in whole, I am quoting Scripture. Secondly, if I use an example of a story, it is something relatable to the Scriptures; the names may have been changed, but the rest is fact.

Scholars will argue over a word and its intended meaning. The Jews say it is out of context because it carried a different meaning—depending on the circumstance. That brings us back to square one and what God is telling Joshua, *"Meditate on my word day and night, don't listen to man, listen to me, seek me, ask me, knock on my door and I will provide the answer."*

CHAPTER 25
THE FIG TREE

God picked Joshua and liked the fact he was a man who took a stand and was committed to Him. Wouldn't it be great to be chosen by God? What a compliment! To know God is always by your side would be quite a confidence booster wouldn't it? Well, there is one thing we need to understand. God IS by our side and has hand-picked each of us; we just have to take a stand like Joshua did and profess that God is our choice to follow.

God told Joshua that he would be **prosperous.** "Keep this Book of the Law on your lips; meditate on it day and night, so that you may be careful to do everything written in it. Then you will be successful wherever you go." Joshua 1:8 (NIV).

Joshua on the other hand, has just tuned eighty-five and God has given him a promotion, a new title, and a great responsibility. He is about to lead the Israelites into the Promise Land.

There were many battles. For the next seven years, Joshua led his men, taking over territories and placing tribes in the land. At age eighty-five, most would not be up to the task, but Joshua's and his closet friend, Caleb, were not only up to the task but anxiously looking forward to it. The agreement between God and Joshua culminates on this word: prosperous.

"Do what I command and these are the results you will receive. I will make you prosperous, I will push you forward, you will go over mightily and you will be profitable."

If that is not enough to make one go around with his chest puffed out saying, "Look at me, but not Joshua." No sir. He went about his duty while honoring God. Joshua "got it" and understood with God all things are possible.

In closing this pep talk with Joshua, God said: "Have I not **commanded** you to be strong, give, enjoin, put in order and not be terrified?"

There are two ways to take the word **command**. If you can imagine, you have been sitting at God's feet listening to Him go through these Scriptures and you may get impatient. Then, you are reminded this is a command.

To someone who is an 'A' personality like myself, there would have been a time when I would have said, "Enough already, I get it." Well, Joshua had been around and understood his mission was to get God's people into the Promised Land. God's directive to Joshua was explicit: it had a purpose with specific end results in mind.

God never gives an order or command without a reward—yes, I said reward. The reward is not always what we would like to have or want but it is always what we need, in the amount we need it.

God told Joshua what he expected: to be submissive, follow His command and He would give him a long and prosperous life. Joshua understood his role and did what was asked of him.

If you were given the privilege of interviewing Joshua after he had hung up his battle gear, it may go something like this. As you ask your first question, He would stand up and say, "Come walk with me." Now, keep in mind you are talking to a 110-year-old man. His walk is crisp and you are in awe to be in his presence. As you walk out on his porch you can see valleys, hills, streams, wooded land and cleared fields.

In the distance you can hear an occasional cow moo nearby, a sheep baa and dogs barking while children play. As you smell the fresh air and feel the cool breeze, Joshua, with the voice of a twenty-year-old and arms out stretched says, "He let me manage all this for Him. So, *as for me and my house, we will serve the Lord.*"

As a reporter you are taught to go after the controversy and create a story-line so I am sure you would ask, "But what about all the ups and downs that have occurred? What about your time under Moses, the battles you have endured and those who betrayed you?" He would just look around, smile and point to all. God has graced him with and repeat, *"As for me and my house we will serve the Lord."*

As my good friend Gordon would say, "If you don't get it, I don't think your elevator goes all the way to the top."

Joshua's life was fulfilled. He had exactly what God had promised and to a measure greater than he expected. The one quality that could be the most out-standing for Joshua was, "Leading is knowing whom to follow."

As we leave Joshua, knowing of the success he had and coming to the conclusion that God was always by his side, we now meet up with a prophet who has a stamina that is probably only matched by Job's. This prophet is Habakkuk and there are those who say his commitment level is off the chart.

The name Habakkuk means 'to embrace' and as we study the selected verses you will be able to see why the meaning behind his name is appropriate. Habakkuk was bold in his attempt to have a clear understanding of such things as injustice and why evil people prosper. He was quick to challenge God as to why so much wrong was allowed to go unpunished. The setting for Habakkuk was 607 B.C. in the Kingdom of Judah.

Like Job, Habakkuk took his questions directly to God, sometimes with clinched fists and gritted teeth not understanding why God was allowing some things to occur. But in the end, we see God not only comes through, but Habakkuk makes a statement that many consider to be beyond absurd.

Starting in chapter 3:17-19 (NIV), Habakkuk, because of his love for God, makes his claim as to what he is willing to go through and still be joyful. He begins by stating, *"Though the fig tree does not bud and there are no grapes on the vines, though the olive crop fails and the fields produce no food though there are no sheep in the pen and no cattle in the stalls, yet I will rejoice in the Lord, I will be joyful in God my Savior. The Sovereign Lord is my strength; he makes my feet like the feet of a deer, he enables me to tread on the heights."*

Tree is our keyword. As we have studied, it represents *carpenter, gallows, fasten, and close.* Jesus' earthly father Joseph was a carpenter and Jesus himself spent his early days as a carpenter. To be a carpenter was a high calling and it was a craft that required you to be highly skilled.

The fig tree was a source of life because of its fruit. It was also a symbol of what was to come. The tree provided many different aspects of life. By providing fruit, which is a form of life—to one day being chopped down and used as firewood, represents the beginning to the end, a complete cycle of life. The tree could be known as the 'Alpha and the Omega,' since it represents much of the same.

We then see the word **fasten**, as the limb is fastened to the trunk. We need to have our life support attached to God or we too will perish. Fasten also says 'to adhere' 'to join together' and 'come close to.' These are words that lend to the thought of two becoming like one. This is how close our relationship with God and our family needs to be.

The final word related to tree is 'close,' meaning, *to come to the end.*

Think About It

How do you think the final chapter of your life will end?

_____

_____

There will be a time when God closes the final chapter on our lives. We have no way of knowing when how and when it will end. We start each day thinking and planning for years to come, not knowing if we will return home at day's end. The beauty of our life with God is that He will let us write the final chapter.

These three verses are full of wisdom as we discover how God works through Habakkuk, and his commitment on how we should live. As stated, at the beginning Habakkuk makes a very strong commitment. Most would call it absurd, but it is a stark reminder of where our life is headed and to which drummer we march.

Though the fig tree does not bud and there are no grapes on the vines, Habakkuk is reminding us the tree or vine will not always produce, so we need to be able to go to the source and see why. The word **'no' means,** *not, nought, of a truth, for want, or without.* It carries a double meaning and requires some research that gives us the ability to understand. As we see 'no' associated with *for want, not, a truth without,* I see a light come on that says, "With God at the helm, all of our needs are met."

To start with, we see there are no buds on the tree or grapes on the vine, and by using the word 'no,' which is associated with the word 'nought,' Habakkuk was making his point, even more dramatic to say, "there was zero evidence of life on the vine."

There are days when we face doubt because at each turn the problems just seem to keep mounting, with no way out. A friend may say, "It will be ok. Just ask God for guidance and He will provide a way." You are thinking to yourself, "There is not a bit of truth in what you are saying." My life is in such a shambles. God has abandoned me and I am on the outside without a way of getting to the inside.

Getting the true meaning of the word 'no' tells us there is no other way. Many have tried, but none have succeeded. I can hear the whistle blow, the referee saying, "Foul, yellow flags coming out of pockets etc."

All the naysayers who know of people who succeeded and had a good life, will say their lives ended ok. First of all, we make those statements not always knowing all the facts. The real truth is, people build walls that are often impenetrable. We don't know. There are those who say, "I am part of the family. I know what went on and it was all good." You may be 100 percent correct. I am not here to rain on anyone's parade, but statistics bare out my statement. This is what the devil (the enemy) wants us to think. He wants us to be weak and vulnerable—to be needy and play right into his hand. Well, Habakkuk had a different mindset.

We next explore the word **vine** and throughout His Scriptures, God is referred to as "the vine, and we are the branch. Without the vine, the branch will not survive, but more importantly, the vine is there to bend and to produce the grape.

Have you ever had the opportunity to visit a vineyard and notice how the vine grows, how it twists and turns and how the pods of grapes hang? The strength of the vine supports them. This is the exact picture of how God is in our life. He maneuvers through our lives and bends to accommodate us. His strength allows us to hold on when we think there is nothing left. He manages to see us through and sometimes we forget to say, "Thanks God, for being there."

He produces the fruit in our life that is necessary for us to survive, but we are so accustomed to being spoiled that is not about having what we need. We are so self-indulged that we think we must have the extras just to survive.

God tells us in Matthew 6:28-30 (NIV): *"And why do you worry about clothes? See how the flowers of the field grow. They do not labor or spin. Yet I tell you that not even Solomon in all his splendor was dressed like one of these. If that is how God clothes the grass of the field, which is here today and tomorrow is thrown into the fire, will he not much more clothe you—you of little faith?"*

In a nation such as ours where we are so spoiled thinking we need all this stuff just to survive, it may for some be difficult to grasp such a simple concept and not really understand how to appreciate what God considers the finer things of life.

Our thoughts of what is considered the finer things is so misconstrued from TV adds, billboards flashing and the radio blaring. We have very little concept of real beauty or peace and quiet.

Habakkuk next mentions though the olive crop fails, the olive was a prominent part of the Roman heritage. The branch was engraved on government buildings and on the heads of statutes as a symbol.

The **olive** meant *illuminating oil, prominent, cheerfulness and brightness.* The olive was a crop that had many uses. The oil was used for lighting lamps and also used for anointing. The olive was used as a food for consumption. It graced the tables of kings and the common man. The olive was also considered a form of wealth. The olive tree is considered to be one of the oldest types of trees known and when it blooms the fragrance for the tiny flower has a wonderful aroma.

Even though the olive tree did not start in Rome, it gets more recognition as being from there. The olive garden at The Mount of Olives is said to have trees over 2000 years old. Interesting coincidence wouldn't you say?

Though the olive crop **fails,** *becomes untrue, disappointment, lying, deal falsely*— these things need not happen with God in our corner. When you fail at something you become a disappointment to those you are dealing with and yourself as well.

Here is a very good example. I was staying with a very good friend and he liked to keep his house cool—especially in the warm months. On this particular day, it was somewhat overcast and the wind was blowing so I decided to turn off the A.C. unit, thinking I could be saving him some money. With the windows open and a couple of ceiling fans running the house was cool and comfortable.

When he gets in from work, he was not happy to see the windows open because in his thinking it was going to take more energy to cool the house down than what I was trying to save. My plan of what I thought was helpful, but actually ended up backfiring on me and made the evening strained and uncomfortable. I, in turn, was beating myself up for doing something I should not have done in the first place.

To '**fail**' also means *to become untrue.* How does that come about? If we are on an assignment, a certain task that is part of a larger project and we fail to keep up our part, our promise has become untrue.

To 'fail' is also a form of lying. If you have made a promise to someone and failed to keep that promise, you have lied to that person. Lying builds walls of distrust and destroys relationships that take a lot of work to rebuild. Sometimes they never get rebuilt and what is so simple to repair never happens and enemies are formed.

When a person is caught in a lie, the accuser and the accused both begin to rationalize the extent of the lie. The accused may feel it is only a little lie. The accuser on the other hand may have been deeply offended and see it as a major infraction of their relationship.

God sees a lie as an untruth. He does not break them down into categories. People have come to blows when one calls the other a liar. There have been murders over being called a liar. Family members never speak again because of that word. We are told to speak the truth in love. How is it such a small word carries such an impact on our lives? If we know the danger this word carries, why do we tread where it can cause such misery.

When we fail, we can be dealt with falsely not giving us the chance to correct our wrong. If this occurs, our relationship can suffer enormous damage, even to the point of being irreparable. These are all negative things that can happen when we fail to do our part or keep our promise. But Habakkuk has a different outlook as you will see.

He says even if the **fields** produce no food, cultivated, spread out, country, and soil, these are all related to God's Word.

CHAPTER 26

PREPARING THE GROUND
TO PLANT A GARDEN

When I was a little guy, I looked forward to Saturday. As he was getting ready to plant a garden, my father hired a man to bring his tractor and plow the ground. The tractor came through the yard, maneuvering past the trees and my mother's flowers up the hill to the garden area. I loved the smell of the fresh plowed soil. I can still smell it like it was yesterday.

The first step to preparing the garden for the planting season was cultivating the soil. God tells us that just as He cultivates and fills us with His Word, we are to cultivate His people and prepare them for the teaching of His word.

The first time the man with the tractor came to our field, all he did was plow the ground. The next time he came, he brought a different tool called 'a disc,' which he used to cut up the big clumps of soil to make it manageable to work.

This is what we are to do with the Word of God: break it down, make His word manageable and understandable and then spread it out and take it to every nation.

Jesus' Great Commission is found in Matthew 28:19-20, which says, *"Therefore go and make disciples of all nations, baptizing them in the name of the Father and of the Son and of the Holy Spirit, and teaching them to obey everything I have commanded you. And surely I am with you always, to the very end of the age."* In essence, we are the soil and we are the basis for God's Word to grow and spread. If we are not growing, we can't help others grow for we are the source to spread His message.

Habakkuk is not through, as he says, even though there are no cattle in the **stalls,** which can mean *resting, slack, slothful and weak*—I will **rejoice.** Does this guy have a positive attitude and trust in God or is he one of the fast-talking motivational speakers? The word 'stalls' tells us it could be a place of resting or a place where we become slack, slothful, and this will cause us to be weak.

Think About It

Have you ever found yourself in a position of rest because you are doing so well that the rest turns to being a little slack?

_____

_____

You begin to coast, your performance starts to slip, you find yourself in this funk, you have lost your rhythm, business is off, and you don't know why. The same could happen to the individual who is an avid jogger. Work happens, routines get changed, they get a little out of shape, become slack in their training and hurt themselves.

I was having a conversation with my good friend, Gordon. He is a police officer and was telling me of an incident while on duty. He was summoned along with another officer to a break-in that was in progress. The intruder had broken out a window then found a sheet of plywood to cover the window and somehow had wedged the plywood in the window while he was still in the house. Gordon not only is a veteran officer but an ex-marine sergeant and karate expert. He lifted his leg and wham! The plywood was gone, but in bringing his leg back he hit his anklebone on the window seal and bruised it severely.

As he was explaining the proper way to kick and regain your stance, because he was not in shape, when he brought his leg back instead of being parallel, he let it drop and thus the anklebone took a severe blow.

We think, "Man, I still have the moves but forgot we have not kept up the conditioning so we really can't compete." Not only should we keep our bodies in shape, but we need "to stay in shape, read God's words daily, seek Him with all our heart and we will always be in condition and up to the task.

Now that Habakkuk has given us a gentle reminder to stay in condition mentally, as well as physically, he tells us to rejoice.

Had I used a term like 'sternly' instead of 'gently,' some of the readers would reject or rebel at reading that sentence. It's funny how the mind works and what it immediately accepts or rejects.

For my morning Bible time, I was reading Deuteronomy. It starts out by Moses telling the people of Israel how blessed they will be when they enter the Promised Land if they fully obey the Lord. *"There, in the presence of the Lord your*

God, you and your families shall eat and shall rejoice in everything you have put your hand to, because the Lord your God has blessed you" Deuteronomy 12:7 (NIV).

Just a few verses before on Deuteronomy 11:28 (NIV), it says: "The curse if you disobey the commands of the Lord your God and turn form the way that I command you today by following other gods, which you have not known."

These are two contrasting verses. As I read these chapters for the first time, it confused me and frankly I got upset. *What is going on? Am I blessed or am I cursed?* I thought. It took me a while to get my head around all that was being said. We are not told it will be easy, but we need to persevere. But then I think, this is the exact attitude that got the Israelites in trouble with the Lord and turned an eleven-day journey into forty years of lessons.

God's word is full of promises as we have seen, but He also never allows us to lose touch with reality. So many preachers, teachers, and people just like you and I only want to fluff the good parts and as we can see, God deals in all aspects of our lives. The beauty is He also teaches us how to handle it, just as Habakkuk is telling us.

Rejoice is *to triumph, exult, and jump for joy.* All of which are ways we are to be elated, overcome, and give praise to our Heavenly Father. There is a place and time for the power of positive thinking, but it needs to be in "total" alignment with the Word of God.

In the middle of all of that has not taken place, Habakkuk still finds it in his heart to give the Lord praise. He chooses to take the high road and stand for the Lord in the midst of all that is happening.

He knows his Sovereign Lord will triumph and He will be a recipient of the Lord's grace and mercy. The words that rejoice reflects are pretty self-explanatory. We will overcome, we will win in the end, God will exalt us, and all who choose to follow him will jump for joy and sing praise to His name. Amen.

Just writing these words has lifted my spirit. My heart is light and it is exciting to think of what God has in store for those who choose to follow him. It is an adventure that is filled with twist and turns. Habakkuk says it will be **joyful,** but there may be fear, cringing, and spin round.

Just when we think we have it all together, we are thrown another curve ball. As we read the Bible we began to see "Joy and fun are a wonderful part of our lives, but we should never become so enamored that we lose sight of our focus."

You can easily be taken advantage of when you become too caught up in the moment. We need to have a healthy fear and don't get caught in a situation where you are spun around and lose sight of your purpose. Habakkuk next reveals his secret. The Sovereign Lord is his **strength,** an army of men, wealth, worthy, and riches all this belongs to the one who relies upon the Lord for their strength.

Habakkuk knew how God worked and he questioned Him but knew where his strength lay. Habakkuk tells us one last thing: God will make His feet like the **feet** of a deer and enable him to go on the heights. **Feet**, meaning *able to endure, journey, and time.*

After seven years of battle, Caleb was ready to take on the occupants of the land and at eighty-five was able to endure because he knew God was on his side. Caleb also knew God was the master of His journey and it was in God's time that all would come to pass.

He had put a desire on Caleb's heart and did not worry about the finances, how it would end, or who would be the hero. He just believed and left the rest up to God. Just to make sure you don't misunderstand Caleb, he was not 'a name it or claim it' kind of guy. He knew he had to put action behind his belief. But most importantly, he believed God would always have his back.

One more comment on time. Forty years earlier, God put a desire on two young men's hearts when they were sent to spy on the Promised Land. Caleb and Joshua were the only two who came back with the desire, vision, and belief they could take the land the Lord had promised them. So when we hurriedly say a quick prayer and ten minutes later as we pat our foot impatiently with head tilted to one side looking and saying, "Ok God, what gives? I have said my prayer. Come on. I have had a hectic day. Let's get on with it, show me some results." If you have not ascertained by now, this prosperity thing is not about you or your timing. While it is true (very true) God is still in the blessing business, it is on His timetable with those blessings applicable to our needs, not our wants. He also wants to make sure we use that blessing for the betterment of His kingdom.

You may be saying, "What do you mean if it is a blessing I "need"—then it is for me, not someone else." While that is true, God expects us to represent that blessing, leaving no doubt this was not our doing. God wants us to make a concerted effort to give credit where credit is due in such a manner to those who witness the blessing are convinced it was God who orchestrated this.

While some may think having this kind of commitment to God is impossible, Habakkuk did it. He had his conversation with God and it only reassured him. Not only was his level of commitment off the chart—it was unconditional. Habakkuk never tried to strike a deal with God. He never said, "God, I will commit."

If God is not a deal maker, He will show you how to break a deal. There will be a point when you will look up and say, "Why is this happening to me?" or

"Why did you let this happen to me?" But, you don't want to hear His answer. Habakkuk was the kind of man any coach would love to have on their team for he was a Rudy Rudiger kind of a guy. A desire so strong, a heart so big, with belief off the chart and quitting was not in his vocabulary. So, if we are willing to get in the game, we first need to get suited up. Make sure we have protective gear on, be in condition, be prepared to get knocked around, don't quit and most of all, listen to the coach for he is the expert.

Did Habakkuk say all that? I think he did, and he said it with love and a whole lot of belief and determination. Habakkuk, like Moses, David, Job, Joshua, Caleb, Joseph, Paul and many others who fought the good fight stayed true to His God. They all traveled different roads to reach the same end result. Even though some never got their reward while in their earthly form, their mission was clear and their commitment was solid.

We will never understand or have all the answers, but God will always be there for us. Kabakkuk and the other men's level of commitment was very high for one reason and one reason only—they had come to the conclusion that God was worthy of whatever it took to develop and maintain their relationship with Him.

As they demonstrated, not everyone is willing to walk the road less traveled and many along the way fall to the temptations of life and short-term thinking. From the beginning of the Bible to its ending, the author lays out His plan and for those who have eyes to see and ears to hear will grasp the understanding.

God's plan is long range and that may be the most difficult thing for man to comprehend. Since our media and all the marketing gurus have trained us to want it now, we as a people, self-included, have made some pretty absurd decisions based on short-term thinking.

Habakkuk, along with a handful of others throughout the Bible, demonstrates in action while pleading their case: "There is a way that appears to be right, but in the end it leads to death" Proverbs 16:25 (NIV). Habakkuk tell us these words are the foundation, God is the cornerstone, *believe, follow, commit*—it will be much better if you take the road less traveled.

CHAPTER 27

TITHING

*"Though the fig tree does not bud and there are no grapes on the vines.
Though the olive crop fails and the fields produce no food. Though there
are no sheep in the pen and no cattle in the stalls, yet I will rejoice in
the Lord. I will be joyful in God, my Savior, for the Sovereign Lord is my
strength. He makes my feet like the feet of a deer and enables me to go on
the heights" Hab 3:17-19 NIV. That's commitment!*

Tithe! You are joking, right? In these economic times? The economic turmoil
that is causing many to abandon belief systems, forgo their plans of any
future and to just hang on for dear life are wondering what lies ahead at the next
turn? When morale is low—money pressures are high, living conditions unstable, and people struggle with the basic concept of what will tomorrow bring?

If you have a conversation with an individual or family about the subject of
finances and bring up the word 'tithing,' the typical response is, "Are you nuts? I
am not sure how I am going to keep this roof over my head, feed the kids, make
the car payment—let alone tithe to God." They will tell you that every penny
coming in is committed to someone and there is absolutely nothing left over.

There are two avenues the Bible puts all it has in: believe there is a God and
have faith in His Word. James 2:26 (NIV) says, "As the body without the spirit is
dead, so faith without deeds is dead." We can have all the faith in the world but
if we are not putting any action behind it, (God's way) then nothing is going to
happen.

Abraham was 90 years old when an angel told him he and Sarah were going
to have a son. They laughed in disbelief, but nine months later out came Isaac.
For the next 12 years everything is cool. Abraham is now 102 years and an angel

appears to him again: this time to tell him to take his son, go to a certain place and offer Isaac as a sacrifice to God.

In Genesis 22:2 (NIV), we read: *"Then God said, Take your son, your only son, whom you love—Isaac—and go to the region of Moriah. Sacrifice him there as a burnt offering on a mountain I will show you."*

In the many times I have read this in the Bible or heard a message about it, I still struggle with those words. As I envision in my mind, "What is taking place?" Abraham gives us all a lesson in faith and action. He never questions the angel. He heads off to do as instructed. You cannot turn from this story for the suspense is too great. You have to read it to the end.

Isaac asks his father, "Where is the lamb for sacrifice?" Abraham calmly says, "God will provide." Abraham binds Isaac to the altar with wood piled around him. As Abraham is preparing to slay his son, an angel appears and stops him. Stating, *"You are a true man of God. There is a ram caught in the thicket that is to be your sacrifice."*

You may be thinking, *If that's what it takes to be a man of God, I am not willing to put a child of mine through such an ordeal.* I, like you, struggle with this as well, but I have read and studied enough that I know the words are for real. Abraham's faith was off the chart. He had been through enough to know God would not let him down.

Our next prophet is Malachi. He tells us more about faith and obedience. In Malachi 3:6 (NIV), we read: *"I the Lord do not change. So you, the descendants of Jacob are not destroyed."* There are several verses that explain how God functions and how we should be thinking. The title in chapter three is called Robbing God, which should give us a pretty good clue. Even though God is unhappy with the Israelites, in verse six He tells them that he does not change. In other words, *the promises I made are the promises I will keep.*

As we look at the word **change,** meaning *to fold, duplicate, speak, strike, pervert, second time.* In the news, in the newspaper, or in a conversation over a cup of coffee, we see that man is constantly changing. He commits to a promise, saying one thing; and then, turning and doing the complete opposite. God, on the other hand, stays committed steadfast and ready to lend a helping hand. And all we need to do is ask. The more you read, the more you understand: God does not change. But man will fold on his commitment—telling you one thing and doing another.

Man will permit his ways to become perverted and will strike out in anger or frustration. Man is easily distracted. He will listen to God, then turn around and do something stupid. We also think just because we messed up, God no longer loves us. We figure, since I am on this road, I might as well take advantage of all it has to offer. Having made the same mistake many times, we figure three strikes and we are out.

What God would like to see happen is that we come to Him, ask for forgiveness, and keep the line of communication open. Our human nature is to think that because we messed up, God is angry with us and does not want to communicate. It is just the opposite. He is always there ready to talk, regardless of the topic. Even if the mistake is repeatedly the same, if He sees progress, He is open to listen. **Progress** is the keyword. If we are careless, continually make the same mistake and do not want to improve, then don't expect Him to be in your corner.

The word **Jacob** means *heel, catcher, patriarch, to seize, and restore*. When one turns and walks away from another in disagreement they have picked up their heel (foot) and departed. If you have ever experienced this you know the feeling of "I would like to have an answer, don't just walk away."

In that moment of confusion, you are very vulnerable, searching to find an answer and feeling abandoned. God is in for the long haul. It is like the wolves that want to catch the sheep. They have two objectives. They want to kill or at least scatter the herd, thus making them weaker and easier to catch. With the sheepherder off trying to round up his sheep, the chances of the wolf being successful are even greater. Jacob, being the last patriarch of Judaism, was like the sheepherder running around trying to reestablish God with the Israelites, who were constantly breaking from their heritage.

But God's heart was to restore His people. *"Ever since the time of your forefathers you have turned **away** from me, from my decrees and have not kept them"* Malachi 3:7 (NIV). God was telling his people by turning **away** you have chosen to decline me, revolt against me, remove me from your presences and withdraw from me.

Throughout the Old Testament, the Israelites were constantly getting into a bind and running to God complaining. But the moment God came to their rescue they turned away and revolted, have orgies, worship idols, and withdraw from Him. This had to be breaking God's heart. Still, he was willing to forgive and forget, if His people would just **return** to Him. He wanted them *to retreat, deny, repent, remove, and withdraw*. God was asking His people to give up their old ways. He wanted them to deny all their selfish pleasures and repent, so the sin could be removed from their lives. He was asking them to withdraw and walk away from their present lifestyle.

Think About It

Does any of that sound familiar as to what we deal with today?

How easily we can get distracted? What we think is pleasurable ends up leading us into a double life and using God as our scapegoat. Doesn't sound like much has changed in two thousand years, does it? God also makes it clear if His people returned to Him, He would return to them. He will just pick up where we left off as if we never missed a beat.

Satan is constantly knocking at our door tempting us. That is his job. Many good people have gone astray because of his enticement. He is a master of disguise, leading his victims down a rosy path that ends in everything from drugs to murder to broken marriages, all because we bought his line. When our conscience starts to bother us, we have only two choices: do the right thing or do what feels good.

God is pleading with the Israelites to return to him. When? How do we return to Him? He proposes a question, "Will a man rob God?" What does this question have to do with returning to God? Keep in mind, we are having a conversation with God. He likes to break it down, keep it simple and get your attention. He will throw us a curve ball that is a perfect strike letting us know, "I am in control, please follow my lead."

Malachi 3:8 (NIV) says, *"Will a mere mortal rob God? Yet you rob me. But you ask, how are we robbing you? In tithes and offerings."*

I don't think anyone would knowingly rob God, but yet we do it constantly. How do we rob God? His reply is, "In tithes and **offering**s and he actually says that we are under a **curse** because of this." Those are some pretty strong words and to some they are fighting words.

Tithes means *tenth, accumulation, and to give.* **Offerings** are *a present, an offering in sacrifice, tribute, and a gift offering.* The **curse** was to execute, bitterly curse and set on fire. God was and is very matter-of-fact in His desire to help and protect His people. But there is a flip side to His promise. He expects us to be obedient.

God gives a command He wants His people to follow. Those who understand and follow will be blessed. Know this: God does not play games. He does not say when you do this, you will get X.

There are many Scriptures that clearly state to bring your tithes and offerings into the storehouse. In biblical times, the offerings were designed in part to feed the Levites, whom God had designated to be servants and to never be owners of land. The tithes and offerings were also a test of man's faith that God wanted the best. Man, being self-centered, would try and slide one by God by giving Him less than the best.

Man is still scamming, fleecing, lying, cheating and being down right dishonest. To make matters worse, when he gets caught, he just stands there like a deer looking at headlights, never offering an explanation. Somehow, he rationalizes the offense he committed is acceptable. What happened to the concept of right and wrong?

In biblical times, man looked at the offerings and considered them as a gift for sin or to gain favor with God. When the law was written, this was a command that God expected to be followed. Somewhere along the line, they lost track of the fact it was God who created everything and He is the owner. That fact has continuously been watered down to the point in some circles that God is not even in the pictures.

The scheme of trying to give less than the best has escalated to not giving, plus taking what does not belong to us. Even the Christian struggles with who it all belongs to and will become defensive when confronted.

Taking all this into consideration, God is still willing to reward those who obey. Rewards are something that is part of our system people expect compensation for their efforts. God does not have a problem with the system. Actually, He invented it. When you plant the seeds, you get the crops. Take care of the garden and harvest the fruit. In other words, be good to those around you and it will be multiplied back to you.

These are all principles God created and enjoys seeing fulfilled. There is one more part to God's plan that we as humans don't measure up to, and that is passing along His love and the gospel to others. The rewards God give us while we are on this earth are just a side benefit of what is yet to come. However, none of this will come to pass if we don't do our part, which is share His word every chance we get.

When I say, every chance, that is exactly what it means. Every chance. This means when you are in line at the grocery store, at the gas pump, sitting in a restaurant at your place of work on break. These are all opportunities to tell someone about this God who has been so good to you.

He tells us in His word that no one will miss the chance to hear His Word. This means, we have an obligation and we are not to put it off on someone else; we all are supposed to do our part.

In addition to giving our tithes and offerings, our main focus is to be disciples for Him and be fishers of men. It says in Malachi 3:9 (NIV): *"You are under a curse. your whole nation because you are robbing me."*

I know this statement gets many riled up because we teach that God is a loving God, and how could He do wrong and be loving at the same time? That is the big misconception. It is not God doing wrong. The wrong comes from the choices we make. If we decide to disobey His command and go off and do our own thing and it backfires or something bad happens, how can we blame God?

When we get caught with our hand in the cookie jar after being told to stay out of it, and there is a penalty, *who* is to blame? His rulebook has never changed—we just want to continually be changing the game to fit our need.

To **curse** means *to execute, bitterly curse, set on fire.* These are drastic measures and are not words to play games with. James 3:10 (NIV) says, "Out of the mouth come praise and cursing. My brothers and sisters, this should not be." Clearly, fresh water and saltwater cannot come from the same stream.

God's anger burned when the Israelites refused to obey, and their actions caused countless deaths. How many times have you been in a bind and looked to God for help? He has opened a door for you and within a short period of time you are right back where you were before.

Yet, we choose to play games with a harsh reality that God has laid before us. He says the **whole nation** of you is under this curse. The whole nation, meaning all, everyone, complete, and nation meaning the gentile. That is you and me.

That was thousands of years ago, how could that apply today? Some would argue. Look at the United States. Its economy is going great, the auto industry is somewhat struggling, and our banking system is in such disarray no one really knows what is happening in that arena. We have CEOs more interested in a bonus than their bottom line, and keeping the doors open.

Greed, short-term thinking, and eyes turned on *"the self"* have caused what was once considered the greatest nation on the earth to be one day up and the next day down. This has all happened because we chose to disengage ourselves from God's principles and to make new set of rules, thinking we know best. Under God's rule there is a clear-cut set of guidelines. There is right and wrong, yes and no, and there are NO gray areas.

The Attorney and the shrewd businessman cannot twist the wording to give the law multiple meanings. Enron cooking the books, Maddoff and his ponzi scheme, AIG carelessly overextending, banks turning their heads to poor loan practices. Do you think these are new crimes? Is this the first time something of this magnitude has occurred?

No, we can go to the Bible and see everything that is occurring now has been done before and God did deal with it much more harshly than He is dealing with it now. This may sound crazy. But it is a simple concept: If you do A + B, = C (God's rule). Any diversion of that simple concept will break His rule and depending on what one does with the diversion will depend on what consequence He receives.

Along comes a congressional lawmaker who says, "I can improve this simple formula." Now, the one who wrote the rule book (God) says it does not get any better than this. He has used all the formulas, worked all the angles, and got all the bugs out. He knows what he is doing. But Mr. Congressman says, "Let's remove part A (God) because all the special interest groups are bothered by him and we will rewrite part B. Just to make it sound a little less direct. You know, make it sound politically correct.

Now that was not so difficult was it? Well let's look at our country and its position in the world as we have gradually changed the rules. We have lost our ranking as a leader, our respect as a country, and our people as a nation.

I know these are harsh words, but we soft pedal God's Word with a feel-good kind of preaching, giving us too many, who are Sunday church goers and week day sinners. I would say God has had enough. We need to take a stand, get on one side of the fence and do the right thing.

He wants us to prosper and says in the very next verse, Malachi 3:10, *"Bring your tithe into the storehouse so that there may be food in my **house** and "test" me in this and see if I will not open the **windows** of heaven and **pour** out such a **blessing** that you will not be room enough to store it."*

Does that sound like a bunch of hot air? That is the kind of a challenge an entrepreneur wants set in front of him, but our next generation is so confused with all the dishonest display of corporate America that they are not sure what to do—let alone believe that there is a God.

All the prognosticators: religious and seculars have given their take on all that is occurring in the marketplace and the economic downturn. Whatever I say would be just as speculative because we don't know where it will go from here. We do know what has caused it: greed, dishonesty, and individual gain without any concern for the well-being of another. God's biggest concern for man is that greed is preventing him from having the ability to love his fellow man. This has shown the dark side of man, as one who can be so cold and will stop at nothing to satisfy his self-driven desire. Since man has fallen for all the trappings that lure one into this false thinking of what is defined as success, his ego won't easily let him admit or walk away saying "I was wrong."

Isaiah 57:17 (NIV) says, *"I was enraged by their sinful greed; I punished them, and hid my face in anger, yet they kept on in their willful ways."* Those who have put themselves in this predicament and are bound by their egos will no doubt discover just how painful being wrong can be.

We can have financial freedom, a good marriage, children who love us and show respect in the work place, but we must be willing to follow the rules that He lays before us, instead of buying into the hype and wrongdoing. God's formula works. "Bring your tithe into my store**house** and test me," He says.

House is related to *family, children, builder, repair, and temple.* The relationship we have with God starts in the home. If man is going to succeed, he must first get his life in order with God, and second, he must get his house in order. By taking his tithe and entrusting it to God he is showing that he has faith in God. This is the first step in developing a relationship with God.

CHAPTER 28
DEVELOPING A RELATIONSHIP WITH GOD

From God's perspective, it is not about the reward; it is about the relationship. He is happy to give us the reward once we develop our trust in Him. He is overjoyed to see us succeed when we do it according to His plan. Understanding we are stewards for God is so important in developing our relationship with Him. Having a clear understanding that we don't own any of this stuff, but we are the keepers of it. How we treat what we have been put in charge of weighs heavily on the outcome of all that we do. The word 'house' means family, God intended the house to be for family, children, and a place to develop and grow as a family.

The old adage, "A man's home is his castle" still represents a level of achievement that has become distorted, and the castle has become a nightmare. This thinking that things are more important than God and the attitude of 'I am the reason for my success' has and is bringing great turmoil to the family.

The pattern needs to be broken. We need to re-establish the relationship with God, get back into His Word and make the house the place God intended it to be. We start by trusting God and giving back to Him what He has been gracious enough to let you and me have in the first place.

Once we grasp this concept of tithing we are told to test him. "I will open the **windows** of heaven"—meaning *to lie in wait, lurking, a dove cot, chimney, and slice.* These words could take us in many different directions, but let's see where God wants us to go. The Bible says our relationship with God is to start with a belief that there is a God.

We then can build on that belief with faith and from there we learn to study His Word. This enables us to become knowledgeable and share His word with others. There is a period of learning and growth that develops patience and strengthens our faith. If we just stop and think for a moment, we can see the parallel between what happens when we plant a seed and what God is asking us to do. *To lie, to wait, to lurk* could also mean *to ambush,* but God is telling us to test Him and see if He will not pour out such a blessing.

Here the *wait* and *lurk* has a good connotation. A dovecot was a place for pigeons to land, to rest and be protected from the storm. God is asking us to rest in the assurance that He is true to His word. The chimney lets smoke escape and the fire provides warmth and a source to prepare food as nourishment for the body.

God's Word is considered nourishment for our soul putting the good stuff in and letting the bad escape. A slice was a means of letting water come into your dwelling to provide a source of indoor plumbing, if you will. Again, the Word of God will refresh us like a cool drink of water and that drink is so powerful you will not thirst again. How much more could we ask from someone who has promised to bless us internally and externally? Why would anyone want to reject this? Why would you not want to follow his guidelines?

Man is known for being the inventor of stupidity—wanting to tweak a good thing and wanting to make it better. As we gain momentum and things start to go our way, invariably there will be a bump in the road and a challenge for the devil is always going to present us with a test.

For many the downfall begins here. The secular world wants us to buy into the instant gratification concept and use the word 'charge' to satisfy that desire. God wants us lurking in. He wants us to be like the dove sitting, waiting for the storm to pass and learning to rest in His peace. God knows we have a real struggle with patience, but He also knows by giving in we will never learn how to overcome it.

My heritage is part Cherokee. The Indian took a tremendous amount of time and effort to learn how to hunt and fish. He learned the ways of the animal and by doing so his success as a hunter was greatly increased that very seldom he came away empty handed. Anyone who is a hunter or a fisherman knows about being patient. Some days you go in the woods and spend the entire day to only come away empty-handed. The key is to go back the next day, and the next, you will succeed. If we are willing to spend countless hours at a hobby or at a job to achieve an end result, why wouldn't we spend time waiting to multiply a blessing from the Creator?

The beauty of waiting on God is by following His instructions we are growing in His Word and thus increasing our knowledge in every area of our lives. That is just like throwing a pebble in a pond—the rippling effect just gets bigger.

CHAPTER 29
OPENING THE WINDOW TO FAITH

God reminds us that once the window is open, we are building our faith, and He will **pour** out such a blessing that our room cannot hold it all. To pour is to make empty and cast out that which seems to be in contrast to what God is telling us He will do. *"I will hold nothing back. I will pour it all out."*

Jesus, our Lord and Savior, sacrificed it all when He went to the cross. He gave himself completely to the point of death. Do we really grasp the depth of his commitment? To have faith and believe He is who He proclaims to be is a giant step, but just give it a try check it out.

Something that seems so simple presents a big problem for the human. We want to be able to touch, see, and feel because our mind is conditioned for these kinds of responses. We teach our children to believe in themselves and develop faith that they can achieve, but yet we are hesitant in doing that for ourselves.

One step to bridge the gap between man and God and we turn it into an insurmountable journey. God is willing to give us His best, pour it all out if we will just follow him. Is asking us to tithe a tenth of what He has so graciously provided us too much to expect? The first rule we must never forget—it all belongs to Him and we are in training to be good stewards. The good news is when we grasp this concept we are promoted to the highest level in the company, so your responsibility is great. If you were to treat this like a business, you would need to do the following. Make sure that those under you are being productive, but not being taken advantage of. The quality of what they do is beyond reproach, your payroll is in line, your people are not being wasteful, and you are making a fair profit. Run it the same way in your household.

Though you are not going to treat your spouse and children like employees, think in those terms when running the house, including the budget, being concerned and protective. Can you imagine how much better your life at home would be? Once you master how to run your household your next step is to treat those around you like lifelong valued customers.

This is where God and godly principles come into play. It is imperative that you, the leader, sets the example to run everything according to God's principles. We know this is totally different thinking but for anyone who has done it will attest to the fact that it works.

Now that we have a handle on what it means to be a good steward we are ready for God to empty His abundance into our room until it is overflowing. But 'pour' also means to cast out or get rid of and that too is a reminder that if we are not being good stewards of what we are entrusted to manage, it will not be given to us. It will be cast out, taken away, and given to another. The Bible says some gains will be for another's pleasure.

Dr. David Jeremiah said, "If we don't give God our tithe we are not good stewards and God will get our attention by some means." It could be a very embarrassing public display, the loss of your job, or shutting down of the place where you work. There are many ways to get our attention. But we choose to look everywhere to justify what has happened—except face the truth. The news is full of daily occurrences of people waking up to "I don't believe this is happening" or "Why me God?" We choose to ignore all the warning signs until they get our attention.

My Pastor did a great teaching the story Joseph, the first son of Jacob with his second and beloved wife Rachel. Joseph ends up in prison for being falsely accused of trying to sleep with Potiphar's wife. While in prison, he had the opportunity to interpret two dreams. "Then the butler and the baker of the king of Egypt, who were confined in the prison had a dream, both of them each man's dream in one night and each man's dream with its own interpretation" Genesis 40:5 (NIV).

We continue in Genesis 40:8 (NIV): *"We both had dreams, they answered, but there is no one to interpret them. Then Joseph said to them, 'Do not interpretations belong to God? Tell me your dreams.'"*

Joseph also figured that when the cupbearer was returned to his position he would mention to the king it was Joseph who interpreted his dream. Well that did not happen for two years until the king had a dream and no one could interpret it. The cupbearer then remembered it was Joseph who helped him and he told the king. This time, Joseph is asked to interpret for the king. "'I cannot do it,' Joseph replied to Pharaoh, 'but God will give Pharaoh the answer he desires'" Genesis 41:16 (NIV).

By Joseph giving God the credit, he was restored to second in command of Egypt. The only one above him was Potiphar. It just took a little longer for Joseph to realize who was in charge and how he fit in God's plan.

The pouring out of the blessing will be so **much**, *increase, abundance, enlarge, exceedingly, great and heap* "that we will not have room enough for it." God's Word tells us to be prepared for what we ask and when we see a Scripture that says, "I will open the windows of Heaven and pour so **much** blessing."

Think About It

Are we ready to handle it?

_____

_____

God's Word is designed to prepare us to live life and to live it to the fullest. You and I have been so distorted by man's thinking our moral is shot, our belief system has no basis, we do what we want when we want and believe it's ok. Murder, shootings, drugs, alcohol, have all become means to unanswered questions and searching for the ultimate high which does not exist in man's world.

We have become so self-centered that we will kill our children, murder our wives, steal from our companies and not be bothered by it. And then, deny we did it. What's up with us that we have come to this place that we can look our fellow man in the eye and say it is cool, turn around and commit a heinous crime with not so much as a blink of an eye? But this is not new either.

These same crimes were committed years ago. "Then the Lord said to him, 'Know for certain that for four hundred years your descendants will be strangers in a country not their own and that they will be enslaved and mistreated there." Genesis 15:13 (NIV).

For some, it worked but for others they thought they had a better way. Similar stories exist today. Those who want to shortcut the system make the fast buck, cheat, steal, murder, slink through the dark of night and say it's cool. Man all in the name of self.

Regardless of how much we mess up God still loves us and wants to bless those who are willing to forgo their old ways.

In Luke 12:48 NIV, we read: *"But the one who does not know and does things deserving punishment will be beaten with few lows. From everyone who has been given much, much will be demanded; and from the one who has been entrusted with much, much more will be asked."*

Have you ever seen a baby as he tasted something sweet for the first time? His eyes lit up as if saying, "Boy! that was good. Can I have some more?" That child will actually go into a rage or throw a fit if they don't get it. We adults act the same. We pout, sulk, go around with a sad face, and have this "woe is me" look to get attention when we don't get what we want. That is not going to work, my friend, because God is going to train us how to handle much.

Does that mean we either enroll in the class on "How to Handle Much 101," or we don't get to participate in the abundance? As we will see later in these verses there is certainly some grumbling that occurs from the sidelines. There are those who prosper and even those who challenge God, and even though they don't play by the rules, they understand the game.

The word **much** is used throughout the Bible. Our lives have been placated with ads from television, billboards, radio and print telling us we need it now. We are told we deserve it and have become consumed with notion of self and the idea of *much* has taken over our life.

We have become a nation of debtors, borrowers, living off of next week's pay check, getting further and further behind while some one on the other end is thinking of new ways to enslave us. This drive of wanting it now, having much, has finally caught up with us. Our country is in financial ruin and our leaders are in denial. We have become the ostrich who buries his head in the sand thinking no one can see him and maybe it will go away. Many are forecasting that God is on the sidelines watching a nation He blessed with abundance (much) who has squandered it. We were not good stewards, good managers, and He is watching to see how we will respond to this crisis.

Think About It

Will we try and do this on our own or will we call on God?

_____

_____

Are we willing to humble ourselves and ask for forgiveness, take the long road back to financial soundness, which is God's road or continue to make wrong decisions that only drive us further in the wrong direction?

In Genesis 9:11 (NIV), we read: *"I establish my covenant with you; Never again will all life be destroyed by the waters of a flood; never again will there be a flood to destroy all life."*

God brought a flood which really cleaned house and He promised He would never do that again. He got everyone's attention by wiping out an entire city. Genesis 13:10 (NIV) says: "*Lot looked around and saw that the whole plain of the Jordan toward Zoar was well watered, like he garden of the Lord, like the land of Egypt.*" This was before the Lord destroyed Sodom and Gomorrah. Hopefully, at some point we will get the message. With all the messages He has sent us through the years and the instructions He left us in His book, why don't we get it? What will it take to bring us to our knees and recognize there is only one God and one ruler?

His book has the answer to that question as well. **Much** when used through-out the Bible is followed usually by abundance, whether in an overflow of crops, in war or victory, in knowledge, and wisdom. Some would travel for days and bring great wealth just to sit at the feet of one of God's chosen to listen to him teach.

The other side of much mentioned in the Bible is going to the other extreme. There has been much pain, loss of entire families and wealth, going from a king to one grazing like a cow. Spending forty years learning a lesson, dying and never seeing the promise fulfilled.

From living in plenty to being put in prison and finally put in exile on an island to die knowing the best is yet to come. These are but a few of the examples of a God who goes to great extremes to please the people He loves so dearly.

Yes, some of His love is what I will call tough love if the words He has writ-ten choose to be ignored by the reader. God has ways of getting our attention. Ironically, He knows our choice before we make it and has planned the lesson ahead of time. He is a good teacher and is always prepared.

Granted, as you and I read these words there are grumblings in our mind saying, "I can live with the good things that come along. I can even tolerate some of the consequences but this thing of going to great extremes, to learn a lesson is gong a bit too far."

We all need to be reminded that the extreme came from a decision we made. It resulted from actions we had or are taking in our lives thinking we know how to run our lives better than the designer.

But then you argue he could stop that tragedy, the bad decision, the loss of the job, the divorce. Yes, he could go around all day long putting band aids on everyone's problem, but what would that accomplish?

What would you and I learn if we had a God who was constantly picking us up, never let us fall? Or worse, we took advantage and said, "It does not matter, God will fix it. Don't worry, be happy"?

The Bible teaches us to be responsible, wise in our decision, to create a union with our Creator and put our trust in Him. It is a relationship we need to develop—not a religion. It is about being in sync with our Lord and Savior Jesus Christ for He is our anchor, our guiding light. Hebrews 6-19 (NIV) says it well: *"We have this hope as anchor for the soul, firm and secure. It enters the inner sanctuary behind the curtain."*

As we leave the word 'much,' it is evident God is a man who keeps His promise. If you are a person who has yet read the Bible and you are confused, I ask you to hang in there for the end is much better than the beginning.

CHAPTER 30
GOD'S BLESSINGS

What does the word **blessing** mean to those who chose to follow God's law? It meant *prosperity, liberal, abundantly, praise and thanks*. These words tell me that a blessing that comes from God is going to be more than sufficient.

God says in Genesis 13:16 (NIV), *"I will make your offspring like the dust of the earth, so that if anyone could count the dust, then your offspring could be counted."* To be followed by, Genesis 17:6 (NIV), which says *"As for me, this is my covenant with you; You will be the father of many nations."*

At one hundred years old, Abraham laughed and thought there was no way he and Sarah could have a child. In Genesis 17:17, we read: *"Abraham fell facedown; he laughed and said to himself, 'Will a son be born to a man who is a hundred years old? Will Sarah bear a child at the age of ninety?'"*

In Genesis 18:14 (NIV), we read God's answer: *"Is anything too hard for the Lord? I will return to you at the appointed time next year, and Sarah will have a son."* It all came to pass because of God's blessing.

While on earth, Jesus healed the sick, made the lame walk, caused the blind to see, and brought the dead back to life. These were all blessings. "And wherever he went—into the villages, towns or countryside—they placed the sick in the marketplaces. They begged him to let them touch even the edge of his cloak, and all who touched it were healed." Mark 6:56 (NIV). We see a similar scene in Acts 5:6 (NIV): *"Crowds gathered also from the towns around Jerusalem, bringing their sick and those tormented by impure spirits, and all of them were healed."*

When we ask for a blessing today it usually involves something of value. "Please, heal me; please, Lord get me a job; help me figure out how to pay this bill!" The focus is on "me."

Think About It

Are we willing to stand the test and display unadulterated faith with no questions asked?

Today, we have a condition tied to our request. "God, I will do such and such if you just get me out of this situation." If you will take the time to read the Bible, you will see where God did His work. There was total surrender and complete unquestionable faith. The individual was not thinking about self and the blessing was usually in a form that was not expected.

The blessing was liberal in the sense that God did not just pick this special person to receive a blessing. It was for whoever was in need and to someone who showed unwavering belief. Read Matthew 9:20, 21, 22 (NIV) and see what I mean.

"Just then a woman who had been subject to bleeding for twelve years came up behind him and touched the edge of his cloak. She said to herself, If I only touch his cloak, I will be healed. Jesus turned and saw her. 'Take heart, daughter he said, your faith has healed you.' And the woman was healed at that moment." She displayed an incredible faith and was healed.

Solomon, David's son, was blessed to be the wealthiest, and the wisest man and God put him on a throne. All Solomon asked for was the ability to discern while ruling this great nation he was put in charge of. The blessing God showed anyone was always sufficient and liberal. God enjoys giving much more than receiving. The message behind God wanting us to tithe is to get us in the mindset that this stuff we want to accumulate is not ours. We are managers and we understand our role as a manager, it is the highest rank God offers.

We don't need the title of CEO, President, or Chairman. God has established our worth and we are confident in Him who gives us everything. Once we understand that these words and their significance, our thinking begins to take shape. Then we must treat what has been entrusted to us with the utmost respect. We then can take the proper perspective to accomplish what God has in store for us because the two have now become one.

Marriage between man and God is the same union God wants between man and woman. Man must understand his purpose and must take the role as leader and do so from a godly perspective. Until we grasp this nothing else will work in God's plan.

As we continue to look at the word 'blessing,' James tells us: *"Consider it pure joy, my brothers and sisters, whenever you face trials of many kinds"* James 1:2 (NIV).

Paul tells us in Philippians 4:13 (NIV): *"I can do all this through him who gives me strength."* That would seem to me to be a pretty clear indicator of who to listen too. If we can just learn to be thankful, regardless of our current circumstance—learn to appreciate where you are and learn to see the good in everything. Taking our eyes off of self will always make a bleak picture become clear. These last few statements are made by choice and if that is not obvious it needs to be. God will take care of us and meet us right where we are. The problem we have and trying to fix should be one we are learning from and grateful to be in.

This is a tough pill to swallow, mainly because we live in a society that wants everything fixed now. If it can't be fixed, we don't want to be part of it. There was a time that the generation before us had to learn how to make do with what was given them. Starting at age eleven, I made spending money by mowing lawns. Every spring, my neighbor who was a year older than I, we would race from house to house in our neighborhood to ask to mow the lawns. The average price for mowing a lawn was three dollars and the size was about one-half of an acre. We did it with a push mower and trimmed with a sickle. My father supplied the mower. I bought the gas, kept it running and fixed it when it broke. That was my responsibility. On top of that, fifty per cent of what I earned went to my mother for my school clothes for fall.

But I was thankful. I always had some change in my pocket and knew how to get more if I needed it. By the time I was fifteen, not only did I mow lawns, but I painted, became a laborer for a construction company and never had a lack of money in my pocket.

Frankly, I am not sure how thankful I was, but I did know I could always work. I went through a stage of life where I felt I could conquer the world on my own. I felt indestructible and I could work as long and as hard as needed to accomplish my goals. Then my life took a turn, and I started to live a double life using God as a front and being unfaithful to my family.

I was burning the candle at both ends. The stress and tension I was putting myself through was unbelievable. The most amazing thing was I would not admit to myself that I was the cause of it all. I blew twenty-one years of marriage and three wonderful sons before I crashed and realized the wrong I did.

After my divorce, there was a three-year period where I went wild. Then, God grabbed me one evening and got my attention. I felt Him saying, "How much longer are you going to push your luck? One day I may not be there for you."

That's when I re-dedicated my life to God. I began to seek His word. I was hungry for it and the more I got, the more I wanted to know. The group I hung out with came from a biblical point of view of 'name it and claim it' and I bought into that philosophy for a few years.

It took some time to overcome the 'I ask, you give (God) attitude.' I started coming around and began to see God was for real. I understood that He did answer prayers but there were some guidelines I needed to follow. I am thankful that even in the tough times, I was able to find it in my heart to give Him honor and glory, not just lip service.

Like my father, I knew how to work. HT also knew how to save. He knew he was required to take care of his family. He knew he was to represent God every time an opportunity presented itself.

Perhaps this sound basic, and it is. God is not complicated. We make it that way all on our own. HT knew to believe in God, have faith, trust God and He would provide whatever the need. Maybe not always literally, but the answer came. HT knocked, and the door opened. You see, this is not rocket science.

Giving praise to God is one way of witnessing to others about what He is doing in our life. This is part of His requirement. We are to be His mouthpiece and in doing so we are blessed. It is like receiving a double whammy—you and God are both getting recognition.

God next informs us He will prevent the pest from **devouring** our crops and the vines in the field will not **cast** off it crops. To **devour** meant *to eat, wise, deed,* and also it meant to *burn up and consume.* God is showing us both sides of what can happen if we obey and follow His law, or if we choose to disobey and do our own thing.

The crop was a source of food and a good crop gave an abundance, which could get you through until the next season. It could also provide an increase, which allowed you to generate an additional source of income. Not only could you feed yourselves and your families, but you gave to God your first fruits and wisely stored up for the winter months as a plus. The key was to always keep an amount of seed for next spring to plant.

We also see the word 'deed' used to refer to devour. There are many ways to relate to deed, but they all kind of fall into a couple of categories. It is an inference to business or been given a command. Since God has put us in charge of His fields, then we are managers (stewards) and this makes our job very simple.

He has His guidelines (procedure manual) that we are to follow. Our duty is to follow the procedures manual, do as instructed and our rewards will be abundant. By making a simple adjustment in our thinking, this is not mine, so, I need to make sure I take good care of what I have been put in charge of.

To some, this is too ridiculous for they are not willing to turn loose of the thought of being in control and using the term *I own it*. To that, God replies: "Fine, then you look at it through this set of eyes. We are business partners. I am (God), the money person and I own the land, but I am very generous. I am going to bring you on as a partner 50/50. I (God) will put up all the money and supply the land, plus the seed to get this venture started. All you have to do is plant the seed, water; keep the weeds out, harvest and save some seed for the next season. I (God) will let you keep ninety per cent of the yield. Give me (God) ten per cent off the top and manage the field the way I prescribe." Is that a cool deal or what?

Is he for real? May be your response. Most people would walk off shaking their head saying, "Man, I met a real winner today. Who does he think he is fooling?" Unfortunately, as simple as it sounds, it is exactly how difficult we will make it.

This is where God will step into the picture "Ok. I offered you a pretty substantial business deal and you are not taking me seriously, so I am going to command you to do the following." He is going to offer us the same proposal; however, since our mindset has been one of skepticism we are probably going to look at the offer through a set of eyes with some resentment and maybe even rejection.

I ran this entire scenario by my friend Gordan and his reaction was almost identical to what has been stated here. In fact, he stated once he is commanded to do this there must be a consequence. My response was "Yes, but not from God, but from your choice."

God only wants good for us, but if we want to be on God's team we need to play by his rules. He goes on to tell us he will not let the vines not **cast** off their fruit, meaning *miscarry, abort, bereave, fruit, deprive, destroy*. This is a very interesting set of words. To 'miscarry' means *to lose before it is ready or to die prematurely*. Ok, so we are being told that the crop will go full term and it will bear fruit.

To 'abort' or 'abortion' means *to take before its time*. The crops, once in the ground will go the designated time and will produce a harvest. No storm, nor drought, will cause the crop to fail. To 'bereave' is *to morn over a loss* and that will not occur for the crop will be bountiful.

He next talks about fruit and He is simply saying the vines will bear their fruit at the appointed time. We will not be deprived of our harvest and the pest will not destroy the fruit. God is the best pest, rodent, bug control person to ever exist—if He says they will not come around you can count on what He says. *"I will prevent pests from devouring your crops, and the vines in your fields will no drop their fruit before it is ripe says the Lord Almighty"* Malachi 3:11 (NIV).

"When God made a promise to Abraham since there was no one greater for him to swear by, he swore by himself" Hebrews 6:13 (NIV).

We next look all the nations will be **blessed.** They will be *happy, straight forward, level, go forward, honest, prosper, guide, lead and relieve.* If there was no explanation it should be apparent of the message behind these words. Just simply by testing God and being willing to do as He asks, He tells you and I we will be happy and in that itself is a blessing. With all the stress and unhappiness that is around us to have some joy in our lives would be great.

Wait, there is more. He is telling us we will move in a straight-forward motion and it will be leveled. In the Bible, it is mentioned numerous times our paths will be level and straight. Isaiah 26:7 (NIV) says, *"The path of the righteous is level; you, the Upright One, make the way of the righteous smooth."*

Straight carries a definite implication in the eyes of God. He can make the crooked straight. Of all the different ways I have heard straight used over the years the one that comes to mind the most is in the form of a question. Is he straight? Meaning honest, trust worthy, in good standing. In my wilder days of partying, if the question was asked "is he straight?" it meant is he sober or is he high? If you heard someone say, "man, be straight with me," they were asking you to tell the truth.

All of these were a form of slang to get a direct answer from an indirect approach. This is a lot like God operates in His teachings, but His terminology is very direct, accurate, and to the point. To be straight, walk straight, make level paths straight, all deals with the same thing: don't let your ways be perverted, be in line with God and follow His commands. It also means there will be some who would be ready to hear and understand His words while others would need more time.

CHAPTER 31
LETTING GO OF THE PAST

God teaches us to always be moving forward and not looking back, which is contrary to man for we have this innate desire to stop, look back, and wonder what if. I used to be guilty of spending wasteful time pondering over a situation that has since passed and getting hung up on what if's. I ran it through my mind countless times replaying it, expecting a different ending to something I could not change.

In Luke 9:62 (NIV), we read: *"Jesus replied, No one who puts a hand to the plow and looks back is fit for service in the kingdom of God."* You can't move forward as long as you are living in the past.

Have you ever met someone, and every time you are around them all they want to do is relive something in their past that caused them pain? There will come a point when you will turn the other way when you see them coming. That is destructive behavior and, if we put our eyes on the prize that is ahead of us we can't move forward while we are looking back. God's blessing doesn't always come through Him, but it will come because of Him.

Think About It

Have ever wondered why you are constantly making new friends because your old ones just keep disappearing? Maybe you are running them away because you continue to relive the past. Are things stale at your job? Do you wonder why or just take it in stride?

These may all be symptoms of hanging onto the last big deal or that painful experience that happened years ago. Progress, God's vision and your sanity, is achieved by focusing on what is in front of you—not what happened yesterday. God is a realist and His ideas work. We just have to implement them.

We have all heard *honesty is the best policy* but not many of us practice it. I know if I said that in a crowded room, one or two would step forward and challenge me. Nobody likes to be called on or question their integrity.

Well, my next question would make a quiet room even quieter if I asked, "Have you ever told a lie?" If the answer is no, then that person is a liar. Now, I know that I would be treading on thin ice and taking a chance of getting punched in the nose but that is a chance I would have to take.

God does not tolerate liars. There is every kind of thought, every kind of reasoning, and every kind of excuse as to why a certain condition requires us to lie. But God will emphatically tell you He hates liars and there is never a reason to lie. The word we are focusing on is *honesty*, and in Job 6:25 (NIV), we are told, *"How painful are honest words! But what do your arguments prove?"* In Proverbs 12:17 (NIV), we also read: "An honest witness tells the truth, but a false witness tells lies."

How painful are the words of truth. That is a serious question, but more important is what was said that led us to tell the painful truth. If we speak honesty in all we do, we will not be confronted with a painful ending. The ending may still come but the truth will not change.

Think About It

So how do we go about dealing with this thing called honesty?

_____

_____

Some definitions of honesty include: *fairness, straightforwardness, and adhering to the facts, integrity, truthfulness or truth*. Now, truth oddly details variations of the truth going from actual facts to miscuing the truth and using a term called a 'white lie' to keep form hurting another individual.

This white lie is established as a lie of lesser moral deception to save pain and not elevate self at the same time, thus it becomes socially acceptable. In Romans 2:2 (NIV), we read: "Now we know that God's judgment against those who do such things is based on truth." And a few versers later, in Romans 2:8 (NIV), it says: *"But for those who are self-seeking and who reject the truth and follow evil there will be wrath and anger."*

The first thing we need to do is decide who we are going to follow and which set of rules we are going to play by. God's Rule Book has one set of rules and those rules apply to Him and everyone who wants to be on His team. As we can see, there are two sets of acceptable rules. If you choose to follow man, there's the moral and less moral. I think the less moral is winning. It is actually now down to a less, less, less, less, moral and dropping. In contrast, God's the same yesterday, today, and forever.

I am interested in a team where I have the opportunity to play and feel good about playing. Once you have been on the field with God's team you are considered a seasoned veteran and there is no way you could ever feel comfortable switching teams. As for me, I'm sticking with honesty, speaking in love and doing what I am being instructed by my coach.

To prosper or to be blessed, we first need to lead—guide others and put aside that kind of twisted thinking that we have to lie to succeed. This leads us to the conclusion that we are to be responsible once we come into His fold. God expects us to step up and take responsibility, be a leader, and harvest the fields. The fields I am talking about are the lost. Those who are hungry searching for answers and following the worldly system to find them. They are continually dealing with frustration, dead ends, using drugs, trying to escape reality, climbing the corporate ladder, only to discover once at the top it is leaning against the wrong wall.

Once we make it to God's team, we need to be willing to suit up and play. He is not looking for benchwarmers and cheerleaders. God needs people at every position and He has one already picked out for you and me.

I played football from the seventh grade through high school and three years of college. I loved the game and was the only thing that kept my interest in high school. I played linebacker and fullback and was a pretty good ball player. I was a walk-on in college and I started on defense. I wanted to play offense and was a star in high school and liked the glory of being the running back. It was an ideal Saturday afternoon for college football.

I remember one Indian summer, with these beautiful fall colors and temperature just right. My high school sweetheart and her mother had driven down from Ohio for the weekend to see me play. She was a cheerleader and loved the game too. I wanted to impress her and noticed the coach was distracted with one of the players on the sidelines, so I put myself in the game.

I told the quarterback what play to run when I entered the huddle. He looked puzzled but called the play. I ran the ball for seven yards and was immediately pulled out after the play. The coach did not say much because I had picked up seven yards. Still, he benched me for a game. Obviously, I did not want to be on the sidelines. I practiced hard and did what was asked of me. I trusted the coaches and had faith they would hold up their end of the bargain but what I did was wrong.

The difference in playing for God is this. We all get to dress and play because He has a spot especially designed for each of us. He does expect us to show up and participate, but the beauty of each position is it is custom designed for our personality, our body type or demeanor, and it is something we will like to do. How cool is that?

However, many people want to be on God's team but don't want to break a sweat, get their hands dirty, talk to people, any of that stuff. God wants more team members. Those of us who really want to play are out there helping drum up new team players who He can bless. How about you?

Since blessings come in many different flavors and disguises, we don't always recognize them. So many of this generation have liberal thinking with their belief system watered down that they are not sure of what to believe in. We put our faith in man and we are continually disappointed each time. We rationalize by saying, "That is life. That is the way it is supposed to be," only to turn and see what or where we can next put our hope in.

Most people are after the superficial—the next thing that comes along that shows promise. God wants to relieve us of this empty feeling of continually trying to find fulfillment outside of Him. How does relieve fit into a nation that God wants to bless?

To relieve one is *to get rid of, do away with*. God speaks of the church as a place where those who are truly widows are to be relieved of their burden. The church is there to help those who are in need. Since God is the Holy Temple, He represents the church of all churches. He is always there for us to lay our burden at His feet and relieve that worrisome load.

Now, setting down our burdens doesn't mean forgetting about them. God tells us in 1Timothy 5:16 (NIV), *"If any woman who is a believer has widows in her care, she should continue to help them and not let the church be burdened with them, so that the church can help those widows who are really in need."*

God is telling us He is not going to take care of everyone who comes to Him with what they consider a problem. First of all, most of what we consume ourselves with, as a problem is not a problem. We just need to sit down with some godly counsel and take a careful look at our situation and come up with a wise godly plan and put it into action. Most people feel this is too much work and it requires sacrifice. Basically, we are spoiled and want our cake and eat it too.

This is the exact reason Paul informs Timothy of seeking the widow who is really in need and let family, friends, and church members help the others. God is a little wiser than most give Him credit for.

In the same way God was trying to get the Israelites' attention, by letting them know they were robbing him, we are to look closely at He's telling us about our relationship with the Church.

The church has a specific function within a community and some do it very well, while others make a mockery of God's Word. "Then all the nations will call you blessed, for yours will be a delightful **land**,' says the Lord Almighty" Malachi 3:12 (NV).

God has dominion over all, and He is willing to turn it over to His chosen people, which includes the gentile. We are to honor the land, not destroy it. The **land** means *firm, field, ground, country, earth, world, and wilderness.* All of it. In Proverbs 4:13 (NIV), we read: "Hold on to instruction, do not let it go guard it well, for it is your life." Psalm 89:28 (NIV) says, *"I wall maintain my love to him forever, and my covenant with him will never fail."*

Firm, is an absolute that God puts before us. Just as He made the ground firm under the priest's feet as they stood in the middle of the Jordan while all the Israelites crossed, He will do the same for us.

We can stand firm on God's Word as the absolute undeniable truth when we choose to follow Him. He provides the field which serves many purposes. It provides game for the hunter, a place to graze the cattle and sheep, a place to plant your crop to harvest to feed for your family and generate revenue.

Just as God is waiting for Israel to return to Him, He is capable of destroying the field. In the Book of Joel, God allowed the locust and fire to destroy the fields. The fields were no longer good for producing food, grain, or the wild animal to use for grazing.

From the ground comes everything. When God created the earth, He created man from the dust, as well as every animal of the field, bird of the air, tree for food, and plant of any kind. We take so much for granted that we don't give much thought to how it all came about.

As we come to a close on these verses in Malachi, I would like to revisit the first word we discussed which was 'firm.' In Proverbs 4:25-27, it tells us, *"To let our eyes look straight forward, fix your gaze directly before you. Give careful thought to the paths for your feet and be steadfast in all your ways. Do not turn to the right or the left; keep your feet from evil."*

The words we have covered in this segment tells about a God who wants to please His people, and will go above and beyond the call of duty to do so. All He asks is for us to follow His formula and the firmness that Solomon refers to in the above verse.

The firmness of his word is the foundation on which we can build our entire life. Because His teaching is rock solid. There have been many a test great and small by those who want to destroy His foundation, but it stands today not weakened. It does show the scars of time, but those marks only solidify and attest to its strength as to the only source of a winning formula to find eternal happiness and true riches in Christ Jesus.

God took care of His people in their country and warned them of the One who created the earth shall be the same Who destroys it to rebuild a new one. Revelation 11:17 (NIV) says, *"We give thanks to you, Lord God Almighty, the One who is and who was, because you have taken your great power and have begun to reign."*

CHAPTER 32

THIS ALL BELONGS TO GOD

From the field to the country, to the world and back, and to the wilderness, God owns it all and wants to share it with those He loves and who chose to love Him. The only thing He asks is we love Him and follow Him.

God's ways are not a cult or some selling gimmick. He is for real. He delivers what He promises. He is open 24/7 and will turn no one down. We can try to shoot His Bible full of holes and make acquisitions, write books, and take His words out of context. Some will buy into it, but there are others who will always be looking for the better deal—the pot of gold at the end of the rainbow. There have been many who have risen to fame going against Him and eventually gave in only to go to greater heights.

God is not about tearing down and destroying. He is about building up and moving on. The destruction that occurs is from man and his choices. God has a heart as big as the universe. He rules and has no problem giving to anyone; we just need to be on the same page with Him.

I get so excited as I write these words. It becomes difficult for me to understand why others don't see what I see and decide to follow this God of mine. I say mine because I have a relationship with Him and I can attest to things that He has done in my life in the past and is doing now. I can't wait to see what He has in store for me in days to come.

This is why having a firm foundation is so important, and in my humble but accurate opinion, there is no Lowe's or Home Depot that can provide any building material that will match the foundation you can build with God. Even those who challenge God, but have a healthy fear of Him are the ones who get His attention.

To **fear** is *to revere, be in reverence, hold in high esteem.* God was more concerned about those who held him in reverence than those who challenged him. He knew the outcome of the ones who did evil and yet prospered. He knew their gain would be short lived or in vain.

Think About It

Do you think a person who gets dishonest gain or challenges God will lose his wealth, suffer, or some other tragedy will come his way?

_____

_____

I don't know, but God knows. You can read what history has written, see what medical doctors say, and watch what is on the news channel. Some people say it is all coincidental and they could be right if it were just an occasional occurrence. However, history is full of detailed events and with a little study it becomes apparent that it is more than a fluke.

Moses was under much stress as he ruled over the Israelites trying to settle disputes from minor incidents to things of a much greater matter. Jethro, Moses father-in-law, came to him after observing the strain he was under and offered a simple solution. *"But select capable men from all the people—men who fear God trust worthy men who hate dishonesty gain—and appoint them as officials over thousands, hundreds, fifties, and tens. Have them serve as judges for the people at all times, but have them bring every difficult case to you, the simple cases they can decide themselves. That will make your load lighter because they will share it with you"* Exodus 18:21-22 (NIV). Jethro offered a system of handling the disputes, which is now known as our judicial court system.

Man is notorious for taking on more than he can handle and then wanting to say, "Look, this is what I did when it is over." Self-seeking was, still is, and will continue to be man's demise. God knows this and has a simple solution but man thinks he knows better and does not like to give up ownership to something he never owned in the first place.

This is where it gets tricky because we want to control not what God has in mind for us. I know the struggle, we all do. It is an ongoing battle and like it or not God is in charge. We are His managers and that is a tough pill to swallow. Because man wants to be in charge until he forgets his boundaries. Learning to fear God and hold Him in reverence is a daily battle we need learn to deal with. It will make us a better person, but we must be willing to submit.

"On the day when I act," says the LORD Almighty, "they will be my treasured possession. I will spare them, just as a father has compassion and spares his son who serves him" Malachi 3:17 (NIV).

To *spare* is *to have compassion, to commiserate, to have pity to spare.* God's greatest desire is to see His people succeed and be prosperous, but they must do it His way. If you want to start an argument tell almost anyone you have something for them, but they must first do such and such. Most will immediately start wondering what is the catch? The minute they hear your proposal they start building a defense and resentment.

We have Adam to blame for this. From the moment they ate the apple things changed. Their vision, their thoughts, and fear entered where it had never been before. Some look at their condition and want pity, but God meant it for good. He knows our broken state which requires compassion and understanding. He will not throw us a pity party but He will give us direction.

God has a desire to see us as whole, complete, and this is not something we can accomplish on our own. But once we understand the compassion He has for us and are willing to submit to His will, then we can develop that same compassion for others. What God shares with us, He wants us to pass on to our fellow man. We don't have a problem developing a passion or drive to have or succeed. That drive will become a burning desire and we live it day and night to the point of consuming us.

God, on the other hand, has a deep awareness of our suffering and has a longing to help us. The dictionary defines the word *spare* this way: "A profound human emotion prompted by the pain of others are more vigorous than empathy. The feeling gives us the rise to an active desire to alleviate the suffering of another."

The dictionary uses the word 'profound' in this case meaning strong, that one is actually compelled to act on another's behalf to help relieve their suffering. This is how much God loves us and why he is so driven to help us for he has this desire to relieve our suffering.

In Matthew 11:28 (NIV), we read: *"Come to me, all you who are weary and burdened, and I will give you rest."* Those who have pain and suffering whether they want to admit it or not, conceal it very well. With time it takes its toll and begins to show through in appearance, conversation, attitude, or body language. We don't want to burden others with our troubles so we keep them to ourselves.

To **serve** is *to work, enslave, bondage, labor, be wrought, and worship.* You say, "What else needs to be said with these words? What more of a definition does one need?" Man, I am tied to a life that does not seem to be much fun if I follow what is associated to the word serve.

The word 'serve' came from two origins: the French *servir* and the Latin *servire*, both meaning to be a slave or servant. Well. maybe this does not sound like much of a way to start out a conversation by telling someone that you expect them to be your slave. After all, that is a pretty primitive term.

In Genesis 22:2, we read how God asks Abraham to serve Him by taking his only son, go to the region of Moriah, and sacrifice him as a burnt offering. It does not say, Moses begged and pleaded with God, or tried to bargain with him. He was not up all night pacing the floor. It simply says, he arose the next morning, got a donkey, gathered some firewood, took his son and two servants and off they went.

In Genesis 22:10 (NIV) we read: *"Then he (Abraham) reached out his hand and took the knife to slay his son."* At the very last moment an angel of the Lord spoke to Abraham Continue to Genesis 22:12, which says, *"Do not lay a hand on the boy. he said. Do not do anything to him. Now I know that you fear God. Because you have not withheld from me your son, your only son."*

This is how much faith Abraham had when he reached the foot of the mountain. The two servants that came with him were told to wait while he and his son went and worshiped the Lord. Geneses 22:5 (NIV) reads: *"He said to his servants, 'Stay here with the donkey while I and he boy go over there. We will worship and then we will come back to you.'"*

That my friend is faith—total faith, no questions asked. Did Abraham get that kind of faith on his first try? No, it took him many years and many mistakes. The agreement between God and Abraham was "we won't quit on each other."

Think About It

What does 'serve' mean to you?

_____

_____

The meaning of serve today has different meanings. It could mean to be in the military and represent our country. Ask any soldier who has been in combat and they will proudly say, "I did it for my country and would do it again."

To serve also means to hold a political office and represent your fellow constituent, which is an honor when done in the proper fashion. To serve can mean to be a waiter, waitress, or a clerk in a retail store. Or, any other profession that serves people. To the one you love . . . serving is about showing that person your deepest gratitude and the love you have for them.

Whatever your profession, you are offering to serve others through it. We find many and myself included looking down our noses at others when we have been in a position of authority tapping our foot in anticipation waiting on an acknowledgment that we are the ones in charge.

God has gotten my attention on many occasions when I've so rudely pulled that stunt. And then I remember Jesus' words: *"I came to serve, not to be served."* This should be a reminder that our position is one of giving, not receiving. If we expect to do God's work, then we need to be relatable to those around us and the best way to relate is to be one of them.

The remainder of the verse in Malachi 3:18 (NIV) says, *"And you will again see the distinction between the righteous and the **wicked**, between those who serve God and those who don't."* To be a wicked person in God's eyes you were morally wrong, a bad person, condemned, guilty, and ungodly. That covers a pretty broad array and does not leave much room for doubt.

One could always argue by what standard is morally wrong, which seems to be a rather common response today. Morally wrong in God's eyes was very straight forward. He had given a set of guidelines and expected them to be followed. The problem with man is he resists being told what to do or have boundaries placed around him in such a manner as to reduce what he thinks is freedom.

In today's society morality has become twisted, and thinking so distorted that violence is used in the place of rational reasoning. God simply says if we are a bad person we will be condemned and found guilty.

We may be able to finagle our way out of a prison sentence with a high price lawyer, but God won't be persuaded. And though He is a forgiving God, sin has consequences, and bares a person's responsibility.

The godly and the ungodly are referred to in different ways in the Bible. The godly seek to follow God and His righteousness, while the ungodly choose to follow the ways of their own lust, greed, or depravity.

Does this mean the ungodly are destined to a life of trouble, torment and damnation? Maybe while on earth all will appear to be fine; however, unless they choose to change their ways, the end is not pretty. Jesus says in Matthew 23:33, *"You snakes! You brood of vipers! How will you escape being condemned to hell?"*

There are those who want to cling on for one more ride while thinking they have plenty of time to get right with God. I was one for a very long time. However, we are not guaranteed tomorrow and what we have learned so far seems to be a much better way to live. We have a much greater reward here in the now by following God's plan.

God has laid out His entire plan for us. He tells us to give back to Him a portion of what He already owns while reminding us we are managers, not owners. He tells us that a manager is the most important position on His team and to not be consumed with what everyone else is doing.

Finally, He tells us to serve Him out of love, not because we think we have to, and He will include us on his scroll of remembrance. One last thing . . . there will be a separation of the righteous from the wicked. One day Jesus will wash His hands of those who have vacillated in and out of His life and they won't be given another chance.

CHAPTER 33
THE POWER OF WISDOM

*"Know also that **wisdom** is like honey for you: if you find it, there is a*
future hope for you, and your hope will not be cut off"
Proverbs 24:14 (NIV).

Throughout the Bible, God refers to wisdom as *understanding, blessing, and prosperity.* In this particular verse, it relates to *skillful, wise in word, teach, and wit.* God teaches His principles through stories and past experiences of others who failed to listen, giving directives, faith, and parables. All that is written about God is a lesson that will pass along great wealth in wisdom.

To be skillful means you are quick to learn, you have an aptitude to grasp, and you will excel quickly. I have worked around people who had this uncanny ability to grasp whatever was being taught quickly. Wisdom is also related to wise in word. God guarded His words. Every word that comes forth from His mouth has power, and so He reminds us not to be foolish with our words or to let unwholesome talk come out of our mouth.

Words are not funny when they are spoken at the expense of others' feelings. Regardless of how innocent we may think our words are, when another person is the brunt of a joke someone is left with a wrong impression. Words are our only line of defense of guilt or innocence and the action that follows those words become our judge and jury. Paul was humbled by Jesus, who chose to let him become a leader. Paul became very wise in word and a teacher to others.

To teach another is a privilege and the Bible informs us to not take it lightly. I have mentioned that I taught an insurance class. My record of students passing the exam was one of the best in the state at that time. It was because I prepared, knew my material, and it was presented in a way the class could comprehend.

I was very seldom challenged, and even though I was not in my walk with God at the time, I was wise enough to understand that many whom I was teaching were smarter than me, so it kept me on my toes. There is always going to be someone lying in wait for you and the moment you slip up they are ready to discredit you.

Matthew 10:24 (NIV) says, *"The student is not above the teacher nor a servant above his master."* That does not seem to make much difference today, as many are bold and think they have the right to challenge the instructor. However, the Bible does warn against false teachers who represent themselves well and are convincing.

Think About It
How do we tell the good teacher from the bad?

Go on a mission, learn the Bible, get in a good Bible-based church, continuously seek God's Word and ask questions until you understand. God expects us to do our homework.

Do not be gullible. Don't take someone's word. If you have a question, then find the answer. The answer needs to line up with God's Word and you need to be able to see that it does. This may seem like it requires a lot of work, and it does. But, do you think making a seven-figure income can be done without working? Everything requires effort.

Wit means *to know, to learn, or to see.* When you are gathering knowledge, it enables you to converse on a topic you can easily over step your bounds and think you are an expert. There is only one expert and the rest of us are amateurs in comparison. But does that mean we quit learning, just give up and let the other person do all the work? No. We are told to seek God as if we are looking for gold.

In Jeremiah 29:13 (NIV), we read: *"You will seek me and find me when you seek me with all your heart."* In the movie "Facing the Giants", the coach admits he is afraid of Mr. Bridges. Mr. Bridges tells him a story of two farmers. Both needed rain badly and so they prayed to God for rain, but only one went out and prepared his field to receive the rain. Which one do you think God blessed?

When the rain came to both fields only one benefited because it was ready to receive the rain. The exact same message God is giving us is we must prepare to accept the knowledge which will get us to a whole new level of understanding and applying God's Word. We read that wisdom is sweet to our **soul**, refreshed, breathing, desire, pleasure and appetite. Just as a summers rain refreshes the flowers, turns the brown grass green and provides a cool drink to Mother Nature, wisdom will do the same for us and will refresh our soul.

Have you ever been working outside on a very hot summer day and longed for a cool refreshing shower? Just to stand under cool water running over your body and feeling a sense of freshness tingle over you. Getting an understanding of God's Word is like a cool drink of water on a hot summer's day, it's better because it will quench your thirst forever.

Wisdom is something no one can take from you. The words imply we will have a desire, an appetite, and it will bring us a pleasure far surpassing anything man can offer. King Solomon at a young age asked God for just one thing: wisdom.

Solomon acquired his wealth through his wisdom. His mind was always seeking to know more and was constantly asking 'why' and then finding the answer. God gave him a desire to gain wisdom. We can develop that same desire, and it is never too late to acquire it.

Hebrews 6:19 (NIV) says, *"We have this hope as an anchor for the soul, firm and secure. It enters the inner sanctuary behind the curtain."* An anchor that is firm and secure makes a pretty profound statement. If you are a visionary person you can picture that big anchor with this huge chain attached to it securely holding the boat in place, not allowing it to move. God is the anchor and chain; we are the boat constantly drifting to and fro. Solomon finishes this verse with wisdom is sweet for your soul, "If you find it, there is a future hope for you, and your hope will not be **cut** off."

To **cut** is *to destroy, alliance, passing between, perish*. As you read each of these words they take us back and forth from destruction to alliance, which are at opposite ends of each other.

To *perish* means *to have no way to flee, to be done away with, and no way to escape*. but Solomon says, *"this will not happen because there is a future hope for you and me."*

By choosing to act on our knowledge and accepting Jesus Christ as our Lord and Savior, the Scriptures we read and internalize become our anchor. They keep us steadfast and develop an appetite of wanting to know more. We are to become skillful, wise in word and have a desire to help others acquire this same knowledge.

This pleases God, enabling him to bless us while we remain faithful to Him. We now go to the Book of Revelations, a book I steered away from for the longest time because of the misconception I had. The misconception came about by listening to others and not reading and discovering for myself.

Revelation came from the Greek word 'apocalypse' meaning the lifting of the veil, or revelation in today's terms means the end of the world. I guess this is why so many choose not to read the Book of Revelation.

It was around 90 A.D. on the Island of Patmos where John was in exile that he penned this message. This one verse will give us additional insight to the biblical view of prosperity.

In Revelation 5:12 (NIV), John's vision is showing him this: *"In a loud voice they were saying: 'Worthy is the Lamb, who was slain, to receive power and wealth and wisdom and strength and honor and glory and praise!'"* From this verse we will get the understanding of *deserving, sacrifice, power, price, reputation* and much more because of the one who gave his life for us.

There has never been anyone who has garnered more attention, had more insults hurled at, more pages written about, caused more deaths, saved more lives and created more controversy than Jesus Christ. Now John is telling us in Revelation that this controversial figure is going to bring it all to an end. We will not be told the day when, but he assures us we had best be prepared.

"Then I heard every creature in heaven and on earth and under the earth and on the sea, and all that is in them saying: 'To him who sits on the throne and to the Lamb be praise and honor and glory and power, for ever and ever!'" Revelation 5:13 (NIV).

The word **worthy** means *deserving and due a reward*. Think of the way Jesus came into the world. He was conceived to a virgin, born in a manger, a was a bright star who led three kings to Him bringing gifts. At the age of twelve, He sat among the elders displaying wisdom far beyond his age. These were all signs of someone special.

John the Baptist said this about Jesus: *"And this was his message: 'After me comes the one more powerful than I, the straps of whose sandals I am not worthy to stoop down and untie. I baptize you with water, but he will baptize you with the Holy Spirit.'"* Mark 1 7-8 (NIV)

God sacrificed His Son so we could have a second chance—something we don't deserve, but have been given. Not only is Jesus worthy of all honor, praise, and glory, but those who choose to accept Him as their Savior are worthy as well.

In Hebrews 9:28 (NIV), we read: *"So Christ was sacrificed once to take away the sins of many and he will appear a second time, not to bear sin, but to bring salvation to those who are waiting for him."*

We are worthy to be accepted into the kingdom; worthy to be in his presence, worthy to walk with Him and talk with Him. It also says this is His due reward. When you have a reward due you that means you completed your task.

The beauty of being in God's kingdom and being under His reign is He uses His power for the betterment of all who serve Him. He does not lord over us as a tyrant. So, in reality we get the best of both worlds: a King who is fair and just, and a chance to experience true freedom while serving.

Granted, that sounds like an oxymoron: King, serve, freedom. As a rule, those words don't go together. But remember, this will be a new earth with a new leadership.

Just as Jesus gets His due reward for the sacrifice He made, we too will get our reward for committing to follow His lead and the sacrifices or what we consider sacrifices will end up being blessings. Pretty cool stuff, right?

Throughout the Bible, the Lamb is used as a sacrifice or referenced to mean Jesus. Revelation 5:13 (NIV) says, *"Then I heard every creature in heaven and on earth and under the earth and on the sea, and all that is in them, saying: 'To him who sits on the throne and to the Lamb be praise and honor and glory and power, forever and ever.'"*

The **Lamb** will *carry away, bear, remove, and be stronger.* In the Old Testament, the lamb without blemish was used as atonement for sins. Remember, God wanted the perfect lamb for sacrifice. He did not want the imperfect. In Leviticus 22:21 (NIV), we read: *"When anyone brings from the heard or flock a fellowship offering to the Lord to fulfill a special vow or as a freewill offering, it must be without defect or blemish to be acceptable."* This small request could have a great impact on the individual who was doing the cheating.

The Lamb will carry away our sins. Because of his death we get the privilege to live. Doesn't seem fair to God, but that is the kind of God he is—always giving more than He expects. The Lamb will bare our sins. To bare someone else's problems is a pretty big undertaking for anyone. An individual who chooses to help in another's time of need. To step up and bear the responsibility for another is a huge burden to put on one's shoulders. God not only took one person's problem, He took on the whole world.

When we read statements like the one just made we can't imagine that any one person can handle everyone's problems. But we, as a nation will buy into the idea that the Federal Government can bail us out of the financial mess that several different entities collectively got us in to.

If General Motors, who was the world's largest auto manufacture, can crumble because they refused to acknowledge they were on unstable ground and continued to do the same thing expecting a different result. We have a government that continues to print money with the expectations of bailing everyone out with minimal chastisement. What's to prevent the government from crumbling as well?

The Roman Empire fell when they thought they were indispensable. Maybe we should start paying attention to what is written. It appears we have two choices: You either accept the responsibility and bear your part, or we will be removed.

In the Old Testament and the New Testament, when the word 'removed' was used it meant to do away with, replace or destroy. This is in exact line with what is offered. Everyone, is invited to receive this great plan of salvation, also known as life everlasting.

CHAPTER 34

THE LAMB

Nobody likes ultimatums. But, take a look at the word Lamb. We know we are not going to get out of this alive. Death is a sure thing, we just don't know when. Granted, God has on occasion pulled a few back and extended their time a little, but with a world population of over 8 billion and rapidly growing, the odds are not exactly in our favor.

The Lamb is the Alfa and the Omega, Rev 21:6 (NIV) says, *"He said to me: it is done. I am the Alpha and the Omega, the Beginning and the End. To the thirsty I will give water without cost from the spring of the water of life."*

We look at a lamb as non-threatening animal. He is cuddly when young but not real smart. God still chose the lamb as a symbol and says it will finish strong. He is always doing the unexpected. He takes the autistic child and says he is special, the little orphan girl and she grows up to do great things for her creator, the blind child becomes a great artist and the deaf person goes down in history as a great musician. God has no limits to what he can do.

There is a price to pay and it was paid when Jesus was put on the cross. He was **slain**, *sacrificed, maimed, wounded, and it was violent.* When God decided to send His Son to earth the story had already been told some six hundred years earlier about his miraculous birth and his violent death. Is God one for melodrama or was it His intent to get our attention? Since the story was told six hundred years earlier. I don't think He was into drama.

When you hear of Jesus' death on the cross, most just picture Him hanging on the cross, maybe a little blood tickling down off His forehead from the crown of thorns or blood coming from the side that was pierced. We don't like to think of the torture He went through before and after He was put on the cross. We don't even like to think about the spikes driven through His hands and feet.

Jesus was jeered when He started His ministry. He was continuously threatened and escaped a stoning and those who opposed him were constantly trying to bring charges against him of blasphemy.

Can you imagine operating in an environment where your life is in constant danger? The movies is the only place I have seen where the one in danger manages to escape unscathed. This was just a matter of bringing a prophecy to fruition. He was slain, it was violent, he was wounded and He sacrificed it all, allowing us the privilege of eternal life at His expense.

If you have not taken advantage of it, today is a good time to just ask God for forgiveness. Accept him into your life and commit to follow Him. And remember, this is not about religion, it is about a relationship with Jesus. Do what is right and join God's team. Amen.

Our verse continues with the word **receive** meaning *to take or to get hold of.* God was making sure that once the death and resurrection of Jesus had occurred, He received full power to finish subduing the earth and reign for eternity. To some this may sound like a fairytale, but if you just take the time and read the Bible you will see for yourself how it all plays out.

The power that Jesus has is for us, providing we are willing to accept Him as our Lord and Savior. Yes, there is a catch! But anything worth having comes with some strings attached. The difference is these strings are eternal and go way beyond the norm in every aspect.

When you combine faith with action then you develop belief, which means Jesus is on inside of you. Just let Him lead and all things are possible with Him at the helm. In the Book of James, we are told, "We have not, because we ask not." But you say, "I ask all the time and still nothing happens." I know what you mean I have been there, also. What this should be teaching us is asking is only part of the formula—there must be faith combined with action.

I am not talking about saying, "I believe now Jesus. Where is my request?" No, it does not work that way. It is a two-part deal. If you want to take hold of whatever you're asking for then you must not only talk the talk you need to walk the walk.

In Matthew 17: 20 (NIV), we read: *"He replied, 'Because you have so little faith. Truly I tell you, if you have faith as small as a mustard seed, you can say to this mountain, 'Move from here to there,' and it will move. Nothing is impossible for you.'"*

Think About It

Did you prepare your field for rain even though it is as dry as a dust bowl? It has not rained for days and your local weatherman says no rain in sight for the next three weeks?

Moses worked on the ark for 120 years before the rains came. Martin Luther King Jr. marched to his death and never got to see his dream come true, but because of what he set in motion the dream came true.

Jesus received what his Father promised because He believed and with that belief He acted upon what was required of Him to fulfill His journey. He took hold of what was charged to Him and it came to pass. We have to do the same and the beauty of this is applicable in every aspect of our lives. We just need to keep in mind God is first, family second, and work third.

It is all about priorities, knowing who is first in the pecking order. God is a God of order.

Jesus was not only to receive the power, it was His to pass on to us. It is ours for the asking—all we have to do is take hold of it. Luke 9:1 (NIV) says, *"When Jesus had called the Twelve together, he gave them power and authority to drive out all demons and to cure diseases."*

Power means *to be able to, be of power, mighty work, abundance, miracle, strength.* These are all part of the package that was given to Jesus. A friend of mine just purchased a new car yesterday and he was like a sixteen-year-old with his first car. We went for a ride and I must say I was impressed. It is a version of the Dodge Daytona R/T Hemi magnum muscle car and it will 'get down,' so to speak. It can pin you against the seat and give you that adrenalin rush, at least until you see the red and blue lights flashing in your rear-view mirror. Anyway, my friend is excited because of all the whistles and bells that came with it.

The back seat is loaded too. It has a DVD player for children, touch screen, GPS optional shift or automatic transmission. The Magnum engine has shiny wheels and more. So, yes, my friend got the full package. But all those whistles and bells are only applicable when he is in the car.

What God has to offer will outlast anything we have. Our cars, our houses, the money in the bank. All our toys and prize possessions will one day go away, but what God offers is forever.

The word **power** reeks of something extraordinary when associated with words like, *be able to, mighty work, be of power, abundance, miracle, and strength.* It has to be put in a category by itself.

There is a lady named Joni Eareckson Tada who at age 17 had a diving accident that left her a quadriplegic. She will be the first to tell you the church played a very big part in her life before and after her accident. Her accomplishments are even more astounding. From artist to author to co-founder of Joni and Friends Disability International, sought after speaker, Christian Book Golden Word Award winner, Hall of Fame for Christian Book Sellers, Co-Chair of the Presidential Prayer Team in 2007 and numerous honorary degrees. She is known and recognized world-wide and all she had was hopes of being on a swim team, but God had bigger plans.

With God at her side, she has been given the power to do mighty works and strength to endure what she could never do on her own. She has experienced miracles way beyond her belief, and abundance so great with humility overflowing, she can and does say, *"With God all things are possible."*

Go to Joniandfriends.org to see all her accomplishments. I could give you example upon example of real life people who have put their faith and trust in Jesus and bought into his whole package, as my father would say 'hook, line and sinker' and are walking the walk.

Can I unequivocally say Jesus will bless you like He has blessed Joni? Here is the short answer. NO. If there was a tragedy in your life what would you do, how would you react and would Jesus be first in your life? These questions must be addressed.

What Jesus does with each of us depends on us and what we are first willing to do for and with Him. This is a two-way street. Do you want power? If so there are two things you need to decide up front: 1) what are you willing to change in your life? And 2) what do you want the power for?

Jesus is the ultimate businessman. You have never met a shrewder negotiator or a tighter budgeted bottom line CEO than Jesus. His rules only seem difficult because we have had too much freedom, been able to get away with too much, make excuses too often and have not been accountable to the right person. All that changes the minute you accept Him as your Lord and Savior.

The rules change. Yes, accountability comes into play, your conscience actually responds when you do wrong, you become aware of your surroundings and develop this strange desire to help others and this is just the beginning.

You get a promotion. That's right, you are now a manager. Remember, that is the highest rank in God's company. Now in the beginning you are a manager in training but that is a far cry better than any previous offer you ever had, and from this starting point the next thing Jesus wants to give you is wisdom.

Wisdom means *clear, practical, cautious, prudent, skill.* Man, does that not say it all? It is so simple, but yet profound. People are either so enthralled with Jesus and His miracles, or of such disbelief that they don't see His practical side. The Centurion understands about giving orders and Jesus commended him by saying in Mathew 8:10 (NIV),*"When Jesus heard this, he was amazed and said to those following him, 'Truly I tell you, I have not found anyone in Israel with such great faith."*

Rahab, the harlot agreed to put her life in jeopardy to guarantee her family's safety when Joshua attacked Jericho. Her decision was based on knowledge she had gathered from her customers. She came to a clear practical conclusion that God had favor with Joshua and that was the team she wanted to be on. Joshua 2:12 (NIV) says, *"Now then please swear to me by the lord that you will show kindness to my family, because I have shown kindness to you. Give me your sign."*

We see in these two examples that wisdom is not always about who is smarter, but where you are getting your information. In each case, the source was a direct line to God, so if you are going to read the book and choose to follow its author, then you must also follow its advice. You don't make choices on half-truths. Your decisions are based on practical applications, not on what ifs or hypotheticals.

You come to conclusions based on prudent sound information. Then use those skills you have learned to prove it works because you have witnessed it. You may say, " This is all well and good," when you have all the time to do all what is necessary, but what if a decision needs to be made now? My only answer is proper training will always give you the ability to make any decision. There is not a situation you will encounter that you can't find the answer for in the Bible. I know you think that this is ridiculous with all this modern technology there is no way you can find answers for that in the Bible.

The technical answer is for a formula, no, but the practical application to achieving that answer is yes. It's there, you just need to be patient. Seek guidance and in the multitude of counselors there is wisdom. In all probability, your answer will be much clearer and more practical and far more prudent.

God's teachings have stood the test of time for those who are willing to take the necessary time to find the answers. That is why the Bible has and still causes so much controversy. Every time a so-called expert tries to disprove the Bible they only expose more of its truth. This in turn gives us strength to move forward.

Jesus was given **strength**, which means *forcefulness, power, possession, ability and condition to reign.* The Lamb will receive the strength necessary to rule this world and over the powers of darkness. There are two kinds of strength: the inner strength and the outer strength. Jesus, while on earth, displayed both types, many times while being tested during His three years of ministry.

His inner strength came in the form of resolve. In the Garden, the night He was captured as He prayed to his heavenly Father. He says in Luke 22:42 (NIV), *"Father, if you are willing, take this cup from me, yet not my will but yours be done."*

Jesus displayed His outer strength in the courtyard as He destroyed the tables and scattered the money of those who was using the Temple as a place of profit. In Matthew 21:12 (NIV), we read: *"Jesus entered the temple courts and drove out all who were buying and selling there. He overturned the tables of the money changers and the benches of those selling doves."*

This quiet, unsuspecting man had the ability to call upon His power given Him to display his Fathers will when it was necessary. Strength has been displayed throughout the Bible several times in the Old Testament from Joshua, David, Samson, Daniel and Job, just to name a few.

These men all displayed an outer strength because they had an inner peace with God. Joshua stepped in and took over for Moses, leading his people into the Promised Land. David displayed disgust at Goliath who taunted Saul's army as he said, *"If my God can protect when I am guarding my father's sheep from the lion and bear, he can do the same for me against this Philistine named Goliath."*

In 1 Samuel 17:37, we read: *"The Lord who rescued me from the paw of the lion and the paw of the bear will rescue me from the hand of this Philistine. Saul said to David, 'Go and the Lord be with you.'"*

David's inner strength kept him focused on God and he came out the other side to be blessed even greater than before. We see in these different men's strengths how God orchestrated their lives and made great men out of them. It's the same with the Lamb of God. He had the inner quiet strength and when needed the strong outer strength, even though he was never pictured as a warrior. But in the end Jesus will rule for a while with the iron hand and His outer strength will dominate. He will use force and power to prevail and He will make His presence known to mankind.

This does not sound like the Jesus we know and read about, does it? We are told there are reasons beyond our comprehension as He tells us in Isaiah 55: 9 (NIV), *"As the heavens are higher than the earth, so are my way higher than your ways and my thoughts than your thoughts."*

Ironically, this display of power will bring **honor** *esteem, highest degree, precious,* but it will come at a price. There are many who have represented God and paid a price. Some with their lives, others going to their graves not seeing their reward. Jesus said in Revelation 22:12 (NIV), *"Look, I am coming soon, My reward is with me* *and I will give it to each person according to what they have done."* The honor that is given Jesus is of the highest esteem, the highest degree and precious to behold.

The modern-day CEOs are seen as gurus. Bill Gates, Tim Cook, Jeff Bezos, Donald Trump just to name a few and are in no way comparable to godly leaders of the Bible. The names mentioned above rose to the top because they developed an attitude of inner strength. It was not about them, it was about who they trusted. Their product was their means to fame and fortune and for the most part it was all about them—very singular in purpose. Granted, they took along a few people as they rose to the top, but it was mostly about them.

Throughout the Bible, when God chose a leader it was for a purpose and the mission He had in mind for the individual was for the good of the people, not for the individual. Moses was chosen to lead the Israelites out of Egypt to a land God had sworn to give to them. It was an honor for Moses to be chosen by God. All the ministers, Sunday school teachers, theologians, seminary professors who esteem Moses today do so because God chose to elevate Moses. He was not out to make a name for himself.

Nehemiah, was used by God in a most peculiar way, to be put in the annuals of the Bible. His burden was to rebuild the wall of Jerusalem where there was severe opposition. Even though God was elevating Nehemiah to do a particular task, it all began with him on his knees asking God to give him direction, courage, and strength.

In Nehemiah 1:11 (NIV), we read: *"Lord, let your ear be attentive to the prayer of this your servant and to the prayer of your servants who delight in revering your name. Give your servant success today by granting him favor in the presence of this man. I was cupbearer to the king."*

Isaiah was considered by most "the greatest prophet of the Bible." God gave him a high calling, to minister to kings. His teachings and proclamations made him unpopular with those kings and in the end, he was sawed in two. His teachings and writings have gone on to influence thousands who have read his words of inspiration.

God chooses those people whom He wishes to esteem and shape. And, not only to handle the calling, but to do it in such a manner that the light shines on God as they stand in the background. Billy Graham may be the most notable modern-day figure who has been elevated by God, prayed with presidents and sat with heads of nations. His face is known internationally, yet he always gave all the credit to his Lord and Savior, Jesus Christ. Graham is exemplary of what every godly man should aspire to be—thirsty for God's Word, willing to step out and do the unordinary and step out of the spot light and give God the credit.

Jesus was the same way. He did what needed to be done, was brave when he needed to be, humbled when recognized, and always gave his Father the credit. When we aspire to live a life that is God-centered, we too will be held by God in high esteem, but the beauty is this, it won't matter because our eyes will be on God, not on ourselves. Wait, there is more because we will be so focused on God. Even more it is like the saying, "the harder I work, the luckier I get." This is the kind of honor we receive when God gets the credit. Amen.

The word **glory** means *to think, be accounted, to please, be of reputation and praise.* When you or anyone has accomplished something worthy and your peers recognize your achievement, you are honored by this recognition. This type of honor to some leads them to believe they should get the glory, and all of a sudden, their thinking changes and their head gets swollen, elevating themselves above others. This kind of glory is destructive because it alienates this individual from others along with the fact they have trouble handling their new-found fame.

The glory bestowed upon Jesus when He returns is not to make Him into some untouchable shrine, but to adorn Him with the praise He deserves.

Think About It

Why does he deserve it?

_____

_____

Jesus deserves this glory because He is following through on what he promised. He is coming back to finish what He started. In our nation today, there's a CEO who says, "I am here for you." However, he takes a new position two days later and everyone else is left holding the bag wondering what he said.

CHAPTER 35

TRUST IN THE LORD

I changed companies a while back. I made the move because after careful research I felt the company was the right fit. I chose this particular office mainly through the recommendation of the corporate office. I immediately started developing a relation with another broker in the new office. We hit it off so when questions arose, I went to him for advice, and a friendship began. One day, I came into work and found he had moded on to work for another company. Nobody knew the reason why he'd left, and that left me unsettled.

I felt betrayed because he in part was my reason for choosing to come to this particular office. As time went on, I discovered he had been planning this move all along while encouraging me to come on board. The trust I put in him was lessoned and his reputation as a person of his word was tarnished. Each time I had communication with him, that picture entered my mind and I inwardly questioned his integrity.

While on earth, Jesus followed through with everything He set out to do. He was worthy of glory. His reputation proceeded Him wherever He went and the praise He received was deserved. Before he ascended to heaven, He told his disciples, "I will be back." In John 20:17 (NIV), Jesus said, *"Do not hold on to me, for I have not yet ascended to the Father. Go instead to my brother and tell them, I am ascending to my Father and your Father, to my God and your God."*

He is a leader who displayed the utmost integrity. He never had a hidden agenda. All who chose to follow Him knew what His purpose was for He never played both ends against the middle. Jesus was the individual who deserved the glory and taught those who were willing to accept His teaching how to handle glory.

Jesus was not conceited. He never said, :I am here with you always," and then two days later was gone. Instead, He left a legacy of men and women who became committed to Him down through the ages. Many have sacrificed their life—others their reputation. Many others left their fortunes and fame behind to follow Him, believing He will be back.

In Revelation 5:12 (NIV), we read; *"In a loud voice they were saying: 'Worthy is the Lamb' who was slain, to receive power and wealth and wisdom and strength and honor and glory and praise."* In Philippians 4:6-7 (NIV) it says, *"Do not be anxious about anything, but in every situation by prayer and petition, with thanksgiving, present your request to God."* And the peace of God, which transcends all understanding, will guard your hearts and your minds in Christ Jesus."

As I left the house one morning to go to the clubhouse for my morning workout, prayer time was on my heart. I had been slack in my time with Jesus and it was bothering me as I was running my day through my head trying to figure out where to work in some prayer time. Philippians 4:6-7 came to me. I must start with some sincere prayer time every day, not just a quick insincere God 'thank you for the day' blah blah blah prayer. I need to spend real time talking to God.

I need to share my inner feelings, my wants, asking Him to fill me with His desires. I am still learning it's okay to ask God for things, to be specific and listen to myself as I talk to God. Only when I learn this fully will I discover how silly some of my requests are while others are so general they should be more like an afterthought.

God is a god of order and very specific, so why should our prayers be any less? This means prayer will take a little work in the sense of not being mundane and not repetitive. Prayer is a conversation, nothing more, and we don't need to be eloquent and use as my father would say fifty-cent words for God is okay with ordinary language.

Anyway, that verse was on my mind during my entire workout, especially the part of *"the peace of God that transcends all understanding will guard your heart and minds in Christ Jesus."* The more I thought about those words the clearer it became to me. If I would just spend sincere time in prayer with God asking (petitioning) Him, He will bring a peace over me.

Anyone who has a prayer, problem, or concern ... if they believe in Jesus, they can go to Him and get that same peace. Perhaps you're thinking that all that sounds good in theory but it doesn't work like that in real life.

My first reaction would be, "Then, you don't really believe." And you would say, "Yes, I do!" But, I would have to disagree with you. James: 8 (NIV) says, "He is double-minded and unstable in all his ways" and you would immediately know what I was referring to.

I bring all this to your attention for one reason only. In the verse we just finished studying, Revelation 5-12 (NIV), Jesus is preparing to wreak havoc on earth and we need to be ready. While Jesus was on earth, every time He needed to talk to His Father, He got alone and spent time on His knees in prayer. His conversations were plain spoken and precise and His burden was always lifted and He came away with a different perspective.

Jesus did not have a problem asking God 'why,' but He understood He was here to do His Father's work. If we don't take the time to present our requests to God, then how do we know if He answers prayers? God wants to help. We just need to realize we need the help and, most importantly, the One who is eager to provide the help.

Once we grasp that little concept, we can all have that peace of God that transcends all understanding and will guard our hearts and minds. Prayer can work miracles. We just have to give it a chance.

To further emphasize this point, let's read Isaiah 55:11 (NIV), which says: *"So is my word that goes out from my mouth; It will not return to me empty (void) but will accomplish what I desire and achieve the purpose for which I sent it."*

As we look at these words we will get an even better understanding of God's spoken word and the power it has when He is in the picture with us. We are not talking about some magical power or mysticism. We are talking real power of the spoken word. You may say, "Do you expect me to believe this?" Well I am not saying this is some hocus pocus stuff, we are talking about establishing a relationship with God and putting our faith to test by not only believing, but putting action behind that belief.

In the movie *October Sky/ Rocket Boys,* a group of young boys from a coal mining community in a small southern West Virginia town wanted to be different. They did not want to be coal miners. Because of a science teacher who believed in these boys, Homer Hickem and his buddies never gave up on the idea they could make a rocket. Through hard work, persistence, and belief they eventually fulfilled their dream. Their dream became a reality only because of faith and action in their belief.

God will give us that same desire of our heart, that same drive once we get our thoughts in alignment with Him and start walking the same path He travels. But let me caution you. Don't be like the Pharaoh who would continually hardened his heart. Each time Moses appeared before Him asking the release of the Israelites, God is not to be deceived.

Rest assured, He knows your true intent. In Hebrews 4:12-13 (NIV) it says, *"For the word of God is alive and active Sharper than any double-edged sword, it penetrates even to dividing soul and spirit, joints and marrow; it judges the thoughts and attitudes of the heart."* Everything is uncovered and lay bare before the eyes of Him to Whom we must give account. No further explanation needed there!

Back to Isaiah 55:11 (NIV), let's look a look at the word, **word** meaning *a matter, thing, advice, business, care, counsel, commanded.* We know how powerful words can be and we also know it can be sharper than any double-edged sword. Once that word leaves your mouth it can never be taken back. *"So shall My word be that goes forth from My mouth, It shall not return to Me void, But it shall accomplish what I please, And it shall prosper in the thing for which I sent it"* Isaiah 55:11 (NIV).

Having said that, it only seems logical that we should carefully choose our words and consider the impact that they have on those receiving them. The more you look at what was said in Hebrews 4:12-13, the better you understand the power of the spoken word and how it can penetrate, divide, and uncover the real intent of a person's heart.

Since God is the creator of the word, who could better understand the power it carries and the impact it can potentially have on mankind? That is why it is vitally important we understand the meaning behind Isaiah 55:11.

Look at the word and you will see that when God brought a prophecy to one of His prophets it was a matter to be carefully considered and carried out. As we read God's words and as it speaks to us, in a certain way this too is a matter that we need to consider and act on. If our day is full of struggle and our heart keeps telling us to stop, take time, and pray, or pick up our Bible and read, this is God's way of telling us we need to address this matter now. He is saying "I want you to deal with this now."

The thing we want to do is push it aside and tell ourselves we will deal with it later, we are too busy, or this is the middle of our work day and we have all this work to do. What we just told God is, "I am too busy right now to follow this gut feeling, this tugging on my heart. I will do it later when I have more time."

Later never comes, and we have missed a great opportunity for God to do great work in us. The best message we can receive from this scenario is God will eventually quit knocking on our hearts because He sees we ignore him, thinking we can do it on our own.

Think About It

How many missed opportunities and missed chances to let God do a great work have you passed up? How many learning experiences have you missed that could have solidified your faith more and allowed you to witness to others more?

When we turn a deaf ear to God's knocking on our hearts and let life get in the way, we miss an opportunity to be filled with His supernatural peace. When we understand God's role in our life, then there is no crisis that we can't take time and listen to God, pray, or pick up His Word and seek His counsel. Jesus assures us that when we honor Him before man, He will honor us before His father. God wants us to lean on Him. He is pleased when we are dependent on Him. This silly notion of independence says we are qualified to do it on our own. Even after we have fallen several times we continue to try and do it on our own.

This is why God will eventually go to the sideline and become an spectator. Some people will eventually get it and let Him back in their life while others will abandon God and harden their heart.

God cares for us and wants to see us dwell in His Word, which is full of hope, promise, and can fulfill that empty feeling we so desperately long for. His book is full of examples of those who chose to disobey and how their actions caused them to self-destruct. Some found their way back, while others were not as fortunate. In reading the accounts of those who never changed and seeing how they ended, some may have thought 'good, they deserved it,' but God wants everyone to have His blessing.

What if you were to treat His Word as part of your business manual and you were having a problem at work. Would you look it up in the manual to find the answer? God's caring is so great He instructs us on how and where to receive counsel. We can talk with fellow Christians, our pastors, elders, deacons and even Christian counselors—all these people have chosen a profession of following God's calling to help us. There's wisdom to be found in a multitude of counselors, but be aware of false teachers, He tells us. His words have power and can soothe the soul at the same time. He is the best friend you will ever have and His advice will never be true.

He says "*the words that come from my* **mouth,** *(blowing, edge, portion, side, puff, scatter to the corners) will not return to me empty (void)."*

I can just picture God talking in a sales seminar to a group of hungry sales people. Those who are eager to go out into the world and make their mark creating a name or elevating themselves to CEO, COO, President, Founder, all because of God's inspiring words. As He explains the power of the spoken word they are hanging on every word, taking notes and sitting on the edge of their seats. Their eyes are glued to His every move wanting more, at the same time thinking, "Hurry up, I can't wait to go and apply what you are teaching me."

To someone who is hungry for knowledge, they are open to learn and accept new ideas and willing to try anything. We would all do well to learn from those who are hungry to learn and not afraid to tackle the world.

Their courage and zeal is not in their degree of vocabulary and fear does not entangle them. They have discovered the power of the spoken word coupled with the One who invented it. We see the young successful person and some of us envy them because we see what we once were. However, as we read God's Word we are reminded he used those of all ages to get his task accomplished—from the eight-year-old King Josiah to Caleb at eighty five.

Simply by confirming out loud what you believe and letting yourself hear those words, it becomes an affirmation, thus increasing your faith and belief. This is why prayer is so important and why Jesus' prayers were recorded. He talked with His Father communicating out loud. He himself needed to hear what He was saying to his Father.

In James 3:10 (NIV) it says, *"Out of the same mouth comes blessings and cursing. My brothers and sisters, this should not be."* This verse is extremely important in understanding Jesus and communicating with Him. Since the Bible is clear in its instruction on how we should live our life, and set the examples for others, we cannot be double-minded and we cannot display actions that send two complete different messages. There will be no blessings and our witness will be ineffective. In the same manner, we cannot go around in a puffed up state pretending to be something we aren't, acting as if we are superior to others.

These body languages that we send out are powerful and if they are the wrong message we can offend others and defeat our mission for which Jesus has equipped us. Not only do we speak with the mouth, our expressions, our look, our reaction to a question or statement is all forms of communication and they all send a message to the intended individual. It becomes imperative that we learn and understand how to communicate God's way. We have all heard the term 'he or she was blown away' or 'I got blown away' when I heard what happened. It has been said our mouth is the pathway to our heart and our real thoughts.

Out of the abundance of the heart the mouth speaks. When our feelings are so strong, the moment we engage our brain, our tongue begins to spew forth our true feelings and those words can be very crippling. Once those words cross our lips there is no retrieving them—the damage is done—the cut has been made and sometimes there is no healing. Matthew 12:34 says. *"You brood of vipers, how can you who are evil, say anything good? For the mouth speaks what the heart is full of."*

As a Christian, we need to guard our heart and be in constant communication with God. To manage our words and control our tongue, replace anger with love, bitterness with acts of kindness and leave the rest up to God.

The mouth is one of the smaller parts of your body. You would not think it could be so much trouble. We have witnessed it can be a source of healing or destruction and it can cause a rippling effect that can carry to the corners of the earth.

I bet you never thought you had that kind of power. Frankly, having power like that is not necessarily a good thing. For Billy Graham, yes. For you or me, probably not. When God spoke it was for one of two reasons; He was either teaching or rebuking because He was not much on small talk. When He appointed a prophet or a disciple, their duty was to carry out a command. Perhaps that doesn't sound like much fun, but God knew man was going to have His fun and His pleasures. God wanted to convey the right way to have the fun and enjoy a godly life in the process.

CHAPTER 36
PRIDE: THE BIGGEST STUMBLING BLOCK

The word **return** means *to turn back, retreat, break, dig, li e down, and come back.* Living in South Florida where it is often said, "if you don't like the weather, wait five minutes"—there can be no clouds in the sky and poof, rain will start like someone turned on a faucet and it will stop just as quickly.

In the verses just previously to the one we are studying, God give us an example of how all that he does has a purpose. The rain falls from the heavens to provide water for the flowers to bloom, the gardens to grow, the trees to sustain life and to replenish the streams, rivers and oceans. It is a cycle we don't give much thought to, unless you live in an area like South Florida where water plays an important role in the daily function of all that goes on.

The planning and zoning boards in every municipality require green space which consists of a certain amount of landscaping, shrubby, trees, and flowers, and this consumes a lot of water. Each development often depends on a man-made lake or canal for their supply of water. When those sources start running low then restrictions are applied and even fines when disobeyed. Just as the areas are very beautiful to look at, they put a tremendous drain on the ecosystem. Because of man's rules, we have taken something intended for good and turned it into something for selfish pleasure.

I have always been a car buff and must admit my car has been my idol. It has to be clean inside and out. I spend hours washing and waxing it only to be disappointed the minute it rains or gets dirty, but can't wait till next Saturday to do it again.

Once the lawn was mowed, the chores around the house were done, the car was cleaned—these were my weekend gods, and I was consumed by them to the point of burn out. I guess you can say that my priorities where way out of line. Church was just another Sunday chore, rushing around, getting everyone ready, and hurrying home to work on the house. My life was all turned around for it, and it was all being done for the wrong reason. I was into things that were all about what I wanted and seeking one more thing for personal satisfaction and none of it was about a relationship with God. I had put Him on a shelf and had completely forgotten about Him.

Divorce came through my own doing. My world changed and all I wanted to do was seek more stuff and party. I pushed God even further away. Just as the Israelites quickly forgot all the hard work and conditions they had left behind in Egypt, when the journey became tough while going through the desert they wanted to turn back, instead of pressing on. *"Didn't we say to you in Egypt, 'Leave us alone; let us serve the Egyptians?' It would have been better for us to serve the Egyptians than to die in the desert!"* Exodus 14:12 (NIV).

The Israelites never considered their current circumstance as temporary. Similarly, I was running away thinking the grass was greener, not wanting to look back as God stood there in both instances, for me and the Israelites, pleading for us to turn back.

God waited for us to retreat, turn our lives around and come back to Him. We were both-stiff necked people not willing to listen, only wanting to do our own thing. In my case, as well as the Israelites, it led to destruction. My marriage of twenty-one years was gone. The Israelites wondered for forty years never getting to see or taste the Promised Land

How foolish we can be simply because we get this notion that our way is better, and refuse to listen or see another's point of view. We become so blind to the obvious and refuse to admit our failures that we will accept a path of total destruction out of stubbornness and spite.

We will dig ourselves a hole that we can't get out of or we realize our wrong and become too ashamed to look back and ask for forgiveness.

Return, for some reason somewhere along the way, we got this all confused. If we (I) *turned back, retreat, lie down break away, come back* and all we see is "If I do that I am showing defeat, I made a bad decision and now I am admitting it to the whole world."

What God means for good we see as bad. How is that? Our pride, our ego is our biggest stumbling block admitting we did wrong. For many it is next to impossible. When we make a bad choice, take a wrong turn, whatever drives us to the point of going over the edge to not turn back is usually our ego. Yet, if we will allow ourselves to hear those tiny little voices in our head we will see Him standing there with arms open ready to receive us.

Such a simple process that we make difficult because of pride, ego, stubbornness, and not wanting to face the truth, in most cases knowing we are wrong from the get go. Making the effort to invest the time to understand the Bible could be the best choice one ever makes.

The word **could** is used because it is a willful choice that we have to make—not to be forced or coerced by anyone. He tells us His words will not return to Him **void**, empty, worthless, vain, undeservedly, without cause.

Had I known this one sentence, do you think my life would have been different? Since only God knows the answer to that question there is no sense in elaborating the point—right? That is the exact kind of attitude that got my thinking years ago to lead me down the wrong path, rather than taking the time to get to know God and His will for my life.

Ezekiel 12:2 (NIV) says,*"Son of man, you are living among a rebellious people. They have eyes to see but no not see and ears to hear but do not hear, for they are a rebellious people."*

Think About It
What do you think the above verse means?

_____

_____

To me, it means that if I want something bad enough, then I should take the time to dig in and get the understanding. Getting to know God requires digging into His Word with a great deal of tenacity.

Using the word **void,** he says, *"My word will not return empty,"* also meaning *worthless, vain, undeservedly, without cause.* When God gave a command, He expected it to be acted on.

"Now go, lead the people to the place I spoke of, and my angel will go before you. However, when the time comes for me to punish, I will punish them for their sins" Exodus 32:34 (NIV). God's words were never wasted and sometimes they were not pleasant. That was not because He set out to do harm, but His people chose not to obey. They reaped the consequence.

Years ago, as a restaurant manager, I ran the largest store in the chain with over a hundred employees. We prepped all of our food, had three shifts and because of its location it was very busy. I made the schedule and when it was posted, I expected the people to show up and do their appointed task. When someone did not show up at any position, whatever the shift, the manager on duty had to fill in. We had to be qualified to do every duty in the store. I trained the assistant managers to know each of the different positions so that we could not only help when needed, but also to make sure those individuals did their job properly. If correction was needed it came from a position of authority and the words were spoken because they would be of help and not because it was coming from a manager.

The store was so busy that time and fluid motion was an absolute must. You could not afford to have meaningless chatter. The manager needed to know at all times what was going on in each department in order to make sure the customer was always satisfied.

HT was the same way. He knew every position in the mine how to run each piece of equipment where his men needed to be at all times. This was a must from a safety stand point to production. It all had to run like a well-oiled machine. Yes, there would be hick-ups but if everyone knew their job, you could overcome a situation much quicker. That is why the company respected HT and why his shift was almost always ahead on production and less down time than the other shifts.

In Exodus 25:10 (NIV), we read: *"Have them make an ark of acacia wood—two and half cubit long and a half cubit wide, and a cubit and a half high."* God gave Moses specific directions on how to build the ark. His instructions were very specific in size and quality. He spent forty days with Moses giving him very detailed instructions. Do you suppose he wanted his words to be empty, meaningless or in vain? I don't think so.

On several occasions during that period, he would remind Moses by saying, *"See that they make them according to the pattern shown you on the mountain"* Exodus 25:40 (NIV). God's word had power and meaning and was never to be mistaken for meaningless chatter without cause.

Those times when we think we are undeserving of God's blessing, it usually is when we have strayed and are having a bad day and wanting a little pity. God is not into sympathy. You may think that's a cruel suggestion, but. He expects us to be responsible for our actions when things go wrong. When we are in alignment with His Word and things don't go according to plan, we still have His protection.

As hard as it may seem to grasp this concept, it works. This is where faith is bigger and belief becomes unshakeable. You read a little of my story, but HT on the other hand, understood God's law. His family was intact. He set the example of a godly man. Yes, there were differences. The road was rocky from time to time, but his God was bigger than his problem. He was willing to do what it took to keep the marriage together. He knew he was not capable of fixing the problem on his own. He relied on God through prayer and godly counsel.

To really understand the full impact of Isaiah 55:11(NIV) we need to have the faith of the Centurion, Joshua, and Job, all wrapped into one. They put their confidence in one greater than them and lived their life for him taking their eyes off of themselves believing God was the only answer and there was no other way. In other words, they sold out to God—lock, stock, and barrel.

We finish up this verse with the word **accomplish**, *to do, advance, become, bring forth, govern, have charge of, finish, warrior, and serve.* Just at the onset I will say, "This is exciting." Look what God has in store for those who choose to listen to Him. Maybe you don't see what I do in looking at these words, but by the time we are finished, hopefully you will.

According to Merriam-Webster 'to accomplish' is 'to complete,' 'to bring about a result', 'to fulfill' or 'reach a certain stage.' This says we have attained a certain level of accomplishment. God's Word will not return to Him empty (void). It will do or become what He says.

That in itself means 'power to know you have the ability,' 'to give an order' and 'it to be carried out.' *Just as you have stated it* means you are in a position of authority. This is where good or bad can occur.

When I was the restaurant manager, I had authority over all one hundred and five employees. It was my job to see they did their jobs. I was responsible to run the store keeping food cost, labor cost, and expenses in line to make a profit. The nice thing about having an operation that large was the volume we did, which gave me some leeway; however, the better I got at my job the less upper management tolerated mistakes.

As you read through the Bible, you get this sense that the better we become at understanding His Word, the less He tolerates our sloppiness. There is too much at stake for us to be lax in our efforts. God is giving us a chance to achieve beyond our greatest expectation and we need to understand and not take this lightly.

Throughout the Bible we are given commands with the expectation of doing that command and seeing a result because we did what was asked of us. In the Old Testament God became frustrated so many times because the Israelites would become impatient, rebel, and go against what Moses had written in the law. God punished them like you punish your son or daughter, but He always forgave them and brought them back into His fold because He loved them.

"For I know how rebellious and stiff-necked you are. If you have been rebellious against the Lord while I am still alive and with you, how much more will you will you

rebel after I die!" Deuteronomy 31:27 (NIV). God tells us He will not be mocked. "Do not be deceived: God cannot be mocked. A man reaps what he sows" Galatians 6:7 (NIV).

If we are expected to accomplish something, we must learn to serve. There is no way getting around this issue. This is where the Israelites faltered by refusing to obey. Many times, they responded like the Pharaoh. When confronted by Moses, he agreed with him but then turned around and did the opposite.

To accomplish something, we must first do what I call the grunt work. We need to learn the basics before we can become a master in whatever profession one chooses. The restaurant chain I worked for was sold to another company by the time I had attained the position of area supervisor. I was over six stores and had become the first regional manager for the company.

I was in my new position less than a year when the sale took place. The vice-president of operations told me I should start looking for another position because the new owner had his own upper level management and I would be replaced. So, I resigned, at the advice of the vice-president of operations. Looking back, I am not sure that was the best choice, but that is what I did. The restaurant chain I worked for was known for having a great manager's training program and other restaurant chains would eagerly snatch up managers.

I was immediately offered a position with a new fast food chain out of Columbus, Ohio that was building several stores in our area. As a manager, I would earn more between base salary and bonuses than before with less responsibility, so I thought this was a great deal. Boy, was I in for a surprise!

The word *accomplish* took on a whole new meaning for me over the next year. My boss turned out to be the *Pharaoh* for this company. Talk about a wolf in sheep's clothing. He often said what needed to be said to lure you in and meet a need. It was all that and more.

Over the next year, I spent time at the doctor's office trying to figure out why I was breaking out in hives, coming home stressed out, dreading to get up in the morning, and learning to hate the very thing I really liked to do and was good at it.

After only four months of training, I was running a new store only to be put back in training a few months later because the Pharaoh's brother had completed his training and was now ready for a store. I was the lucky one to be demoted.

I survived those days and moved on, remembering the lesson but not carrying the bitterness that went with it. The Israelites, on the other hand, wanted to continually remind Moses that even though the Pharaoh was a hard man, the conditions were better than their current situation. The Israelites wanted to always bring up the past as a reminder that they were not willing to move forward and focus on today and plan for tomorrow.

They were always complaining about something, never happy about where they were, or excited about life. They continually looked for a reason to complain. God, on many occasions got tired of listening to them complain and threatened to destroy all of them. Had it not been for Moses intervening, God would have ended it.

To *accomplish* means there will be labor and sacrifices. In my situation, while under the boss I call the Pharaoh, I did all that was required of me, and then some! However, it turned out to be all for nothing. But, that was not the big picture—that was only a bend in the road which would later be used to help me excel. We never know what tomorrow will bring nor will we get to experience it if we are not prepared. God was trying to prepare the Israelites to be ready to take over the land that had been promised them, but they did not want to prepare— they just wanted to complain. Because of their attitude and what they said, they got what they said and never made it to the Promise Land. God's word has power. His words are filled with promise and they accomplish the purpose for which they were intended.

CHAPTER 37
THE BOOK OF JOB

Job loved God, and no one held a higher place in his heart. His wealth was great, he had seven sons and three daughters, thousands of sheep and camel, hundreds of oxen and donkeys, and many servants. But as most know, God allowed the devil to test Job.

> *"Then the Lord said to Satan, 'Have you considered my servant Job? There is no one on earth like him; he is blameless and upright, a man who fears God and shuns evil'"* Job1:8 (NIV).

As you read the Book of Job and really understand what he went through, it becomes difficult for the human mind to conceive why anyone would be allowed to go through so much. Yet there are books full of stories, the five-o-clock news reminds us almost daily, and some have witnessed for themselves, but we never really understand why.

Again, we are reminded in Isaiah 55:9 (NIV), *"As the heavens are higher that the earth, so are my ways higher than your ways and my thoughts than your thoughts."* Let's examine Job 42: 10-17 (NIV) and see if we can get a better understanding of why God does what He does. Let me remind you even though we may come away with a better understanding of God's thinking, the carnal mind of man will still question as to why.

We will be left with this question—do you choose to believe the Bible and its teachings or go on questioning His words and wonder why? Just as you see Job make a decision and chose a path, we too must come to a conclusion and choose wisely.

The verses we are going to cover are after Job has suffered much tragedy and devastation, including friends turning on him, and even his wife showing signs of giving up. The only one left on Job's side is God. In chapter 42, even after everything he has suffered and been through still is willing to recognize that the Lord is the one in control. He humbles himself and says, *"I know that you can do all things, and no purpose of yours can be thwarted"* Job 42:2 (NIV).

It is like saying, "I have heard and seen what you are capable of. Please, forgive me for thinking I could question or doubt you." The beauty of this is that God already knew Job's heart. This was to allow Job to discover his own integrity.

When we are put to a test and our back is against the wall of decisions, we make the priority in which we think will be the true measure of the person we are. Our honesty, our love, and commitment will show through in our actions as to whom and what matters in those times.

Job was willing to forgive his best friends and his wife and start anew, not knowing what was in store for him except that God was by his side. Talk about starting over from zero—this is what Job was about to do. Job's life was about to take a drastic turn for the better. God blessed him with twice as much and he lived a full life to enjoy those blessings. It is like the successful businessman who was ready to retire. He and his wife were preparing to sail on their boat and travel the beautiful waters of the Caribbean and a judge asked them for a favor just for one week.

That favor turned into a twenty-five-year journey of helping troubled young men turn their lives around. With the support of other successful businessmen, even though their boat never left the harbor, the lives they have touched has been immeasurable.

As Jesus prayed that historical night in the garden, "Not my will but thy will be done," knowing it would be great if He did not have to go through with dying on the cross, but He was willing to do whatever His Father asked of Him.

Obedience and the willingness to listen and take instruction when we would rather do it our way is the one character trait God wants us all to have, but knows only a few are willing to sacrifice to get. Job's trials are a lesson for all of us. He was down completely, stripped of all he had, stricken with health problems, finances depleted, no roof over his head . . .what else could go wrong?

As Job sat in misery from the boils that inflicted his body, he said to his three closest friends, *"What I feared has come upon me. What I dreaded has happened to me. I have no peace, no quietness. I have no rest, but only turmoil"* Job 3:25-26 (NIV).

Think About It

Do you suppose Job thought he was being punished, and if so why?

In reading the Book of Job, we get a clear understanding of what integrity means and the one who displays it. Though shaken, Job does not abandon his God. Though confused, he does not make excuses or look to lay blame, even in anger he still holds onto the one thing he knows for certain—that His God can do all things.

The fear Job speaks of is one that so many of us encounter. It is like speeding through a school zone and praying you don't get caught. You know what you are doing is wrong, but you are trying to make up for lost time or not be late for an appointment all the while continuing to break the law praying, "Lord don't let me get caught."

That is an oxymoron! You are asking God to get you safely to your destination, while breaking the law. Well, He is not going to have any part of it. You may arrive unscathed, no tickets, no accidents, but think of all that you caused to happen inwardly.

The stress, anxiety, wear and tear you put your own body through all because of improper planning. Years ago, after my divorce, my finances were in shambles, caused by a lot of deb. I had a car dealer friend of mine who wanted me to come to work for him, so I did. I had been in the insurance business and felt a change may be good for me. After starting my new job as a car salesman, I still retained my insurance license and was doing that on the side. I made appointments after I got off work from selling cars and I had a goal to have at least one appointment every evening. I was in debt pretty deep and thought the insurance commissions would get me out pretty quick. I had scheduled an appointment for 8:30 one evening about thirty miles away and knew I would have to push it but figured I could make it.

I had to make a choice as to how I would get to the appointment. I could go by interstate to a certain point and a back road, which I did not know all that well, or through a couple of small towns where the road was narrow and had two lanes with lots of twist and turns. I chose the small towns and winding roads because I knew them well. I made sure I left work on time, maybe even a few minutes early, and off I went.

I made it through the first small town, past the police, red lights, etc. with no tickets and believe me I was pushing my luck. Once I got through the first town, there were some straight stretches in the road and man, I was moving! I kept watching in my rearview mirror and noticed every time I would pass a car there was this car behind me and it would do the same, but no flashing lights so I figured it was someone just following me.

Me being young, and cool, I figured I could shake this person. So I went faster, but they hung with me. As I was getting close to the second small town and knew had to slow down, which would cost me some time. I dropped over a hill and started down the other side almost to the city limits and it was like someone had turned on the Christmas tree red and blue lights behind me, in front of me, and all around me. I was in deep trouble.

The cops pulled me over in a church parking lot. Imagine that of all places—or was that a good thing? I got out and immediately was surrounded by police saying, "Let me see your license," firing questions at me, like why was I speeding like a mad man . . . reckless driving and putting others' lives in danger . . . passing in curves.

So many questions at one time I could not answer any of them. I was thinking, *Man, they are going to put me in jail.* As I stood there trying to compose myself, my mind and heart both racing, blood flying though my veins, this throbbing headache appeared out of nowhere, and nothing would come out of my mouth. I realized there was dead silence and figured I had better say something and thought, *Lord, don't fail me now.*

I engaged my brain, opened my mouth, and started to explain, telling them I was on my way to an appointment still about twelve miles away and I stretched the truth to the limit as they all stood there and listened. Come to find out it was an undercover policeman that was following me and they had an APB out on a car similar to mine, but I was driving so fast he could not get close enough to me to read the tag so he had the boys meet me.

Believe it or not they let me go. Remember, the church parking lot . . . I wonder. Needless to say, I was late for my appointment, but I got there and made the sale. Still, I drove like a mad man on the way home. Being young makes one think you are indispensable, believing you can do anything, overcome any obstacle, not taking the time to plan just going in a mad rush. You put yourself in a situation not thinking of the damage you may cause or the stress you create.

As I recalled that night, it brings me to this thought: It's time to slow down and let God be involved in the process of our lives. It's time to ask Him for counsel, to go to His Word and find answers to life's situations that apply to us. How would that have made any difference on the night I was traveling to my appointment? Where would God fit into that evening?

Let's see. My day would have started with reading His Word. Since I knew what I had planned for the day, I would have looked for a verse or verses that applied to my day.

Since I was working to get out from under debt, it would have been wise to see what God had to say. In Matthew 6:32-34 (NIV) we are told, *"For the pagans run after all these things and your heavenly Father knows that you need them. Therefore do not to worry about tomorrow, for tomorrow will worry about itself. Each day has enough trouble of its own."*

The Bible supplies us with supporting verses to help us get a better understanding of what I just read. My day would have taken a different turn had I taken the time to look up those verses and the answers I needed to plan my day, and not jeopardize my health, my life, and get much more accomplished in the process.

The Bible leads us on a journey of learning and developing a relationship with God. By changing our ways and committing our lives to Him the changes are remarkable. It is a process that provides us daily growth. Through the growth, we gain inner strength and peace that gives us the ability to endure life, knowing that someone much greater than us is leading us. Amen.

In his life, HT must have read these verses as well. The lifestyle he and the family lived were a fruit of that. The patience he developed, the struggles he stopped—all played a very important role in how his life and lifestyle changed after he committed his life to Jesus.

HT knew if all else failed, his anchor would always be there. He had encountered enough difficulty and trials in his life, and so he knew where to turn to get his guidance.

Back to Job.

Think About It

Why do you think God permitted Satan to do as he pleased

"The Lord said to Satan, 'Very well, then he is in your hands; but you must spare his life" Job 2:6 (NIV). Imagine this conversation taking place. God and Satan sitting

side by side, in a sort of business meeting discussing who has the better product and how they can put it to the test and get the publics opinion. I am not so sure I would want the same test that Job was given. But, then again, Job was not asked if he wanted to participate in the study he was chosen.

When Satan presented his proposal to God he had been in pursuit of a participant for his experiment. God suggested Job and Satan knowing God was a shrewd businessman proceeded to qualify Job by a series of questions.

Satan asked, "Have you not put a hedge around him and his household and everything he has? You have blessed he work of his hands, so that his flocks and herds are spread throughout the land" Job 1:10 (NIV). It is as if Job was a pawn in a game that he knew nothing about.

Satan thought he was in the same category as all the other idols that were symbols of worship and he wanted to elevate himself to the same level as God. However, God has made it very clear that he is a jealous God. *"Do not worship any other god for the Lord, whose name is Jealous, is a jealous God"* Exodus 34:14 (NIV).

CHAPTER 38

LIVING LIKE JOB

Just imagine Job sitting on the ground, physically spent. He is perplexed, tired, has absolutely zero possessions, has just finished venting to God, and in the dead of silence God begins to speak.

God rebukes Job for questioning his goodness and justice by telling him how little he knows, how little he really understands the complexity of all the creation, its vastness separating the light from the dark, morning from evening, the warm summer sun from the cold winter's day. All that occurs . . . and Job has the audacity to question God.

I can imagine Job slinking even lower as he listens to God go through two chapters of rebuke. As God finishes his time with Job, he asks will the one who contends with the Almighty correct him? He expects for one who accuses God to answer him.

God went on to rebuke Job a second time. Job received the message loud and clear and he replied to the Lord.

God was angry with Job's friends Eliphaz, Bildad, and Zophar. *"After the Lord had said these things to Job, he said to Eliphaz the Temanite, 'I am angry with you and your two friends, because you have not spoken the truth about me as my servant Job has.'"* In the end, God was pleased was Job's humbleness.

"After Job prayed for his friends the Lord made him prosperous again and gave him twice as much as he had before." Job 42:10. The key here is not what God gave him but what he did for his friends, thinking of them instead of himself.

There are six keywords in this verse. See the impact they had on Job's life and how they can impact us as well. **Prayed** in this context was *to judge, intercede, entreat, make supplication.* In the context of which Job prayed for his friends, we see the word **judge** being used to remind us of two things. First, God pray for his friends, which meant God had judged their actions and pronounced a sentence.

They only way the Supreme Justice was going to have mercy on these three men was that someone he respected would have to pray and that prayer would have to intercede for them. To intercede, according to Miriam-Webster, is to intervene between two parties with the purpose of reconciling their differences. It is interesting how today's definition fits exactly into what God wanted Job to do around the year 2000 B.C. We read God was angry with these boys so He used someone He trusted to intercede and make it right. God allowed Job to judge his friends through prayer and not stand before them and pronounce sentence, but to intercede and save their lives.

The next verb or action word we see is **entreat**. When looked at in modern terms this word still carries the same implications it did in biblical times. It meant *to negotiate, to plead,* and this was exactly what God was requiring of Job. God had already pronounced sentence on these three men and Job was their "ONLY" hope.

As Job prayed his prayer it became a prayer to negotiate and to plead for mercy from the court of the Supreme Justice to have mercy on these men. Finally, to pray is *to make supplication.* This is really cool. When you look at the modern-day definition of supplication it means *to make a humble and earnest request,* most especially to God.

Job's prayer is a supplication for his three friends. As you read his book, you can see Job is humbly and earnestly seeking favor from God to save his friends. Do you think they knew the trouble they were in or realized what a real friend Job was? This gives us an inkling of the power of prayer when it is done according to God's will.

The next word is **friend**, and in this passage, it is related *to brother, associate, husband, tend a flock, keep company with, and companion.* In Miriam-Webster's Dictionary we find the definition for friend to be *one attached to another by affection or esteem and considered a favored companion.*

When I was eleven years old my best friend, Bruce, drowned. Bruce and I were best buddies, as we were six months apart in age and did everything together. For me, the worst part about his tragic accident was that I was away visiting my sister and came home to discover his funeral was the next day.

Somebody mentioned to me that if I had been there that it probably would not have happened because we were inseparable. This laid a heavy burden on me and being only eleven-years-old, I never learned how to handle it or how to talk to anyone about it. I buried it, and to this day, I wonder how different our lives would have been had I been there.

The Bible says in Proverbs 18:24 (NIV): "One who has unreliable friends soon comes to ruin, but there is a friend who sticks closer than a brother." How did Job's friends relate to him about what had occurred? They each took their turn at consoling him and suggesting their own version of what they felt happened. These three guys were Job's best buddies, as I would call them. The friends he could call on anytime about anything and they would be there rain or shine.

From a worldly view, they proceeded to give their rendition of what they thought was happening and why. Hey, this is what friends do. They counsel, provide a shoulder to lean or cry on, as well as a tentative ear. A true friend always has a word of encouragement, they feel your pain, and just want to help make it all better.

Think About It

Do you have a friend like that?

_____

_____

Job's friends came and sat with him in silence for some time, just listening as they formulated their analogy before offering their opinion. There is one part of friendship that does tend to cross the line. When friends get so personal they put themselves in your shoes and begin to offer advice based on their personal feelings. True friends know when to listen and when to speak, and when they do speak it is from the perspective of clarifying what has taken place—not giving opinions or remedies.

God knew the intent of Job's three friends, but their advice went beyond the boundaries when they offered their theories. As they counselled Job through their companionship, they ended up mudding the water. In this case, even though their intentions were meant to be good, they dug a hole that Job ended up having to pull them out of.

A friend is someone like a husband, a brother, an associate, or one who attends to your flock. These are all words that tell me this is an individual who is close to us. Someone that over time we can develop a relationship with and put trust in. Having said that it only seems natural that God is one we would call a friend. He fits the mold perfectly. He wants to be our friend. He has said, "I will always be there for you. I will never leave you or forsake you." Isn't that what friendship is all about?

Our next word is **Lord,** which is another word for God or sacred name. After Job had prayed for his friends, the Lord made him twice as prosperous as before. In chapter 40, the Lord speaks with Job and the conversation is quite frank. The Lord asks Job, *"Would you discredit my justice? Would you condemn me to justify yourself?"* Job 40:8 (NIV).

I have many times done this to justify myself and the circumstances I was in. Making up lies to cover our path of mistakes and blaming everyone else seems to be commonplace.

"In today's society, most people just don't care about anything or anyone except themselves, and that which can make something work to their benefit—not caring how it may affect other fellow workers."

Job realized in venting his frustration to God, he was in the wrong. but the one thing he did not do was make excuses and look to others to place the blame. Job realized he came into this world with nothing and when his time came, he would leave it with nothing. God appreciated Job for his honesty and his desire to not turn his back on him, and so He rewarded Job accordingly.

God's ways are higher than our ways, and we certainly don't understand them or His reasons as to why some things happen; however, if we will have the faith of Job and just continue to believe in God's Word, it will work out in the end. Job had no idea that he would be blessed with twice as much but he had made up his mind he would not give up on the Almighty—the one he had always found solace in—the Lord, the scared one.

The word **give** means *to continue to do, exceed, prolong, and more.* A few weeks ago, I was talking to my oldest son, who's in sales and management with a national food service company. He was telling me of a call he decided to make on his way home. It was after 5pm and traffic was bad. He was tired and looked forward to getting home. But something inside him said to get off the interstate at the next exit and make one more call. Needless to say, the last thing he wanted to do was get off the highway to make a call, most especially since chances were the owner was gone for the day. Still, his gut told him to get off the highway. As he drove to the restaurant, his mind was not on the call, but the next thing he knew, he was sitting in front of the restaurant. He got out and headed to the office, where he found the owner, and not in a good mood. After some conversation, my son discovered his competitor, who was servicing this account, had failed to make a delivery that put the restaurant in a big bind.

The restaurant had a large party in two hours and the main dish was not going to be able to be prepared. My son offered to go to his warehouse and pick up the necessary items and deliver them. The owner was very thankful and ended up giving him the account, which turned into multiple stores.

One more call and it paid off big time. My son chose to follow his gut feeling, exceeded his own expectations, and the reward he received was more than he expected. Is that going to happen every time? Probably not, but we don't know that unless we try. The same goes with the reward God has in store for us. By following His plan, we will receive it great or small. By choosing to do it our way we will never know what we missed out on. Is the reward going to be monetary? It may, but we need to keep in mind God rewards us according to what He knows. What we think we need usually is not what God has in mind for us.

Society programs us to want for stuff. God, in turn, may not respond to our liking but we are told He will supply our needs according to His riches in glory. That in itself tells me monetary may be in the mix, but may not be His first choice. Still, we shouldn't rule it out, as even though God may not reward us with money, He may open a door that will. It may be a promotion, a new job, or a business opportunity. Who knows what He will send our way? The key is are we in touch with Him and ready to receive His gift?

Prolong is another word related to **give**. We discover there are two ways to view this word. Whether good or bad, they both have the same implication meaning *to lengthen, defer, make long, draw out, live long.* Since God's promise to Job was of a good nature, can you see what He meant by prolonging His reward? It only gets better. He will not only prolong the reward. It will exceed anything Job may have thought and it will be more—much more—than he could ever expect.

In the end, after God had spoken to Job, all he could say was, "I despise myself and repented in dust and ashes." Job felt ashamed knowing he could never comprehend all God was capable of and how foolish he was to complain. God was not finished with Job. He knew people had to be able to see miraculous things before they would believe.

This second chance was like a new start. And because Job loved God and He showed Job how much He loved him, God gave Job more and prolonged his life to allow him time to enjoy all the favor that had been shown him.

The word **twice** means *to duplicate or twice as much.* The dictionary says twice means to double the degree or be doubly rewarded, and that is exactly what God did. He gave Job double the reward over what he had before it was destroyed. When we see an advertisement in the supermarket where it says, "Buy one, get one free," it's usually not a bargain. If you know your prices and know the normal price of that item, what they do is raise the price and then offer the second. What they call free usually is not the case.

But when you go shopping with God, and he offers what I call a 'two-fer,' believe Him because it's the real deal. You will get all you ask for and more so be prepared to be blessed and keep in mind to have your radar antenna up because you never know how or in what form the blessing will come.

The blessing was twice as much as **before** meaning *countenance, turn, face, heaviness, and prospered.* Before all this tragedy came, Job was what everyone would consider a very wealthy man and blessed by God.

Before all the devastation, Satan asked God, "Have you not put a hedge around him and his household and everything he has? You have blessed the work of his hands, so that his flocks and herds are spread throughout the land" Job 1:10 (NIV).

The first word related to **before** is countenance, and looking at countenance tells it all. It is used in a variety of applications and here are just a few: *anger, battle, endure, favor, please, was purposed, by reason.* It appears God chose Job purposely for Satan's test because he knew Job would withstand it. God also knew that Job would not turn from God but would face the challenge and endure all that Satan would throw at him.

Job did encounter some heaviness during his trial under Satan. Those closest to him: his wife and friends challenged him, pushing him to turn against God, but his fear for God was greater. His love and loyalty to God far surpassed all the tragedy that he was encountering. Not knowing how the end would be, he never wavered in his love for God.

Franklin Graham spoke at our church one evening and he gave a very simple but powerful message. His message came from the Gospel of Luke, chapter 14. He titled it "CEO—Cost Excuses Obedience." This meant it cost Jesus his life to pave a way for us and we "must" understand he wants everything from us. He expects our love for Him to be greater than for that of our spouse, our children, or ourselves. To most this is difficult to comprehend.

Think About It

Can you love God more than your children, your spouse, or your parents?

Let's follow the rest of Franklin's message and you will see. Through obedience, when you enter into the presence of Jesus, and He asks you to give it all up and completely surrender, you will be amazed as to how full He will make your life. Take that little snippet of Franklin's message and see how it applied to Job and how his life turned out.

Job's family came to counsel him, his brothers, sisters, cousins, but the source of the **all** was from God. God was prepared to give the *whole, manner, any, and everything* to Job. We can sum the word **all** up to mean *to complete and make perfect.* God completed with Job what He set out to do. He made perfect an ending that seemed hopeless. God is the creator of *all* and He can do all things for those who put their trust in Him.

His brothers and sisters came to console him and spend time with him to make him feel better in his time of grief. It is good to have loved ones around you in time of trouble or sorrow for their support is comforting.

Years ago, when my best friend passed away the number of people that came to show their support to the family was amazing. The casket was brought to the home, so for three days the viewing was done in the home. I remember the cars parked on the side of the road, the flowers on their front porch, people streaming in and out all day long till late into the evening. The support that was given the family was in creditable.

Job's family was showing that same kind of support. Their comfort stemmed from what they felt was all the trouble the Lord had **brough**t, *to come or go to befall, besiege, be against* what had Job done to cause all this. They felt God had singled out Job believing he had disobeyed God and this was why all this tragedy was upon him.

When we heard of someone's misfortune, the first thing we think about is, "What in the world did this person do to deserve all this misery and why are they being punished so severely?"

When we are not seasoned in God's Word, it is a natural process to think God is punishing that person. We, as humans, are taught if you do something bad you will be punished. It took me a long time and a lot of reading to understand that God was not punishing that person. And, yes, God can change that persons' circumstance if He chooses.

What I have learned is to not try and figure out what is going on in that situation unless it is something external that I may have a possible answer to. I can come alongside and console, comfort, pray, and do what I can as a friend.

These things can mean a great deal to their emotional well-being in a time of need. God commands us to comfort those in time of need, especially the children and the widow. We have a tendency to think in terms of what kind of bad things this individual did to cause all these problems in their life when in fact with a little insight we see in a lot of cases why this happened.

In the Old Testament, God was not beyond bringing some pain to a situation to get their attention, whether it was on the individual or circumstance. But once He sent His son to earth to walk among us for a period of time and eventually die for our sins, that all changed.

His mode of operandi changed and His method of delivery became one of ministry, seeking to make disciples and spread His word to tell everyone who will listen to accept His name as the Holy One, worthy of all praise and honor. Those who believe in Him shall have everlasting life. Having said all that, God had a plan for Job and as we read of all his tragedy, we see the *spoken word* did have a big impact on Job's life. But when we are at our weakest and walking in God's way, He is at His strongest. Look what happens next.

We come to the word **gave** again, and this time it means *to appoint, restore, charge, ordain, and yield to God.* God let Satan use Job knowing his true character and in the end he would remain standing. These were inner qualities that God gave Job knowing he would withstand the task. Job did yield to God and the charge that was put on his shoulders proved to be worthy as he did not let God down.

God offers the same qualities to all of us; we just have to be willing to lay down our agenda and follow the one He has for us. Job was doing what he had always done, following the one he had always followed, although he did not understand all that was happening in his life.

The one thing he knew for sure was his relationship with God. His faith remained unshakable while realizing how weak he was and willing to stand before God having no idea how much strength could be displayed through him. Proverbs 3:5 says it well, *"Trust in Him and lean not on your own understanding, acknowledge him in all your ways and he will make your path straight."*

As Job sat in the ashes and sackcloth covered in boils (not a pretty picture) I am sure he figured death was knocking at his door, and why not? He had lost everything else. "So Satan went out from the presence of the Lord and afflicted Job with painful scores from the soles of his feet to the crown of his head" Job 2:7 (NIV).

But in his weakness, as he turned to God, Job gained strength to endure and hang on. And, as he communicated with God, his circumstance began to change. His body healed, the family came to console him, and God did miraculous things. Job did not try to analyze all that had happened. Instead, he accepted it all and let God do a work in him.

The word **every** has significance in this verse. It means *champion, mighty, worthy, and steward.* These words are very appropriate for a man such as Job. In chapter 1, we are told of a man who was blameless, upright, feared God, and shunned evil. It goes on to say he was the greatest man among all the people of the East. He was always concerned if one of his children may have cursed God in their heart or sinned, so he offered a burnt offering for each of them.

The Lord asked Satan, *"Have you considered my servant Job? There is no one on earth like him, his is blameless and upright, a man who fears God and shuns evil."* Satan is just arrogant enough to think he can get one over on God, and he accepts the challenge.

I wanted to give you some additional insight into Job's background enabling us to have a better understanding of the feeling's God had for Job. Now as we look at the word **every,** it makes a great deal more sense when we see phrases such as *champion, mighty, worthy,* and *steward.* Job could certainly be considered a *champion* for God. He held tight to God's law and feared Him with reverence. Ask most people to define the word champion and your answer might vary only a little. They would give answers such as the college football champion or basketball champion. They may tell you the World Series baseball champion or national league football champion or the world heavy weight boxing champion, and the list could go on. Do you think you would hear anyone say, "he or she was a champion for God?"

Tony Dungy retired after seven years in the National football League as the head coach of the National Champion Baltimore Clots. He said, "I want to do more than just coach men." He is a strong Christian and his influence on young men, he felt could be of a greater good outside that arena.

Dungy has a two-minute radio program called an Uncommon Moment where he tells God stories of individuals who unashamedly put God first. It may have been in an arena or on a quiet street, but God came before they got the glory. Job was one of those uncommon men who championed for God and the few times the word champion is used in the Bible it is related to words such as *discern, inform, concerned intelligence, and wise man.* Solomon spends a lot of his time talking about or displaying wisdom. It was the only thing he asked of God.

There were many great men listed in the Bible and most messed up along the way but because of the desire to please God and follow His law, they all attained a level of wisdom as they championed their cause for God.

On Sunday mornings, pastors all across the nation quote these champion's verses and chapters, time and time again. They remind their congregations these men held the National League title that far surpassed any title or trophy that will sit on a shelf and collect dust.

Job was not only a champion, he was worthy, and a steward. God said there is none like him in the land and for God to give anyone that kind of a compliment, he must be pretty close to the top of the pecking order. Since God is not one to hand out awards frivolously you can rest assured Job deserved the praise he received. Jobs' relatives and friends who came to console him each brought him a piece of silver and a gold ring.

Our focus is on the word **gold,** meaning *shimmer, clear sky, and fair weather.* The value of the day was in what a person had in land, animals, the size of his family along with the number of servants he had. Gold was used to adorn the person, to make into fine ornaments. Gold was a symbol of wealth and with it you had the power to purchase, trade, obtain, and acquire.

"Aaron answered them, 'Take off the gold earrings that your wives, your sons and your daughters are wearing, and bring them to me.' He took what they handed him and made it into an idol cast in the shape of a calf, fashioning it with a tool. Then they said, 'These are your gods, Israel, who brought you up out of Egypt" Exodus 32:2-4 (NIV).

Much of the gold was used to create idols. When an individual has the ability to gain wealth, they usually want to display that wealth in various ways. It may be seen in the clothes they wear, the diamonds that adorn their hands, neck or ears. It may be seen in the houses they live in; their collection of paintings, fine china at their table or the cars in the drive way. In many of those homes somewhere there will be a display of statues shimmering of gold to let the onlooker know, "I have wealth which translates into power."

This is where things start to get fuzzy for man. He begins to get this idea of, what I call the "I" syndrome. He thinks, "I did all this, it is mine and I am the reason this occurred."

It is because of me. Without fail, his world will come crashing down, and everyone says, "Oh, what a shame."

Many kings and great leaders throughout history have had this "I" syndrome and their worlds have come crashing down around them. Gold carried the same significance in Job's day, and today, it has the same destructive tendencies if you let it rule your life. Job had a pretty good handle on his life and that was not a problem for him. His friends and family came to reconnect and the gold they brought represented a new start. They were trying to say, "All the bad things are behind you; it is time to move forward."

For the sailor, clear skies mean it is good sailing weather. For the farmer it means, he can get a lot of work done that day. For Job it meant a fresh start. The clear sky and the fair weather meant he would now be able to move forward. All the past was just that—the past. This was not a time to moan or complain, the clear skies were there for a season, he must get busy and take advantage of the fair weather to plant the fields and prepare for harvest.

Yes, the harvest. Job did not know the storm he had just endured was preparation for the bountiful harvest he was about to receive. The clear skies and fair weather were a sign for Job, just as the sailor checks the sky to know it if is ok to sail. The great thing about Job was he had his house in order, he knew who was first in his life. God was at the top of his list and always would be.

The Lord **blessed** Job the in latter part of his life more than the first. To be blessed was *to kneel, to bless God, benefit greatly, and to praise.* Job was no stranger to praising God, as he had always offered sacrifice and prayed to God. Job's life took a drastic turn for the better—much more than he expected. His live stock was twice as great as before. After the tragic loss of his children, he was blessed with seven sons and three beautiful daughters. It says nowhere in all the land were there to be found any women as beautiful as these.

Job did his part, which was obeying God, praying, offering sacrifice, working his fields and raising his family, putting God first. Job's estate had such an increase that he broke tradition and gave an inheritance to the daughters along with the sons. An **inheritance** was a portion of the estate. It meant *to divide, to give.* As it was not a tradition for the daughters to receive an inheritance, Job's blessing was so great and God had blessed him with such beautiful daughters, Job's keeping was not with the norm. Job lived a hundred and forty years and got to see his children and their children to a fourth generation, and he **died** old and **full** of **years**.

As we close the Book on Job and his life, these last three words carry a great deal of significance and lessons we can all benefit from. He died *old and full of years.* In the sense of dying, he was worthy of death, and **wise** meant to *satisfaction, having enough, to suffice, and plenty.*

Finally, **years** meant *a revolution of time, double, report and return.* The implication behind these words is powerful and says a lot about Job and his relationship with God. How does one become worthy of death? I have heard people make the comment when someone passed away that he deserved to die, but that usually meant they did not like that individual and was glad they were gone.

God had blessed Job and his death was worthy, carrying with it an honor of being a champion, a great and mighty man, a husband, and a steward. Prior to

Job's trials, he was considered a blessed man by God, but he lived such a God-centered life that at his death his legacy remained vibrant and lives to this day. These words speak of honor to this man, words that any man would want to have said about them.

My best friend who drowned at age eleven, I heard people say things about him where he had impacted their lives. He was only a little boy, but his presence was felt in that small community.

Job was a wise man and with time his wisdom grew. He understood his role with God and he lived it out setting examples for his family and friends. He was not ashamed of who he followed or in his belief. God was number one in his life and by making that known publicly as he confessed before man, God honored him with a long life and abundance.

The blessings abounded again in the end. As we notice it says *to satisfaction, enough to suffice, plenty.* Job was not greedy and God was not a stingy god. Job not only had plenty in his late years, he was able to enjoy it, all of it, and was greatly blessed at his death.

Knowing whose side to be on while we are in the game of life is very important. Those who choose to buy into this idea that there is no God have a very big surprise coming when their lives come to an end. There are two paths. On one, you will have to choose and if you wait till you die then my friend, you will lose.

Job died **full of years**, *a revolution of time, double, do a second time.* In Job 42:10,16,17 (NIV), we read: "After Job had prayed for his friends, the Lord restored his fortunes and gave him twice as much as he had before. After this, Job lived a hundred and forty years; he saw his children and their children to the fourth generation. And so Job died, an old man and full of years."

Job, as many others we have looked at, chose a path that led them on a journey that was full of twist and turns. They faced trials that tested them, strengthened them and they grew. They were men who aligned themselves with the Almighty God of the universe. The legacy they left to some seemed impossible and to others unbelievable. If you chose to believe what is written in the Bible then you must accept what it says in 2 Co 5:7, 9-10 (NIV), *"For we live by faith not by sight. So we make it our goal to please him, whether we are at home in the body or away from it. For we must all appear before the judgment seat of Christ, so that each of us may receive what is due us for the things done while in the body, whether good or bad."*

Life offers us choices daily, decisions that require us to be honest, faithful, trustworthy, and fair. Many will be between you and God and no one else will ever know.

Think About It

What will you do?

This test will be presented throughout our walk on earth and how we handle them will be recorded in the record books. The beauty of being on God's team is that the minute you join, He wipes your slate clean. Just as He did for Job in giving him a life full of years, He offers to do the same for us. But we, like Job, have to be prepared to do the uncommon, to do more, not less, to step up and accept responsibility, step back, and let others get the credit.

When we join God's team, it is no longer about I, me, or mine. God showed us how His system worked when He told Job to pray for his friends. When Job's eyes were taken off himself and fully focused on another's needs and his heart fully ingrained in that process, then God blessed him.

In God's world, it is not about us. He knows what we need and He is prepared to supply all of it. It is my prayer that you will turn your heart to God, take that leap of faith, walk the road less traveled, learn from the lessons given and become a leader on God's team. All who come forward are greatly welcomed and you, my friend, will be used in a mighty way and it will not go unnoticed. Amen.

What happened to HT?

At twenty-eight, his mother died. At thirty-five, the son he wanted was born, and at age forty, he had already put twenty-nine years in the coal mine industry. Before it was all said and done, he had fifty years in the mine and if it weren't for health issues, it would have been fifty-three.

A fifth-grade education, a lot of hard work, a whole lot of Bible time, prayer, faithful to his family, and following God's Word gave give him a full life. He loved to hunt and fish. He loved to work in the garden and had a green thumb that would not quit. He was a good steward, saved his money and planned his life according to God's will.

HT was respected in his community and the men that worked for him thought he was the best. His superiors respected his work ethic and felt he always gave more than was expected. He knew how to lend a helping hand and he believed God was always there when he called on Him.

For the person who has to know, where did he end up financially? Here's a quick rundown. He had two homes, paid for two cars in the garage that were both newer models. There was a little over quarter of a million dollars in the bank plus the value of the two homes and two cars. To HT, it wasn't about the money, the homes, or the cars. It was about knowing he did the right thing, as he followed what he believed from what he learned through the Bible. Why make something difficult out of something so simple? After all, it was easy for a man with only a fifth-grade education.

The disciples once asked Jesus who was the greatest in the kingdom of heaven. Jesus said: *"Truly I tell you, unless you change and become like little children, you will never enter the kingdom of heaven. Therefore, whoever takes the lowly position of this child is the greatest in the kingdom of heaven"* Matthew 18:3-4 (NIV).

HT started working in the mines at age eleven. He never had a childhood, working two jobs by age sixteen. He was a prime candidate for Jesus. He humbled himself, was hungry to learn, and had that childlike faith. His daddy (Abba Father) taught him well. If HT were alive today, he would say, "God took good care of me."

Let God do the same for you.

Dad an Mom shortly after marriage

Dad as a baby with his parents

www.ingramcontent.com/pod-product-compliance
Lightning Source LLC
LaVergne TN
LVHW081327060426
835513LV00012B/1210